THE MANCHURIAN CRISIS

1931-1932

THE
Manchurian Crisis

1931-1932

A TRAGEDY IN
INTERNATIONAL RELATIONS

By SARA R. SMITH

GREENWOOD PRESS, PUBLISHERS
WESTPORT, CONNECTICUT

To My Mother and Father

FOREWORD

FEW EVENTS in world history can match in importance that with which this volume deals. For the Manchurian crisis which grew out of the Mukden incident of September, 1931, was the opening phase of the second World War. Therefore this detailed history of that crisis, based upon a thorough analysis of all the documents available when the book was written, should be of lasting interest not only to historians but to all students of international affairs.

Like the shot fired at Sarajevo seventeen years earlier, the shots fired in the railroad yards at Mukden constituted the overt act which led to war. But in both cases the real cause of the war lay in the subsequent failure of diplomacy to prevent the tragic consequences of that act in the breakdown of the structure of peace. In 1914 it was the state system of Europe, based on the balance of power, which, in the face of determined aggression, had no adequate means of self-defense. The first World War was largely due to the fact that in the hour of crisis there were only divided councils, especially as the aggression had been so definitely provoked. It was to prevent such confusion among the nations anxious for the preservation of peace that the League of Nations was established, with its provision for collective security. But in 1931, almost the same kind of confusion prevailed at Geneva as had been the case in the tragic days of August, 1914. This, however, was due, as this volume so clearly shows, not merely to the inadequacy of the machinery of the League of Nations but also to the fact that the United States was not a member of it. With the best will in the world toward the League, Secretary Stimson found himself in the critical opening hours of the crisis more or less in the position of a rival to the League Council. This at least was the view taken by the Japanese who made much of any divergence of points of view between Washington and Geneva. The lesson from this failure to coordinate a power outside the League with the collective security which it was supposed to offer is obvious.

The strategy of peace must be as direct and effective as that of war, and this cannot be the case so long as there are separate directives, for the inevitable result of such confusion is either delay or inaction.

There is, however, one further lesson to be learned from the Manchurian crisis which is even more pertinent to the issues of today. It is to be found in the dilemma in which the liberal Foreign Minister of Japan, Baron Shidehara, found himself when the military element in the Japanese Government forced his hand owing to the fact that there was dual control by the civilian and military elements in the Japanese Cabinet. This situation was reflected in the diplomacy of the Japanese at Washington and Geneva. Mr. Stimson's attitude towards Japan was motivated by his desire not to cause any loss of face upon the part of the Japanese liberals, which he thought might result from an insistence upon an international investigation of the Mukden incident. But this was the one procedure which the League of Nations would have to employ if it were to undertake the pacific settlement of so grave a dispute. Before anything else could be done, it was necessary to find out exactly what were the facts in the case by an examination of the evidence on the spot. More than once before, the League had successfully carried out this procedure, and at least on one occasion, that of the Greco-Bulgarian war scare of 1925, it actually prevented war. Such an intervention, however, must take place without delay, because the first overt acts are bound to be followed quickly by others, so that the situation to be investigated no longer remains the same. It was unfortunate, therefore, that the Japanese initial objections to a Committee of Enquiry by the League of Nations were strengthened both by the news from Washington during the first hours of the crisis and by the fact that in the Secretariat at Geneva there was evidently developing a strong anti-Japanese sentiment. Under these conditions delay, difficult to avoid at best, became inevitable, and when at last Japan itself was ready for the Lytton Commission, the Japanese conquest of Manchuria was practically assured.

It is a distortion of perspective, however, to concentrate entirely upon the failure of the United States and the organization of the League of Nations to cooperate in the critical hours when such cooperation might have been effective. For both the French and the British governments, which had been the mainstay of the League up to that time, were loathe to assume their full responsibilities under the Covenant for the maintenance of peace in so remote a part of the world as Manchuria. The French had always concentrated upon the League as an instrument of European peace. The British had no desire to be the sole instrument of League sanction in the Far East. In other words, the situation revealed a fundamental weakness in the actual working out of collective security, a failure to realize the full implication of that article of the Covenant which stated that any war or threat of war anywhere in the world was a matter of concern to all members of the League, which "should take any action that may be deemed wise and effectual to safeguard the peace of nations." Unfortunately, when this obligation of the Covenant was for the first time tested by a great Power, not only was the incident in a distant part of the world, but the European nations were face to face with grave economic and political crises at home. Under these conditions it was almost inevitable that coordinated international action should be difficult and slow. The Japanese militarists had evidently calculated their initial moves with these factors in mind. In any case, the situation played directly into their hands, with the result that they were able, in the succeeding years, to seize and maintain the power in their own government which led them to attempt the conquest not only of China, but of all Asia.

The narrative which follows is therefore much more than a study in the history of diplomacy. It also brings to light some of the most essential elements in the future maintenance of international peace.

JAMES T. SHOTWELL

Columbia University
December, 1947

AUTHOR'S PREFACE

ACKNOWLEDGMENT is gratefully made to Dr. James T. Shotwell for his continuing interest in my work, for his constructive criticism and his encouragement; to Professor Nathaniel Peffer for the insistent but friendly way in which he presented opposing points of view, thereby making me examine my own more thoroughly; to Mr. Arthur Sweetser who read the first draft of my manuscript and whose comments illuminated many an obscure situation; to Mr. Clarence Streit for an invaluable interview in the early days of my study and to Mr. Benjamin Gerig for a similar interview. There are others, of course, too numerous to mention by name, to whom I am deeply indebted for encouragement and criticism. To my sister Elizabeth, however, goes a very special word of appreciation for the long hours of typing and proofreading, and for the gentle prodding about details which needed attention. To Miss Matilda Berg, my long-suffering editor, my sympathy and my thanks!

SARA R. SMITH

Parkersburg, W. Va.
December, 1947

CONTENTS

Foreword, by James T. Shotwell   vii

I. The Stage Is Set   3

II. The 65th Session of the Council, September, 1931   22

III. First Interlude: October 1 to 12   81

IV. Prentiss Gilbert Sits with the Council   93

V. Second Interlude: October 24 to November 16   128

VI. The Paris Meeting   170

VII. Anticlimax   225

Index   263

THE MANCHURIAN CRISIS

1931-1932

MANCHURIA, 1931-1932

BASED ON THE LYTTON REPORT MAPS

I
THE STAGE IS SET

INTRODUCTORY.—In the field of international affairs the years between the first and second world wars may be divided roughly into two periods. The first was an era of promise, the second of failure: the first was highlighted by the development of machinery for peace and by the signing of special treaties looking toward the avoidance of war and the eventual removal of many of its causes; the second was marked by ever deepening gloom, by rapid deterioration in almost every phase of relations between nations, by the violation of treaties, by the growth of aggressive policies and by the continual undermining of the agencies of collective security. The year 1931 is the dividing line between these two periods and the Mukden Incident of September 18–19, the first of the steps leading downward to the abyss of global war.

Much has been written about the Manchurian crisis thus precipitated into the lap of a world not only unwilling but unprepared psychologically to meet and control the situation. There has been little attempt, however, to bring together the whole story as it concerns the League and the United States in the crucial period of the 65th Council meeting. To most Americans this story has been more or less a closed book, a seemingly impenetrable mystery, accompanied by misunderstanding and misinterpretation and clouded by lack of knowledge. Out of this confusion have grown two legends, two myths, which through their constant reiteration have become all too firmly fixed in the minds of radio listeners and newspaper readers in this country. The first is that we went out on a limb in 1932—in Secretary Stimson's note of January 7th and his letter to Senator Borah of February 24 [1]—that Great Britain left us there high and dry, and that this failure to back us up in our attempt to solve the problem is the real and only reason why Japan was not

[1] See Chap. VII.

stopped at the inception of her march of conquest. The second is that we cooperated to the fullest extent with the League of Nations, and the subsequent failure to settle the Manchurian question satisfactorily proved that the principle of collective security was unsound. Anything approaching continued general acceptance of these two myths by the American people is dangerous to our future policy regarding world organization for peace and security. They have furnished and will continue to furnish ammunition for the isolationists—who are not all dead, nor were they all converted by Pearl Harbor; on the contrary, they are, perhaps, all the more menacing because they have been driven underground by public opinion and must therefore seek their goals by secret and devious means. The first myth is even now effective propaganda for those who would divide the United States and Great Britain. It becomes imperative, therefore, to study these legends carefully and to make the real situations known.

Even within the restricted scope of this study—the case as it was handled by the Council of the League and the United States in 1931 and 1932—there is no claim that the whole story is here revealed. Much of the material is still not available in published form since the State Department files were closed to research in 1939. Moreover, there are many intangibles to be considered which add difficulty to the study, factors of personalities, of domestic political and economic situations in various countries, and of conflicting national interests. In many cases it has been necessary to read a great deal between the lines and this may have led to mistaken conclusions. Such conclusions are open to criticism but they have been honestly reached and not made to prove a predetermined point.

ALL THE WORLD'S A STAGE.—Annus Terriblis! So Arnold Toynbee characterizes the year 1931;[2] and it is against the somber backdrop of this tragic year that the Manchurian crisis must be considered. Perplexing at best, the failure to stop Japan becomes utterly incomprehensible unless one keeps in mind the catastrophic economic and political conditions which prevailed the world over.

[2] Arnold J. Toynbee, ed., *Survey of International Affairs, 1931* (London, 1932).

No detailed discussion of these situations is needed here; merely to mention the outstanding events of those months is to bring them back all too clearly to those who lived through them. It was in this dark year of 1931 that the decrease in world trade, the growth of tariff barriers and exchange restrictions became so marked as to alarm the general public as well as those whose vital interests were concerned. It was in this same year that the unstable and tottering finances of Austria and Germany finally collapsed, carrying with them the whole structure of international payments and causing serious financial crises in every European country. In vain had President Hoover tried to prevent this by means of the moratorium, a device which might well have succeeded had the collapse been caused by a local rather than a world-wide dislocation.

In Great Britain the summer and early fall were marked by a series of internal crises whose far-reaching influence on later world events cannot be too greatly emphasized. The attempt to balance the budget by decreasing pensions and unemployment benefits brought about the repudiation of MacDonald and Snowden by the Labour Party and the setting up of a national government with Mac-Donald as Prime Minister, backed by a small minority of Labourites and Liberals, plus almost the entire Conservative membership of the House of Commons.[3] This was late in August but not until the last of October were conditions deemed sufficiently settled to make an election desirable, an election which, in the words of Lord Cecil,[4]

smashed the Labour Party and handed over the Government of the country to groups which as the months went on became more and more conservative in their political complexion. . . . The result of what has happened has, in fact, been . . . in foreign affairs, disastrous.

Even though MacDonald remained as Prime Minister and nine out of the twenty members of the new Cabinet were either National

[3] The deficit at this time was approximately 120 million pounds. Governmental salaries were also to be cut and a slight increase in taxes was provided. Labour repudiated the measure as economy at the expense of the working classes.
[4] Viscount Cecil, *A Great Experiment* (London, 1941), p. 218. The national government as distinguished from the Conservatives won a majority of nearly 500 seats; the Conservatives, with a total of 471 seats, had a majority of 325 over all other groups and became the dominant partner in the national government. Labour had a meager 52 seats as opposed to 265 in the previous Parliament.

Liberals or National Labourites, this was truly a Conservative government and the change was almost immediately reflected in a new attitude toward Geneva. Perhaps even more disturbing to the English spirit were two events of mid-September for these struck at the very heart of English pride and tradition—-the navy and the stability of the pound sterling. On September 15, almost on the eve of Mukden, there was serious insubordination, if not mutiny, in the fleet at Invergordon, and on September 21, the day China appealed her case to the Council of the League, Great Britain went off the gold standard.[5] The two events were not unconnected and together they shook the stoutest of British hearts, while the second rocked the entire financial world to its very foundations. Small wonder that the average Briton paid as little attention to the fate of China in 1931 as to that of Czechoslovakia in 1938.

As to the United States, only the very young among us need to be reminded of the deepening depression and the staggering number of bank failures in September and October of 1931. Faced with the actual or prospective loss of his job, watching with anxious eyes the rapid dwindling of his savings or the loss of his investments, seeing also the growing lines of the unemployed, the "no-men-wanted" signs and, finally, the lengthening bread lines, the average American was as indifferent to what was happening on the other side of the Pacific as was his British cousin. A factor in the situation not so readily remembered, however, nor so easily recognized as significant, are the elections of the preceding November. Midterm elections frequently show a trend away from the party in power, but in 1930, as had happened with the Democrats in 1918, the swing was so great as to destroy entirely both presidential leadership and Republican party control in both houses of Congress. As a result, Congress was so badly split that little effective action could be taken even on vital economic matters. The effect of these elections on President Hoover was unfortunate; the evidence of a general turning away from the party of "normalcy" in these decidedly "un"-normal times dimmed his prospects for reelection in 1932, while the split in Congress made it next to impossible for him to put through

[5] For an excellent acount of these events and the close relation between them, see Toynbee, *op. cit.,* pp. 109–10. See also p. 28, below.

any of his policies and increased his hesitancy about offending the isolationist group which showed increased strength in both parties.

Personalities are frequently as important as world conditions. It is men who make and administer laws, who formulate and carry out policy. No constitution, no treaty, no covenant, is entirely proof against the fallibility of human beings. Therefore the men who handled the case in Geneva and those who were at the helm in the world's capitals are vital to our story.

Let us look first at Geneva where the Assembly was about to close a long and difficult session and the 65th Council was about to open when the Far Eastern powder keg blew up. Heading the British delegation was Lord Cecil,[6] foremost advocate of the League in his country, one of the authors of the Covenant, and a recognized authority on League procedure. His personal prestige in Geneva was always great but as an exponent of British policy his position was much stronger in September and October than after the general election of October 27. With the debacle of the Labour Party and the advent of Sir John Simon at the Foreign Office, Cecil's influence in Downing Street waned. In the October session Lord Reading, who was Foreign Minister from August through October, headed the delegation but Cecil was present and was the actual head most of the time. Lord Reading did not tie Cecil's hands to any extent, but rather followed his lead. In marked contrast to this is the situation in Paris in November and December. Again Cecil was deputy for the Foreign Minister and met with the Council more often than not, but this time it was Sir John Simon who, whether he was in London or in Paris, determined British policy. Certain shifts in Cecil's position relative to China and Japan can be accounted for most easily by this changing attitude toward the League in administration circles in London. Commenting on an incident which oc-

[6] Concerning his appointment Cecil writes (*op. cit.*, p. 219): "The resignation of the Labour Government took place on August 24th and the Assembly was to meet on September 7th. Evidently outgoing ministers could not take part in the British delegation and the new Government were too much harassed to do so either. Accordingly, I was asked to go to Geneva, my own political attitude being one of reluctant support of the new Government. I agreed, provided I was given adequate assistance, and Lords Lytton and Astor, with Mrs. Alfred Lyttleton and Sir Arthur Salter were appointed as members of the delegation."

curred in 1923 when he took office under Stanley Baldwin as Lord Privy Seal in charge of League Affairs, Lord Cecil writes:

> I have mentioned this incident because it illustrates the official Conservative attitude to the League, then and thereafter. It was not that my colleagues, then or thereafter, were hostile to the League. The Prime Minister, Mr. Baldwin, was temperamentally in its favor. But both he and others regarded it as a kind of excrescence which must be carefully prevented from having too much influence on our foreign policy. Geneva, to them, was a strange place in which a new-fangled machine existed in order to enable foreigners to influence or even control our international action. For us to do anything to help it either with money or diplomatic action was, in their view, an effort of national altruism which could rarely be justified. It is true that those Ministers who actually visited Geneva and took part in the work of the League, like Lord Balfour, Mr. Edward Wood (now Lord Halifax) and, later Sir Austen Chamberlain, usually took a different view. But most of them never went there, and among that number were both the Prime Minister, Mr. Baldwin, and Foreign Secretary, Lord Curzon.
>
> To me this attitude was heartbreaking.[7]

Lord Cecil might have added that although Sir John Simon was a member of the Liberal party when he took office, he was a strict conservative as regards this view of the League and later contact with Geneva did not change his attitude in the least.

Side by side with Cecil as an advocate of collective security and as an untiring worker for world peace stands Aristide Briand, then Foreign Minister of France. Despite his great personal prestige at home and abroad, Briand was hampered by the fact that as regards both the League and action against Japan he lacked the support of the permanent staff of his office at the Quai d'Orsay. These officials, together with almost the whole of the nationalistic section of the French press, looked upon Japan as "the good policeman" of Asia.[8] Tied by pressing problems and by his own personal illness—the shadow of death was on him even in September—he did not attend the first sessions of the Council but most fortunately served as president during the second and third. In September he was represented by René Massigli, chief of the French Foreign Office at

[7] *Ibid.*, pp. 145–46.   [8] See p. 132, below.

the League of Nations, of whose high qualities Hugh Wilson, American Minister to Switzerland, writes: [9]

René Massigli was the right hand man of the French delegation. An exact mentality, a retentive memory, an inexhaustible capacity for hard work, coupled with participation in nearly every French delegation to international gatherings since the Treaty of Versailles, gave Massigli a competence and authority in League discussions out of all proportion to his official position in France.

Spain, in order of rotation, held the office of president in the 65th Council and was represented by her Foreign Minister, Alejandro Lerroux. This was not a fortunate circumstance, for Lerroux was a poor presiding officer, ineffectual and hesitant; unacquainted with League procedure he leaned heavily on Cecil during the Council meetings and on his colleague, Salvador de Madariaga, for aid and direction between meetings. The German and Italian delegations also were headed by their Foreign Ministers, Dr. Julius Curtius and Count Dino Grandi, respectively, both of whom apparently would have followed any clear-cut lead from Cecil and Massigli in support of the League. The latter in turn looked to Washington for the same sign; but this, unfortunately, did not come at the right moment.

Representing China was the veteran diplomat, Dr. Alfred Sao-ke Sze, Chinese Minister to London. Educated in the United States he spoke English fluently. Suave, keen-eyed and keen-witted, he was never caught off-guard, never fell into the many traps set for him by his opponent, Kenkichi Yoshizawa, Japanese Ambassador to London and head of his country's delegation to the League. Superficially the contrast between the two men was striking, but there is a wide divergence in the estimates of Yoshizawa and his ability. Contemporary accounts refer to him as halting, inept, mumbling, speaking poor English and poorer French. Lord Cecil supports this view [10] but others say that when he so desired Yoshizawa used very precise English, that he was a careful and exact but slow thinker, and his halting speech was a technique to cover up and gain

[9] Hugh R. Wilson, *Diplomat between Wars* (New York, 1941), p. 235.
[10] Cecil, *op. cit.*, p. 222.

time. That he was not without great ability in diplomatic negotiations is evidenced by his later career, which also showed that his loyalty was to the army group rather than to his chief, Baron Shidehara, the Foreign Minister. Outside the Council, but just as important were several others who also played a vital part in the proceedings. Heading the permanent staff of the League was the able and efficient Secretary-General, Sir Eric Drummond (now the Earl of Perth). Ten years' experience in directing the work of the Secretariat had taught him all the pitfalls to be avoided, developed his natural administrative bent and proved his devotion to the organization to which he gave the prime years of his life. Constantly on guard to prevent mistakes in procedure he was accused by Tokyo of being strongly anti-Japanese when, as a matter of fact, he was probably only pro-League. Ably seconding him was Arthur Sweetser, senior American member of the staff and official liaison between Ambassador Dawes and the Council at the Paris meeting.[11] Not so much in the public eye as the members of the Council, these men and many others like them worked night and day, untiringly, to prevent a breakdown in the machinery for collective action against an actual or potential aggressor. That their efforts were not successful was not their fault, for in their hands was not the making of policy but only the administration of it after the States Members of the League had decided on a course of action.

Mention has already been made of Salvador de Madariaga, whose place in the history of the disarmament movement is comparable to that of Cecil and Briand in the development of the machinery of peace. This brilliant Spaniard not only played an important part behind the scenes in the September sessions of the Council but became an active member in the October and the November-December meetings. There the rapier shafts of his quick mind penetrated the guard of Yoshizawa's stolid exterior on more than one critical occasion and ably supported the efforts of his British and French colleagues.

Since the United States was not a member of the League, this

[11] For further details of Mr. Sweetser's very important contribution to the case see p. 158, below.

country had no active part in the September proceedings. There were present, however, two very capable observers, Hugh Wilson, Minister to Switzerland, and Prentiss Gilbert, American Consul in Geneva.[12] Mr. Wilson was in Geneva for the meetings of the Preparatory Commission on Disarmament and as an observer at the sessions of the Assembly's Third Commission (on disarmament) when the news of Japan's adventure in Manchuria startled the world. Of his own position and that of the United States he writes:

> I was not a member of the Council, of course, but I might as well have been one since I usually met with Eric Drummond and members of the Council in the room of the Secretary General either before or after the Council's sessions, and sometimes both. The position that the United States might adopt was of overwhelming importance to these members of the League, an importance which makes somewhat ironic our inherent fear of commitment and involvement; we were certainly involved and, equally certainly, we were not committed. . . .
>
> These were eventful days not only in history but to me personally. I was dragged out of the Assembly to answer the telephone from Washington. I had constant conferences with members of the Council, the press was clamorous. Without appearing at the Council table it was obvious that I represented the decisive factor in decisions which might be taken, telegrams had to be sent and deciphered at all hours of the night. As usual our staff was entirely inadequate but they worked at a feverish pace.[13]

In Washington the four men most concerned with formulating and directing our policy in this affair all had some degree of first-hand knowledge of the Far East. President Hoover's experience was that of the engineer on professional trips in various parts of the world, during one of which he was caught in the siege of Tientsin by the Boxers; Secretary of State Stimson served as Governor-General of the Philippines from 1927 to 1929 and had made visits to both China and Japan. The Under Secretary, William R. Castle, Jr., had gained his knowledge through six months' service as Ambassador to Japan, while Dr. Stanley Hornbeck, Chief of the Division of Far

[12] Inasmuch as Mr. Gilbert's part in the October meetings is dealt with in detail in Chap. IV no further discussion is needed here. The same is true of Mr. Dawes and the Paris meetings, for which see Chaps. V and VI.
[13] Wilson, *op. cit.*, p. 260.

Eastern Affairs, had back of him years of teaching in Chinese government colleges. Except to note that Mr. Hoover's Quaker background probably influenced him more than isolationist sentiment did in holding Secretary Stimson back from any action which even remotely threatened the use of force, nothing more needs to be said here of either the President or his Secretary of State. The greatest conflict of personality and of opinion, however, was in the two subordinate officials, of whom little was known at the time. Castle was born in Honolulu, the grandson of missionaries, who bought land, became sugar planters, and gained considerable wealth and position in the Islands. Educated at Harvard he was appointed special assistant in the State Department and had risen to the position of Assistant Secretary when he was sent to Japan to replace Ambassador Cameron Forbes for the period of the London Naval Conference, the latter being attached to the American delegation to that conference as special advisor on Japanese affairs. When Castle was recalled to Washington at the end of June, 1930, he became Under Secretary of State; and it was from this vantage point that he wielded an enormous and, in the eyes of many persons, a pernicious influence on the course of events. While in Tokyo he seems to have become an admirer of all things Japanese and was a strong advocate of nonintervention in the affairs of both Asia and Europe. Through his background of education, rank and wealth, he moved in the same official and social circles as the Secretary of State and the President; with the latter he was on terms of considerable intimacy and appears to have been the usual medium of communication between the White House and the State Department, at least during the early weeks of the Manchurian crisis. Hardworking, capable Dr. Hornbeck had taught American history and political science in Chinese colleges and Chinese history and political science in American colleges before he entered the State Department. Better versed in the Far Eastern situation than the others, he knew what neither Stimson nor Castle seems to have known: that the time was ripe for trouble in Manchuria; that if Japanese plans for the expansion of their control in that area were to be carried out they must be got under way before the consolidation of Chiang Kai-shek's position in China and the growing cooperation between that General and Chang Hsueh-liang in Manchuria made it impossible. Hornbeck bombarded the Secretary of State with memoranda to that effect. But the difference in diplomatic rank plus Castle's friendship with the President gave the Under Secretary the inside track and this had unfortunate results in the making of policy, the issuing of statements to the press, and in the very different attitudes adopted by the Department toward Katsuji Debuchi, the Japanese Ambassador, and Yung Kwai, the Chinese Chargé d'Affaires.[14]

In Tokyo, a Minseito cabinet had been in office since 1929, succeeding that of Baron General Giichi Tanaka. The Prime Minister, Reijiro Wakatsuki, had been the leading delegate to the London Naval Conference and had succeeded Yuko Hamaguchi as Premier after the latter's assassination in November, 1930, at the hands of the younger army group who opposed the signing and ratification of the treaty. Both Wakatsuki and his Foreign Minister, Baron Kijuro Shidehara, were liberals, advocates of international friendship and diplomacy rather than force as the means of realizing Japan's goals in East Asia. Far from liberal, however, was the Minister of War, General Minami, whose peculiar position resulting from the dual control exercised by the civilian and military elements of the cabinet is discussed in some detail in the following chapter.[15] Another figure, known in contemporary accounts only as the Foreign Office Spokesman, who played an important and complicating part, is Toshio Shiratori. Country bred and well educated, with diplomatic training in posts in Washington and London, Shiratori became the spokesman at the time of the Japanese invasion of Manchuria. Until then the office had been an inconspicuous one; Shiratori made it not only conspicuous but dramatic; more than that, he made it an agency for undermining the policies and plans of the liberals in the cabinet and particularly of the department of which he was supposedly the mouthpiece. Closely tied to the army group, with connections so influential that it was impossible to remove him no matter how disloyal to Shidehara he proved to be, he spoke "with

---

[14] See pp. 85–86, below. See also Stimson, *The Far Eastern Crisis* (New York, 1936), p. 4, for an expression of the Secretary's high personal regard for Debuchi.
[15] See pp. 26–27.

such freedom and disregard for higher officials of the Foreign Office and Japanese envoys abroad that he became known as the 'outspokesman' of the Foreign Office." [16] Ardent disciple of Baron Tanaka he was also an advocate of the policy of dividing Great Britain and the United States, a policy which was followed with considerable success down to the outbreak of World War II.

In China the situation at this time was not so much of personalities as of general conditions. As has already been indicated, under the leadership of the "Young Marshal," Chang Hsueh-liang, Manchuria was drawing closer to China,[17] while China was drawing closer together under Chiang Kai-shek. It was now or never for Japan, but whether it was the young officer group in the army or the army itself which took the bit between its teeth we may never know. Wilfrid Fleisher says it was the former and that they had to persuade General Honjo, commander in Manchuria, to their way. This is not borne out, however, by another statement of Fleisher's regarding "proof" in his possession that the army in Manchuria had been preparing for this move for weeks. Such preparations could

[16] Wilfrid Fleisher, *The Volcanic Isle* (Garden City, N.Y., 1941), p. 252. Some excerpts from Fleisher's colorful account of Shiratori's career (pp. 252–56) are given.

"Shiratori's meetings with foreign newspapermen were held daily and produced such sensational items at times that no foreign correspondent could afford to be absent from any of the conferences. He had a better judgment of news value than any other Japanese official I have ever met." . . .

"Outside the government, Toshio Shiratori had been a powerful figure and his views have largely governed Japanese foreign policy in the last year [1941]. He was one of the original negotiators of the Anti-Comintern Pact, the strongest advocate of the axis alliance, and he urged Japan to make a non-aggression treaty with the Soviet Union so that she might turn her attention to her 'southward expansion policy.' He has said that the Dutch East Indies are a matter of life and death to Japan 'economically and strategically' and he has urged a 'determined policy in southeast Asia.' " . . .

"Shiratori is one of the most ambitious men in Japanese life and has long hoped to become Foreign Minister and to be able to direct foreign policy openly and at his will."

[17] The "Old Marshal," Chang Tso-lin, had, during the greater part of his life inclined toward a policy of collaboration with Japan but he came to resent the increasing attempts of that government to control his actions, especially in regard to the factional strife in China in the twenties. Disregarding Japanese advice to steer clear of the situation he became head of the northern militarists alliance. Returning to Mukden after a defeat at the hands of the Kuomintang Army his train was wrecked by an explosion just outside the city and the Marshal was killed. The guilt of the Japanese was never established, but there was every reason to believe that it was a maneuver to get rid of a troublesome factor in Manchuria. If they expected the son to be more amenable to discipline they were greatly disappointed.

have been made only with the knowledge and consent of Honjo.[18]

Probably more important than any other single element in the background, with the possible exception of the world economic crisis, was the absence of the United States from the scene when the tragedy opens, when the Council met on September 21 to consider the case formally. Consider for a moment that crowded room in the old Palace of the League on the Quai Woodrow Wilson with its bronze plaque in memory of the American President, "founder of the League of Nations." It is not a large room nor is it so imposing as the Council Chamber in the new Palace on the hill overlooking the city. Here are gathered the representatives of the States Members of the League, the observers, the press, and as many interested visitors as could be jammed into the corners. There is an air of excitement, of tension, a craning of necks accompanied by whispers as the members of the Council enter: "There's Cecil. See him? the tall one!" . . . "Who's that?" . . . "Where's Briand?" "He's sick, didn't you know? But there's Massigli, he's all right. He knows what to do." . . . And they take their places at the long table— Spain, Great Britain, France, . . . China, Japan. Only Russia and the United States are not there.

The spectators drawn to this international capital for the meetings of the Assembly did not fail to grasp the significance of the scene, and even the presence of Hugh Wilson sitting in friendly proximity to the Secretary General could not remove that sense of the absence of the United States at a time when great events were in the making and decisions as vital to us as to any nation represented at the Council table were to be made. Nor was it merely that, in a major crisis where our own interests were concerned, we were not present. That would have been dramatic enough, but heavy in the air lay the cumulative effect of the years of estrangement between the League and the United States—our refusal to join, then our gradual but grudging recognition of its existence, the ever-present uncertainty as to what we would do, all resulting in a psychosis which could not be overcome in a few short weeks in the autumn of 1931.

[18] Wilfrid Fleisher, *Our Enemy Japan* (Garden City, N.Y., 1942), pp. 25–26.

PROLOGUE.—Like the economic collapse of the preceding summer, the Mukden incident was not the result of a temporary crisis, of a flare-up between Chinese and Japanese troops, one outside, the other inside the railway zone indicated by the treaties of 1906.[19] To review even briefly the background of this situation would be to review the whole history of the Far East since the Sino-Japanese war of 1894–95. Suffice it to say that because of this war, the conflicting economic and political interests of the Great Powers in eastern Asia, the Russo-Japanese war and its resulting treaties (some of which China never acknowledged as legitimate and binding), and the Twenty-one Demands forced upon a helpless China by Japan during World War I, Manchuria had become the tinder box of Asia. To be kept in mind also, are the treaties growing out of the first World War, in which the nations of the world not only made an honest and sincere attempt to prepare the way for peace but exerted a special effort to prevent China from becoming the prey of any one power or combination of powers. Then, as now, a strong, independent China was an essential to peace in the East, and the fact that they had in mind the risks they themselves would run if, out of the explosive situation, there should occur another such scramble for territory as that in Africa during the nineteenth century, does not lessen the value of what they tried to accomplish through the self denying ordinances of the Four Power Consultative pact and the Nine Power Treaty. Having agreed not to build further fortifications in their Pacific possessions as compensation to Japan for the renunciation of the Anglo-Japanese alliance and the return of Shantung to China, the Western powers trusted that country to keep both the spirit and the letter of these engagements, with results all too well known.

That Manchuria was the common back yard of Japan and Asiatic

---

[19] The Report of the League of Nations Commission of Enquiry on Manchuria (cited hereafter as the *Lytton Report*) has an excellent short account of the railway and other treaties giving Japan special rights in Manchuria in Chap. III, Secs. 3 and 4, pp. 42–55. For longer discussions see Walter C. Young, *The International Relations of China* (Chicago, 1929) and *Japan's Special Position in Manchuria* (Baltimore, 1931); W. W. Willoughby, *The Sino-Japanese Controversy and the League of Nations* (Baltimore, 1935); Owen Lattimore, *Manchuria, Cradle of Conflict* (New York, 1932).

Russia as well as an integral if not an integrated part of China added to the inflammable character of the situation. And the summer of 1931 found the fuel piled high for the bonfires of the autumn. The unsettled political conditions in China throughout the twenties, the strong nationalistic and antiforeign sentiment evidenced in the student strikes and numerous kidnapings which marked the later years of that decade, the divisive influence of the war lords, all must be kept in mind. Yet, as has already been said, China was growing closer together under Chiang, just as Manchuria under the Young Marshal was growing closer to China. It was the need for haste because of this growing tie rather than any increase in the activities or numbers of bandits and war lords which precipitated the inevitable crisis in 1931.

In Japan, too, matters were coming to a head in that internal political struggle which marked the years from 1920 on. Those who favored the "strong policy" of Baron Tanaka had apparently lost so much ground to the liberals in recent elections that there was not only the probability that the army would have its appropriations cut but there might even be a constitutional change which would do away with the dual control of the government and subordinate the army and navy to the authority of a civil administration as in the United States and Great Britain instead of having the cabinet at the mercy of the armed services. Thus, to those groups which felt that the army and navy should control the destiny of Japan it seemed absolutely necessary to embark upon some adventure which would arouse the nationalist fervor of the people and swing important interests such as those of the Mitsui and Mitsubishi clans into the reactionary column. Events in Manchuria and China played into their hands.

The already great tension between the two countries was heightened during those summer months by anti-Korean riots in Manchuria, by anti-Chinese riots in Korea and by the death of Captain Nakamura at the hands of Chinese soldiers in a remote section of Manchuria. Of the last event the Lytton Report says:

Captain Shintaro Nakamura was a Japanese military officer on active duty and, as was admitted by the Japanese Government, was on a mission under the orders of the Japanese Army. While passing through Harbin, where his passport was examined by the Chinese authorities, he represented himself as an agricultural expert. He was at that time warned that the region in which he intended to travel was a bandit-ridden area, and this fact was noted on his passport. He was armed and carried patent medicine which, according to the Chinese, included narcotic drugs for non-medical purposes.

On June 9th, accompanied by three interpreters and assistants, Captain Nakamura left Ilikotu Station on the western section of the Chinese Eastern Railway. When he had reached a point some distance in the interior, in the direction of Taonan, he and the other members of his party were placed under detention by Chinese soldiers under Kuan Yuheng, the commander of the Third Regiment of the Reclamation Army. Several days later, about June 27th, he and his companions were shot by Chinese soldiers and their bodies were cremated to conceal the evidence of the deed.

The Japanese insisted that the killing of Captain Nakamura and his companions was unjustified and showed arrogant disrespect for the Japanese Army and nation; they asserted that the Chinese authorities in Manchuria delayed to institute official enquiries into the circumstances, were reluctant to assume responsibility for the occurrence, and were insincere in their claim that they were making every effort to ascertain the facts in the case.

The Chinese declared, at first, that Captain Nakamura and his party were detained pending an examination of their permits, which, according to custom, were required of foreigners traveling in the interior; that they had been treated well; and that Captain Nakamura was shot by a sentry while endeavouring to make his escape. Documents, including a Japanese military map and two diaries, they stated, were found on his person, which proved that he was either a military spy or an officer on special military mission.[20]

The incident aroused the Japanese army and press to fever pitch, and the utmost use was made of it to incite the Japanese people, who were told only that one of the Son of Heaven's officers had been treacherously killed by the barbarous Chinese, without the added information that he was traveling in plain clothes and carrying narcotics. But in spite of all the hullabaloo a satisfactory conclusion was on the point of being reached between Shidehara and the Nanking Government—satisfactory, that is, to all but the army—when

[20] *Lytton Report*, pp. 63–64.

the military coup at Mukden threw the fat into the fire again.

For the most impartial account of the events of September 18–19 with whose after effects we are to be concerned in the following chapters we again have recourse to the words of the Lytton Commission:

On the morning of Saturday, September 19th, the population of Mukden woke to find their city in the hands of Japanese troops. During the night sounds of firing had been heard, but there was nothing unusual in this; it had been a nightly experience throughout the week, as the Japanese had been carrying out night manoeuvres involving vigorous rifle fire and machine gun firing. True that, on the night of September 18th, the booming of guns and the sound of shells caused some alarm to the few that distinguished them, but the majority of the population considered the firing to be merely another repetition of Japanese manoeuvres, perhaps rather noisier than usual. (P. 67.)

According to the Japanese versions, Lieutenant Kawamoto, with six men under his command, was on patrol duty on the night of September 18th, practising defence exercises along the track of the South Manchuria Railway to the north of Mukden. They were proceeding southwards in the direction of Mukden. The night was dark but clear and the field of vision was not wide. When they reached a point at which a small road crosses the line, they heard the noise of a loud explosion a little way behind them. They turned and ran back, and after going about 200 yards they discovered that a portion of one of the rails on the down track had been blown out. The explosion took place at the point of junction of two rails; the end of each rail had been cleanly severed, creating a gap in the line of 31 inches. On arrival at the site of the explosion, the patrol was fired upon from the fields on the east side of the line. Lieutenant Kawamoto immediately ordered his men to deploy and return the fire. The attacking body, estimated at five or six, then stopped firing and retreated northwards. The Japanese patrol at once started in pursuit and, having gone about 200 yards, they were again fired upon by a larger body, estimated at between three and four hundred. Finding himself in danger of being surrounded by this large force, Lieutenant Kawamoto then ordered one of his men to report to the Commander of the No. 3 Company, who was also engaged in night manoeuvres some 1500 yards to the north; at the same time, he ordered another of his men to telephone (by means of a box telephone near the spot) to Battalion Headquarters at Mukden for reinforcements.

At this moment the south-bound train from Changchun was heard approaching. Fearing that the train might be wrecked when it reached the damaged line, the Japanese patrol interrupted their engagement and placed detonators on the line in the hope of warning the train in time. The train, however, proceeded at full speed. When it reached the site of the explosion it was seen to sway and heel over to the side, but it recovered and passed on without stopping. As the train was due at Mukden at 10:30 p. m̀., where it arrived punctually, it must have been about 10 o'clock p. m., according to Lieutenant Kawamoto, when he first heard the explosion.

Fighting was then resumed. . . .

Lieutenant Kawamoto's patrol, reinforced by Captain Kawashima's Company, was still sustaining the fire of the Chinese troops concealed in the tall kaoliang grass, when the two Companies arrived from Mukden. Although his force was then only 500, and he believed the Chinese army in the North Barracks numbered 10,000, Lieutenant-Colonel Shinamoto at once ordered an attack on the Barracks. . . . When the Japanese reached the North Barracks, which were described as glittering with electric light, an attack was made by the 3rd Company, which succeeded in occupying a corner of the left wing. The attack was vigorously contested by the Chinese troops within, and there was fierce fighting for some hours . . . by 6 o'clock a. m. the entire barracks were captured at the cost of two Japanese privates killed and twenty-two wounded. (Pp. 67–68.)

According to the Chinese version, the Japanese attack on the Barracks (Peitaying) was entirely unprovoked and came as a complete surprise. On the night of September 18th, all the soldiers of the 7th Brigade, numbering about 10,000 were in the North Barracks. As instructions had been received from Marshal Chang Hsueh-liang on September 6th that special care was to be taken to avoid any clash with Japanese troops in the tense state of feeling existing at the time, the sentries at the walls of the Barracks were armed only with dummy rifles. For the same reason the west gate in the mud wall surrounding the camp which gave access to the railway had been closed. The Japanese had been carrying out night manoeuvres around the barracks on the nights of September 14th, 15th, 16th and 17th. . . . At 10 p. m. (of the 18th) the sound of a loud explosion was heard, immediately followed by rifle fire. This was reported over the telephone by the Chief of Staff to the Commanding Officer, General Wang I-Cheh. . . . While the Chief of Staff was still at the telephone, news was brought to him that the Japanese were attacking the barracks. . . . As soon as the attack began, the Chief of Staff . . . again reported to General Wang I-Cheh by telephone. The latter replied that no resistance was to be offered. (P. 69.)

The only resistance was offered by the 620th Regiment quartered in the north-east building and the second building south of it. . . . [In the course of their retreat they] found themselves cut off, and had no option but to fight their way through. They started to break through at 5 a. m., but did not get completely clear until 7 a. m. This was the only actual fighting that took place in the barracks and was responsible for most of the casualties. (P. 70.)

. . . the Commission has come to the following conclusions:

Tense feeling undoubtedly existed between the Japanese and Chinese military forces. The Japanese, as was explained to the Commission in evidence, had a carefully prepared plan to meet the case of possible hostilities between themselves and the Chinese. On the night of September 18th–19th, this plan was put into operation with swiftness and precision. The Chinese, in accordance with the instructions referred to on page 69, had no plan of attacking the Japanese troops, or of endangering the lives or property of Japanese nationals at this particular time or place. They made no concerted or authorised attack on the Japanese forces and were surprised by the Japanese attack and subsequent operations. An explosion undoubtedly occurred on or near the railroad between 10 and 10:30 p. m. on September 18th, but the damage, if any to the railroad did not in fact prevent the punctual arrival of the southbound train from Changchun, and was not in itself sufficient to justify military action. The military operations of the Japanese troops during this night, which have been described above cannot be regarded as measures of legitimate self-defence. In saying this the Commission does not exclude the hypothesis that the officers on the spot may have thought they were acting in self-defence. (P. 71.)

II

THE 65TH SESSION OF THE COUNCIL
September, 1931

SEPTEMBER 18 TO 21.—At ten o'clock on the night of September 18, 1931, the so-called Mukden incident occurred. Approximately twenty-six hours later [1] the affair was brought to the attention of the Council of the League of Nations and within three days China had appealed to the Council under Article 11 of the Covenant and to the United States under the Kellogg Pact.[2]

It was recognized from the start that this was to be an important case in League history, one which would strengthen or weaken the whole structure of collective security so painstakingly built up since the first World War. Press correspondents in Geneva and in the world capitals left the reading public in no doubt as to its significance. Statesmen and diplomats were keenly aware of its implications.[3] Supporters of the League began to marshal their forces while those more concerned with the special interests of certain countries seem also to have gone to work. This is not to say that these latter forces were trying to destroy world peace or even the League, but merely that they saw the world through different spectacles. Had the word appeasement been in general use then as it is now it would certainly have been applied to the work of those in Paris and London who undermined the influence of Briand and Cecil in this crisis.[4]

The situation in Geneva was favorable. The Assembly was in session and had unanimously elected China to a seat on the Council so that both parties to the dispute were equally represented. In

[1] The differences in time between Washington and Tokyo, Geneva and Tokyo, and so on, must be kept in mind.
[2] *Conditions in Manchuria*, U.S. Sen. Doc. 55, 72d Cong., 1st Sess., p. 3. This document is hereafter referred to as *Conditions in Manchuria*.
[3] See Mr. Stimson's account in the *Far Eastern Crisis* (pp. 4 ff.) for the situation in Washington, his own consternation at the news, and Debuchi's canceled passage.
[4] I have no documentation for this statement; it is based on undercurrents running through contemporary accounts in newspapers, periodicals, etc. See Constantine Brown, "French Policy in the Far East," *Asia*, May, 1932.

view of Japan's later insistence that China did not deserve recognition as an organized state it is interesting to note that China had Japan's full support in this election. *Ad hoc* representation would have been extended her as an interested party, but her undisputed election placed her in a stronger position.

The sixty-fifth session of the Council opened at five o'clock on the afternoon of September 19. In private meeting the agenda was adopted and the newly elected members, China and Panama, were welcomed. The Council then went into public session and Kenkichi Yoshizawa took the floor. He said that

according to information which had appeared that day in the press, an incident had occurred on the previous evening in the neighbourhood of the town of Mukden. He was anxious immediately to communicate to the Council—in accordance, moreover, with a desire expressed by the President—the first information he had received that morning. Unfortunately, it contained very few details. A collision had occurred between the Japanese and Chinese troops in the neighbourhood of Mukden, near the South Manchuria Railway. Immediately on hearing the news, the Japanese Government had taken all measures possible to prevent this local incident from leading to undesirable complications. Mr. Yoshizawa had asked his Government for additional information, and was sure it would do everything possible to relieve the situation.[5]

Mr. Sze then said he "would not conceal from the Council that he had been greatly disturbed by the news from Manchuria regarding the incident mentioned by the Japanese representative. The information he had received so far seemed to indicate that the incident had not been occasioned by any act on the part of the Chinese. He would not fail to keep the Council informed of any authentic news he might receive regarding this highly regrettable incident." [6]

President Lerroux brought the brief discussion to a close by saying "he was sure the Council had heard with satisfaction that the Japanese Government would take the necessary measures to deal with the situation. His colleagues would certainly desire to join him in expressing the most sincere hopes for a prompt settlement of the question." [7]

[5] League of Nations, *Official Journal*, Dec., 1931, p. 2248 (hereafter referred to as *Official Journal*).
[6] *Ibid.*   [7] *Ibid.*

The Council then turned to other items on the agenda.

These laconic statements, quoted here in full, took only a few minutes of the Council's time and were followed by no comment from the other members. This might seem to belie the assertion that all were alive to the significance of the occasion, but back of the statements lay hours of anxious discussion and painstaking diplomatic effort. All Geneva and much of the world had been asking whether the League would take notice of the affair, or whether, one of the Great Powers being concerned, it would be allowed to go unheeded. That question had been answered and a sense of relief was felt everywhere. Mr. Yoshizawa did not bring the matter to the Council of his own free will—note his words, "in accordance, moreover, with a desire expressed by the President." Diplomatic pressure had been brought to bear upon him during the morning, and probably only the certainty that if he did not act someone else would caused him to bring the Mukden incident officially before the Council in the name of Japan.[8] Salvador de Madariaga of Spain seems to have been an active agent in this. In his Geneva letter of September 19, Clarence Streit describes the situation as follows:

Behind the scenes was Salvador de Madariaga, Spanish Ambassador to Washington, who was literally the chief go-between in getting both sides to agree to today's steps.

Back of this, Secretariat officials had been on the job since they learned of the trouble early this morning. This time the League did not have to depend entirely on press reports or diplomatic channels. There are several Secretariat officials now in China on League reconstruction work and there are several more who lately returned from China and Japan. They were thus able to establish very smooth and valuable liaison, for naturally they were in telegraphic communication.[9]

In Washington Mr. Stimson was sufficiently stirred to call the Japanese Ambassador, Katsuji Debuchi, and ask him to defer his triennial leave; the Ambassador replied that he had already canceled his passage. At the same time the State Department informed the

[8] W. W. Willoughby, *The Sino-Japanese Controversy and the League of Nations*, pp. 30–31.

[9] New York *Times*, Sept. 20, 1931, p. 28. This fact of League liaison in China is very important. It may account for the part played by Drummond, who was always active and whom the Japanese held to be unfriendly to them.

press that the Administration saw no reason for invoking the Kellogg-Briand Pact as a means of preserving peace between the Japanese and Chinese governments inasmuch as information from its own agents indicated that both Japanese and Chinese soldiers acted against the orders of their governments.

Quoting from his diary of September 19, Mr. Stimson says:

Trouble has flared up again in Manchuria. The Japanese, apparently their military element, have suddenly made a coup. They have seized Mukden and a number of strategic towns centered all along and through southern Manchuria. The situation is very confused and it is not clear whether the army is acting under a plan of the government or on its own.[10]

This confusion to which Mr. Stimson refers is important, for out of it grew many of the mistakes and much of the delay in proceedings which in the end resulted in the failure to settle the Manchurian crisis. This confusion was not caused by a simple lack of knowledge as to who was responsible for the outbreak of the Mukden incident, that is, whether Chinese or Japanese soldiers started it, with or without orders from their governments. It seems to be based on a lack of comprehension of the practical consequences of the parliamentary set-up in Japan, of the respective positions of the civil and military arms of the government. When Mr. Debuchi and Mr. Yoshizawa told Mr. Stimson and the Council of the League that their government had taken steps to control the situation their words were taken at face value for the reason that if Mr. Stimson or the Foreign Minister of any Western nation represented at Geneva had made a similar commitment it would have meant conclusive action by his government. Certainly Mr. Stimson was fully aware of the facts in the case and the only alternative to the explanation given is that he understood but for some reason failed to outline and consistently follow a policy which took cognizance of these results.

The general belief in Geneva and Washington seems to have been that the whole affair hinged on whether the action around Mukden was that of junior military officers or whether it represented a set-

[10] *Far Eastern Crisis* (New York, 1936), p. 32.

tled policy of the government. Practically everyone believed that it was the former and could therefore be localized and ended; the statements of Debuchi and Yoshizawa bore out this belief. What many seem not to have realized was that this desirable conclusion depended not on Baron Shidehara, the Foreign Minister, but on General Minami, who as Minister of War not only had the right of independent access to the Emperor but could, through his constitutional position, cause cabinets to stand or fall. If he supported the Manchurian officers then all of Shidehara's efforts would be of no avail. And General Minami had made it clear in August that he was in thorough agreement with the group which dominated the army. In a speech to division commanders he denounced Shidehara's conciliatory attitude toward China, pointed out the vital importance of Manchuria to Japan, and intimated that, if the civil government could not, the army could and would find a solution for the existing friction between the two countries. It was a belligerent speech and called forth protests both from the liberal press and from the civilian members of the cabinet. Writing on "Japanese Dual Diplomacy" some months later Hugh Byas says of this incident:

This military excursion into foreign politics made the diplomats of Tokyo rub their eyes. The vernacular press criticized General Minami. The Chief Secretary of the Cabinet saw Lieutenant-General Sugiyama, Vice-Minister of War, and pointed out the impropriety of the publication of such a speech without the knowledge or consent of the cabinet. General Sugiyama vigorously disputed this view of the political proprieties. Manchuria and Mongolia, he said, are strategically important to Japan, and it is the War Minister's duty to keep divisional commanders informed of conditions there. The Minseito, the party in power, raised a demand for the withdrawal of the War Minister, which influential peers supported. The War Minister consulted the chief of the General Staff, General Kanaya, and declined to withdraw. An experienced European diplomat in Tokyo expressed the opinion that, if Baron Shidehara did not assert his rights, as foreign minister, to be the spokesman of his government on foreign affairs, he would find that the control of foreign policy would pass from his hands into those of the army. Baron Shidehara ignored the slight to his authority, however, and the situation developed as the Ambassador had foretold. Within a month a "military situation" had come into existence in Manchuria, and the initiative was held by the army, who used it to carry out a great political plan, which has since altered the map of Asia.[11]

Despite the prophetic words of the European diplomat to whom Mr. Byas refers, the incident seems to have made little impression outside of Japan. Certainly there is no reference to it or to General Minami in the early discussions of the Manchurian crisis. It is important that this situation be kept in mind throughout the whole story of the attempted settlement of the crisis by the League and the United States.

The excellent reports of this same correspondent in the New York *Times* during these days throw light upon the situation in Tokyo. On September 19 he cabled:

Officials do not try to conceal the extreme gravity of the affair, but there are still hopes that it may prove a local incident capable of settlement as such. The atmosphere of Manchuria for weeks past has been of the kind in which guns go off of themselves. . . .

Hurried inquiries here tend to show that it was not foreseen and, as far as the Japanese Government is concerned, unpreventable.

The official theory is that the Mukden commander imagined an attack on the bridge at Hokutaiei, otherwise Peitayang, was the commencement of a concerted attack on Japanese troops. Anticipating that the cutting of the bridge was the prelude to a general assault he determined to get his blow in first and immediately attacked Chinese headquarters.

The Chinese did not offer serious resistance and the casualties were few.[12]

A later message with the same Tokyo date line says the Japanese Government will make every effort to localize the incident and does not intend to hold the city of Mukden as a pawn in the negotiations soon to begin regarding the attack on the Japanese railroad or for general settlement of the Manchurian problem. Mr. Byas continues:

Japanese troops will be withdrawn as soon as panic in Mukden subsides without waiting for progress in negotiations.

[11] *Asia*, May, 1932, pp. 317–18. See also Seijii Hishida, *Japan among the Great Powers* (New York, 1940), p. 292 and note.
[12] New York *Times*, Sept. 19, 1931. This contradicts Yoshizawa's statement at Geneva both as to casualties and Chinese resistance.

These assurances were given your correspondent tonight by a Foreign Office spokesman. They were confirmed by an official statement issued after an emergency Cabinet Council today. . . .

While this is the Foreign Office attitude the actual question now is whether the Foreign Office or the army is in charge of Japan's policy. Some Japanese circles which are usually well informed believe the army will not give up that trump card until assurances are obtained that Japanese grievances in Manchuria will be redressed. . . .

The question which dominates the entire situation is whether the army has taken the bit in its teeth and is trying to force a war policy on the government. Excited agitation in the army for the past month and hints in the press that if diplomatic authorities failed to obtain satisfaction for the murder of Captain Nakamura [13] in Manchuria, the army had its own plans ready, have not only alarmed the Chinese but have prepared the public to suspect the incident as premeditated.[14]

And on September 20:

The reaction of foreign opinion is awaited with some anxiety. . . .

The theory that the Mukden commander feared the railway outrage was a prelude to a general attack is now discredited in favor of one which says that the Japanese army, exasperated not only by the murder of Captain Shintaro Nakamura, but by the prolonged disregard of Japan's rights had determined to give the Chinese a severe lesson at the first opportunity. The attack on the railroad found them prepared. The "button was pressed" and the plan carried out.[15]

On the third day of the dispute, little more than forty-eight hours after the alleged explosion took place, China brought the case before the Council of the League under Article 11 of the Covenant and at almost the same time appealed to the United States under the Kellogg Pact. The New York *Times* of that day, Monday September 21, carried two headlines: BRITAIN SUSPENDS GOLD PAYMENTS; CHINA APPEALS TO THE LEAGUE. To the average American citizen as well as to the world's statesmen the gravity of the British decision to go off the gold standard far outweighed in importance what was happening in the Far East, a point of view not unnatural in that year of world depression when one economic crisis had followed another in such swift succession. It is

[13] See *ibid.*, Sept. 19, 1931, for a report from Tokyo on probable settlement of Nakamura case; also *Trans-Pacific*, Sept. 24, 1931.
[14] New York *Times*, Sept. 20, 1931.   [15] *Ibid.*, Sept. 21.

not surprising, therefore, that China's two actions of that day received less than the attention they deserved in Washington, and that in Geneva the representatives of both great and small powers were unable to concentrate on the Mukden incident and its settlement without giving too great weight to the possible repercussions on their own immediate interests. And Japan was not unmindful of this.

In submitting her appeal to the Council, China asked three things: that the Council take immediate steps (1) to prevent the further development of a situation endangering the peace of nations, (2) to reestablish the *status quo ante,* and (3) to determine reparations that might be found due the Republic of China; she promised at the same time to act in conformity with the League decisions in all respects. From the position thus taken China did not deviate throughout the entire proceedings, whether before the Council or the Assembly, whether under Article 11 or under Article 15. This was immediately circulated to all members of the Council which was called to meet the next morning at 10:30.

Of the United States, China asked that this government "take such steps as will insure the preservation of peace in the Far East and the upholding of the principle of peaceful settlement of international disputes." So far as this writer has been able to discover no answer of any sort was made to this appeal, though there may possibly have been a verbal answer conveyed to the Chinese chargé d'affaires. The note itself apparently did not see the light of day until the publication of "Conditions in Manchuria," early in 1932.[16] Mr. Stimson does not mention it in *The Far Eastern Crisis,* and implies in his statements to the press and throughout all the negotiations that China's case had been submitted to the League only.[17]

The State Department again expressed itself as opposed to invoking the Kellogg Pact, preferring to use the consultative clauses of the Nine Power Treaty if circumstances should require outside action.

[16] Submitted to the Senate, Jan. 26, 1932; see note 2, above.
[17] The text of this document is not included in *War and Peace, United States Foreign Policy 1931–1941,* published by the State Department in 1945, although the telegram of Nelson Johnson, our Minister to China, referring to it and giving his personal reaction to the crisis, is included. See Chap. VII, below.

The State Department is not disposed to make any move that might be misunderstood in Japan or that might needlessly complicate the problem.

Apparently there are fears that should the Kellogg Pact be invoked this might be construed as a move looking to place the blame upon the Japanese Government for aggression in Manchuria. This might make more difficult the task of the Japanese cabinet in striving for a satisfactory solution of the crisis. . . .

Should a Chinese appeal for assistance be received here the indications are that it would be taken under sympathetic consideration but not acted upon until the situation has been clarified further. No such appeal had been received when the State Department closed today.[18]

On this same date, September 21, the State Department received its first communication from the League. Since this is not included in the documents submitted to the Senate or in those published by the League it is impossible to say whether it was a formal note or an informal communication through our Minister to Switzerland, Mr. Hugh Wilson; it was, however, a message from Sir Eric Drummond, Secretary-General of the League, to Mr. Stimson "evidently to sound out our attitude and views particularly as to whether we thought the Kellogg-Briand Pact was involved. In my reply," writes Mr. Stimson,

I tried to make clear an attitude on our part of cooperation and frankness, giving him such information as we had received from Manchuria and telling him that we were following closely the development with a view to our treaty obligations under both the Nine Power Treaty and the Kellogg-Briand Pact, but were still embarrassed by lack of information. At the same time I called to his attention the evident issue between the Japanese military chiefs and their Foreign Office and my own impression that, while prepared to uphold treaty obligations, it would be wise to avoid action which might excite nationalistic feeling in Japan in support of the military against Shidehara.[19]

At this juncture two points should be made clear: the position taken by Secretary of State Stimson in regard to the Mukden incident, and the importance of that position as regards the solution of the problem. Mr. Stimson's analysis of the situation and the consequent attitude of the State Department has been fully set forth

[18] New York *Times*, Sept. 22, 1931.   [19] Stimson, *op. cit.*, pp. 41–42.

by the Secretary himself in his *Far Eastern Crisis*. Discussing the reasons for our initial policy, he says:

I do not recall that there was any difference of opinion whatever in our group in the State Department [20] as to the policy we should follow in the face of this diagnosis of the situation in Manchuria.[21] The evidence in our hands pointed to the wisdom of giving Shidehara and the Foreign Office an opportunity, free from anything approaching a threat or even public criticism, to get control of the situation. We were well aware of the incomplete development of parliamentary government in Japan and that the Japanese constitution, instead of placing the army under the direction of the Cabinet, gave it direct and independent access to the Emperor as chief of state. We of course knew of the imperious economic problem Japan faced in the necessity of providing a livelihood for a constantly increasing population and we were well aware that in grappling with this problem during the period of the great war she had sought to use the tactics of conquest and colonization over China for its solution. But for nearly ten years under the guidance of Shidehara and his fellow liberals she had been "studiously and persistently sailing on the opposite tack to the militant course" [22] which she had previously followed. All through the decade from the Washington Conference to September, 1931, instead of seeking markets by force, she had been following the entirely opposite plan of "commercial expansion and political good neighborliness." She had been seeking to supply her growing population by the development of friendly trade with the outside world instead of by forcibly acquired outlets for emigration. She had followed this course patiently and in the face of considerable difficulty and provocation. She had withdrawn her troops from Siberia and from Shantung despite the severe opposition from her militarist party. She had acquiesced in the lapse of her alliance with Great Britain and had thus made possible the settlements which followed the Washington Conference. She had exercised great self-restraint in the presence of what seemed to her the needless and insulting methods in which our American

[20] In their *American Diplomatic Game* (New York, 1935), pp. 300–301, Drew Pearson and Constantine Brown give a very different picture of the situation in the State Department. According to their story there was a violent difference of opinion from the beginning between Under Secretary of State, William R. Castle, Jr., and the Chief of the Division of Far Eastern Affairs, Dr. Stanley Hornbeck. Inquiries by this author support the story but the sources of information unfortunately cannot be quoted.
[21] In previous pages Mr. Stimson has stated that diagnosis—that all evidence pointed to the fact that the incident was the work of the military and neither planned nor acquiesced in by the civil authorities in Japan. See *Far Eastern Crisis*, pp. 33–34.
[22] Arnold J. Toynbee, ed., *Survey of International Affairs, 1931* (London, 1932), p. 400.

Congress had treated the subject of Japanese immigration, and she had exercised a consistent policy of non-retaliation to a continuing series of Chinese provocations during the progress of the Chinese civil wars.

More than that, we had witnessed a very recent example of Japan's spirit of responsibility and fidelity to modern views of international relations in the course which the Minseito Cabinet had followed in the ratification of the London Naval Treaty of 1930. In that matter they had quite the most difficult task of any of the nations involved. That treaty was highly unpopular with the naval authorities in Japan. But Premier Hamaguchi had carried it through to ratification in the face of tremendous opposition as a result of which he had lost his life.[23] Mr. Wakatsuki, who had been chairman of the Japanese delegation in London and had been active in securing the ratification of the treaty, was now Premier.

The Japanese Government had thus for ten years given an exceptional record of good citizenship in the life of the international world. Shidehara was still in office. We knew he had been laboring hard for moderation against the pressure of the army leaders in Manchuria. We had reached the conclusion that those leaders had engineered the outbreak probably without his knowledge and certainly against his will.[24] It seemed clear to us that no steps should be taken which would make his task more difficult because certainly our best chance of a successful solution of the situation lay in him.

History is full of lessons which point to the dangers of an opposite course. A century and a half ago the intervention of the European allies had only served to fan the flame of nationalism in revolutionary France and, by rousing the patriotism of her armies, had strikingly demonstrated the danger of outside interference in a domestic struggle such as was now going on in Japan.[25]

At the same time, while the importance of great caution in order not to inflame the passions of the Japanese people was thus in our minds, the other side of the picture of necessity was also clearly before us. If the military party should succeed in having its way, if Shidehara eventually should yield to them, the damage to the new structure of international society provided by the post-war treaties would be incalculable. There was no danger of our losing sight of this. Two years before there had been presented to us in the same locality a similar problem. In the summer and autumn of 1929, just as the nations of the world were on the point of celebrating the ratification of the Pact of Paris renouncing war,

---

[23] For a Japanese account of this see Seijii Hishida, *Japan among the Great Powers,* pp. 277–82. See also Charles G. Dawes, *Journal as Ambassador to Great Britain* (New York, 1939), and Pearson and Brown, *op. cit.,* p. 304.
[24] See Wilfrid Fleisher, *Our Enemy Japan* (Garden City, N.Y., 1942), p. 25.
[25] There is at least a question as to whether these cases are parallel.

hostilities between the Russians and the Chinese had flamed up in northern Manchuria which threatened to throw discredit on that treaty at the very moment of its birth. Acting under the newly born treaty the American State Department had then promptly taken the lead in mobilizing a very general expression of world opinion cautioning those two nations against a breach of the Pact.[26] The memory of our efforts at that time at once rose in our minds now.

Thus in the face of those two opposite dangers I find as early as September 23rd I had jotted in my diary the following entry:

"My problem is to let the Japanese know that we are watching them and at the same time do it in a way which will help Shidehara who is on the right side, and not play into the hands of any nationalist agitators." [27]

In this analysis Mr. Stimson fails to mention that during this decade of liberal effort an extremely conservative ministry was in office for two years (1927–29) with Baron Tanaka at its head. Regardless of the authenticity of the memorial which bears his name, there is no question as to Tanaka's advocacy of the strong policy in Sino-Japanese relations. There is also no question that General Minami, Minister of War in 1931, was Tanaka's follower and this should have thrown doubt from the very beginning on the probable success of Shidehara. Mr. Stimson may have overlooked the Tanaka Cabinet but not his own use of the Pact of Paris in the Manchurian crisis of 1929, Russia and China then being the parties concerned. "The memory of our efforts at the time at once rose in our minds now," he writes: but he offers no valid explanation as to why he thought it right and wise to caution these countries against a violation of the Pact yet would not use the same means two years later in similar but more critical circumstances. There was, naturally, no need to consider Russia's feelings in 1929, as we were not then on speaking terms with her. A variety of views as to the propriety and effectiveness of Mr. Stimson's action have been expressed. By some it has been held that he was largely responsible for settling the dispute. I, myself, heard that opinion freely expressed in Geneva in 1930, but the majority view seems to be quite the contrary. It is not unreasonable to assume, however, that a similar course in Sep-

[26] For very different views of this intervention see A. Whitney Griswold, *Far Eastern Policy of the United States* (New York, 1938), and Hishida, *op. cit.*
[27] *Far Eastern Crisis*, pp. 34–37.

tember, 1931, might have been exceedingly helpful. Such a policy was strongly advocated by Nelson Johnson in his telegram of September 22.[28]

To what extent Mr. Stimson helped Foreign Minister Shidehara is open to question. There were competent observers at the time who believed that he would have given him far more effective support in the early days of the crisis had he let it be known unequivocally that the United States would not acquiesce in a regime of force in Manchuria. In those days, during the September meeting of the Council of the League, Shidehara still had a chance to lead Japanese public opinion against the radical military group. In those days that violent nationalism to which Mr. Stimson refers had not been aroused, nor was it foreign interference which eventually inflamed it but pride in the victories scored by the army in Manchuria and skillfully played up in the press by the War Office along with stories of alleged Chinese atrocities against "helpless" Japanese and Koreans.[29] Had Baron Shidehara been able to point to a strong position taken by the United States and the League there is at least a possibility that the military would have withdrawn from the position tentatively assumed. As it was, each success which went unchecked made them bolder, and it was Shidehara who had to withdraw step by step until the War Office and not the Cabinet became the real director of national policy in Japan.

That the position adopted by the United States would be a determining factor in any attempted settlement of the problem was made evident from the start: by the note of the Chinese Government to the Government of the United States on the same day she submitted her case to the League, by Sir Eric Drummond's message to Secretary Stimson sounding out the views of this government even before the League Council held its first meeting for the consideration of that case,[30] by the reaction of the press throughout the world. The policy of the United States concerning the League had always been doubtful; the uncertainty as to what this government

---

[28] See Chap. VII, below.   [29] *Trans-Pacific*, August–October, 1931.
[30] It was on September 22 at the second meeting of the Council that China's case was formally taken up.

would do in an emergency had been a constant hindrance to the development of League jurisprudence. In minor cases, strictly European in scope, this had not been an obstacle to settlement, as we were completely isolated by our own will; but in this, the first case of world-wide importance to come before the League, the United States was vitally concerned. Her economic stake in the Far East was large; her territorial interest made her one of the foremost Pacific powers; the policy of the "open door" and of friendship for China had become traditional in the minds—and perhaps in the hearts—of the American people; she was a signatory of the Nine Power Treaty guaranteeing the territorial and administrative integrity of China, and both a sponsor and a signatory of the Kellogg-Briand Pact for the renunciation of war. There was no possibility of complete isolation; nevertheless, so far as the League was concerned, American policy was unpredictable. Whatever the State Department at Washington said or did in those crucial days was closely watched; every word, every inflection of the voice, every move was weighed, in Tokyo as in Geneva, in London and in Paris, by those who wanted the League to act decisively and by those who opposed such action. In a special cable from Geneva, September 21, the New York *Times* correspondent writes:

What action the Council should take is subject to delicate negotiations going on tonight. According to one influential school, it should begin by recommending that both sides return to their previous positions—which, of course, really means telling the Japanese to evacuate Mukden and other points occupied, pending a settlement of the dispute. *There is a strong desire*, however, first *to know that the Council can count on at least the moral support of the United States if it takes such a step, and expressions of American opinion, official, public and press are awaited eagerly.*[31]

SEPTEMBER 22 TO 24.—On September 22 the Council sat formally to consider the case, and a heated argument ensued between Mr. Yoshizawa and Dr. Sze. It was a fascinating spectacle to those who thronged the Council room and sat for hours while these men discussed the conflict then being waged by their countrymen

[31] New York *Times*, Sept. 22, 1931. Italics mine.

thousands of miles away. To many observers it seemed one of the highest points of League achievement that this open discussion was possible. But the surface smoothness and courtesy of the debate did not conceal an underlying bitterness which became more and more evident in the verbal sparring that went on throughout the morning and in the constant attempts to throw doubt on the meaning and accuracy of the statements made. By the close of this, the first public session for the consideration of China's appeal to the Council under Article 11, there had emerged, in outline at least, the issues on which each party was to take its stand.

From the beginning, Mr. Yoshizawa put the stress on the entire Manchurian situation—Japanese treaty rights there, the broad question of Sino-Japanese relations stretching back over a long period of years, recent outbreaks such as the Nakamura case, and so on. Dr. Sze attempted to keep the discussion on the local incident at Mukden and its extension, contending that the Nakamura and other cases were irrelevant, that if Japan had grievances against China she also had access to means of relief, "diplomatic means, or failing them, judicial means, or finally an appeal to the Council."[32]

Dr. Sze stated that Chinese troops had no part in precipitating the Mukden affair and on that basis claimed reparations for China; Mr. Yoshizawa denied both these claims and implied that Japanese action was justified on the grounds of self-defense, an argument which Dr. Sze met with a reference to the Council report in the Greco-Bulgarian case of 1925.[33] The Chinese representative requested immediate action by the Council on the first and second of the three steps suggested in the Chinese note of September 21,[34] while the Japanese insisted on direct negotiations between Nanking and Tokyo. Since this question of direct negotiations as opposed to League action became one of the outstanding points of difference not only between the two parties but in the minds of those who were called upon to find a solution for the problem, it has been thought wise to follow this part of the discussion in some detail.

In his first remarks to the Council Mr. Yoshizawa stated that ac-

[32] The full discussion between the Chinese and Japanese representatives is found in the *Official Journal*, December, 1931, pp. 2266–69.
[33] See p. 40, below, and footnote 40.   [34] See p. 29, above.

cording to his information a proposal had been made from the Chinese side that the solution should be sought by direct negotiations between the two governments. Dr. Sze countered by saying there could be no direct negotiations until the *status quo ante* had been restored:

I do not think that any self-respecting state can agree to open diplomatic negotiations so long as a considerable portion of its territory is under forcible military occupation by the party which requests a diplomatic settlement.

To this Mr. Yoshizawa replied:

. . . not only the Japanese Government but the Chinese Government as well is inclined to settle the question in this way. I have received official information from my government to the effect that one of the highest officials in the National Government at Nanking spoke to the Japanese Minister to this effect.

Dr. Sze was evidently without official information with respect to this and contented himself with pointing out that "at this present moment, there are no direct negotiations in progress. Moreover, I doubt whether a person can make statements in the name of his Government unless he is authorized to do so." Mr. Yoshizawa repeated his statement that the person in question was one of the highest ranking officials in the Nanking government and there was no reason why the Japanese Minister should regard his statement of policy as of no official importance.

The mystery regarding this alleged proposal was cleared up by two cables from Nanking; one, dated September 22, was distributed to the members of the Council that same afternoon; the other, dated September 23, differing largely in that it is a fuller statement, was read into the minutes of the fourth meeting of the Council on September 25. [35] The first message read as follows:

(1) Mr. Shegemitsu called upon Mr. T. V. Soong on Saturday morning September 19.[36]

Owing to seizure by Japanese of all wires and wireless in Manchuria only information available pointed to a purely local incident. He dis-

[35] *Official Journal*, December, 1931, p. 2284, and Annex 1334, p. 2463.
[36] Shegemitsu was Japanese Minister to China, Soong at that time was Vice-Chairman of the Executive Yuan.

cussed advisability of setting up a mixed Sino-Japanese commission to adjudicate matter so as to prevent this incident from threatening friendly relations between the two countries.

Mr. T. V. Soong expressed personal opinion that feasibility of such a step might be considered at both capitals.

(2) At noon September 21,[37] Japanese consul called on Mr. T. V. Soong at Nanking declaring that Japanese Government favoured speedy constitution of such a commission.

(3) Mr. T. V. Soong replied officially that when matter was discussed between Mr. Shegemitsu and himself it was believed that it was a mere local clash. But now it can not be denied that Japanese troops have started warlike operations on a large scale and invasion of Chinese territory still continues and therefore situation is entirely changed and establishment of such a commission could not be considered.[38]

From this it would appear that what Mr. Yoshizawa called a "proposal from the Chinese side" was, according to the Chinese version, a feeler put out by the Japanese. Other instances of the same tactics will be found in the later history of the case, notably in the matter of the neutral zone around Chinchow.[39]

In making his first statement as to this alleged proposal Mr. Yoshizawa warned the Council to keep its hands off the controversy:

The Government, I am told, has welcomed this proposal. Premature intervention in these circumstances would only have the deplorable effect of needlessly exciting Japanese public opinion, which is already overexcited.

Two further significant points were made in the course of the discussion. Early in the session Dr. Sze pointed out that the Japanese representative questioned the accuracy of his statements and added,

As far as accuracy in regard to facts is concerned, I am prepared in behalf of my Government, to agree to an enquiry being carried out by a commission appointed by the League and I am willing to leave the matter in the hands of an impartial commission.

This is the first mention of a commission of enquiry before the Council and it was answered only by Mr. Yoshizawa's insistence on

[37] A footnote in the *Official Journal*, December, 1931, Annex 1334, p. 2458, says that the figure 21 was mutilated and the second cable gives the date as September 22, noon.

[38] *Ibid.*, p. 2458.   [39] See Chap. VI, below.

direct negotiations between the parties. The Japanese representative did not refer directly to Dr. Sze's suggestion nor did Viscount Cecil in his remarks which brought the morning meeting to a close.

China also made it clear through her representative that she would act "in conformity with whatever recommendations it may receive from the Council" and would "abide by whatever decisions the League may in the circumstances adopt" and left the case in the hands of the Council. Mr. Yoshizawa, on the other hand, warned against "premature intervention," reiterated the need for direct negotiations between the two parties, and asked for adjournment until he could receive instructions from his government.

The morning session was brought to an end by Viscount Cecil in an adroit and diplomatic speech in which he first tried to pour oil on the troubled waters by complimenting both China and Japan for their long interest in and cooperation with the League. "Japan," he said, "has always been pre-eminent amongst the nations of the world in her strict and rigid adherence to all international obligations," thus offering that country an opportunity to withdraw from a difficult position not only without loss of face but with heightened prestige. Lord Cecil continued:

In the meantime there are, I think, certain preliminary steps which we may hope to take. This is not the first international dispute of this nature. There have been several clashes of arms which have taken place and where there has been, I hope, no question of a resort to war, and as we are assured by our Japanese colleague and our Chinese colleague is the case at this moment. The Council has now established what I think may be regarded as a settled procedure in these matters.

The first thing that has always been done has been for the Council, through its President, to issue an earnest appeal to both sides not to do anything to aggravate the position and to avoid further fighting of all kinds. Our Japanese colleague has already given assurance that his country will do everything it can to avoid this, and, although I am not sure that I heard any specific assurance from our Chinese colleague to this effect, the whole tenor of what he has said goes to show that he is ready to give the same assurance.

Another step has been taken, I think, in every case. Where it has been established that the troops of either party have entered the territory of the other, it has been customary for the President to issue an earnest appeal to the troops of both sides to withdraw from the territory of the other party and to avoid anything which might lead to a clash.

Subject to anything which may be said, I hope our President may feel it possible to issue such an appeal in that sense. Obviously, each case differs, and it may be necessary to word that appeal in one form in one case and in another form in another case; it may be necessary to take some precautions in one case which would be unnecessary in another. On all those details of form I am quite content to trust to the discretion and judgment of our President, in communication with the two parties.

I do feel, however, rather strongly that any troops which are on the territory belonging to the other party ought to be withdrawn without delay. That is the course which has been taken in previous cases, and I hope we shall not make any difference in our dealings with one country rather than another.

There are two other matters I would like to mention. In the first place, our Chinese colleague has referred to certain statements which have been made in the Council, indicating the general principles which the Council thinks ought to be adopted in cases of this kind. I have before me the statement made by the then President, M. Briand, at the session of the Council held in Paris in October 1925.[40] The statement reads:

". . . He had understood the representative of Greece to indicate that all these incidents would not have arisen if his country had not been called upon to take rapid steps for its legitimate defense and protection. It was essential that such ideas should not take root in the minds of nations which were Members of the League and become a kind of jurisprudence, for it would be extremely dangerous. Under the pretext of legitimate defense, disputes might arise which, though limited in extent, were extremely unfortunate owing to the damage they entailed. These disputes, once they had broken out, might assume such proportions that the Government which started them, under a feeling of legitimate defence would be no longer able to control them.

"The League of Nations, through its Council, and through all the methods of conciliation which were at its disposal, offered the nations a means of avoiding such deplorable events. The nations had only to appeal to the Council. It had been shown that the criticisms which had been brought against the League of Nations to the effect that its machinery was cumbersome and that it found it difficult to take action in circumstances which required an urgent solution, were unjustified. It had been proved that a nation which appealed to the League when it felt that its existence was threatened, could be sure that the Council would be at its post ready to undertake its work of conciliation."

[40] *Official Journal,* November, 1925, p. 1709.

This statement was approved by my predecessor, Sir (then Mr.) Austen Chamberlain, on behalf of the British Empire, by Viscount Ishii, speaking for Japan, by M. Scialoja, speaking for Italy, and by a number of other members of the Council. I think it may be regarded now as the locus classicus as to the policy and procedure of the Council in cases of this kind.

One other matter I ought to mention. We are all aware that there are certain treaty obligations—or international instruments, let me call them —beyond the League of Nations, which affect the dispute; for instance, the Pact of Paris and the Treaty regarding the Principles and Policies to be followed in matters regarding China, signed by the United States and other Powers. In both these instruments the United States of America are very closely interested—in the first place, as one of the promoters of the Pact of Paris, and in the second, as one of the signatories of the latter treaty. It seems to me that we should do well in these circumstances to communicate to the United States a statement of all the proceedings of this Council, and of all the discussions which have taken place within it. The United States Government will then be fully informed of what we are doing and will be able to take any action it may think right in connection with this matter.[41]

In this lucid statement Viscount Cecil did four things: First, he outlined League procedure as it had been previously established in similar cases. Second, he made it clear that in his opinion troops occupying territory of the other party—and this could mean only Japanese troops—should be withdrawn "without delay." Third, he supported the position taken by the Chinese delegate in regard to the lack of justification for aggressive measures under the plea of self-defense. And, finally, he brought before the Council the question which had been uppermost in the minds of many members, the question which overshadowed to some extent even the immediate issue between China and Japan, the important question of the cooperation and support of the United States in finding a solution of the issue.

At the request of the President, the Council then adjourned to give time for the drafting of a resolution along the lines proposed by Lord Cecil.

When the Council met that afternoon Mr. Yoshizawa again referred to the general situation, stressing Japanese interests in Man-

[41] *Ibid.*, December, 1931, p. 2267.

churia—more than a million Japanese nationals [42] and investments of more than two billion yen—while Dr. Sze emphasized the increasing seriousness of the conflict then taking place. Time, he said, was the essential element and he asked the Council to order the immediate withdrawal of Japanese troops to their treaty zones. At this time he distributed copies of the message from the Nanking government concerning the alleged Chinese proposal for direct negotiations.[43] He expressed the hope that his request for a commission of inquiry would receive immediate assent; Chinese territory under occupation was being extended and this must be stopped immediately and troops withdrawn.

President Lerroux then asked the Council to authorize him:

(1) To make an urgent appeal to the Chinese and Japanese Governments to refrain from any action which might aggravate the situation or prejudice the peaceful settlement of the problem;

(2) To endeavor, in consultation with the Chinese and Japanese representatives, to find adequate means of enabling the two countries to withdraw their troops immediately without the lives of their nationals and the safety of their property being endangered;

(3) To forward the minutes of all the Council meetings and the documents relating to the subject to the Government of the United States for its information; [44]

(4) To ask the two parties concerned to meet immediately after the meeting of the Council together with certain other members of the Council.[45]

Dr. Curtius was the first to speak in support of the Resolution as a first step, a provisional measure looking toward other steps for the final settlement of the highly complex dispute. This, he said, was a duty which the Council could not evade as it was of the greatest importance to show the world that such conflicts could be amicably settled by that body. Foreign Minister Grandi of Italy, among others, endorsed his words and appealed to the two parties to help in finding a satisfactory solution.

[42] This figure includes 800,000 Koreans. See *Lytton Report*, p. 25.
[43] See pp. 36 ff., above.
[44] The correspondence exchanged with the Government of the United States in this connection is reproduced in Annex 1334 of the *Official Journal* for December, 1931; also in *Conditions in Manchuria*.
[45] *Official Journal*, December, 1931, p. 2272.

Dr. Sze approved the proposal as a first step but as a first step only. He hoped and expected it would be followed promptly by such other action as the circumstances demanded and trusted the discussion would be resumed on the following day.

Mr. Yoshizawa expressed appreciation of the sentiments of his colleagues and of the attention given the matter by the Council. As to when the Council should meet next, he was making every effort to supply the Council with information but he could not say whether he would be in a position to ask the President to convene another meeting on the following day. He would make the request as soon as he was in receipt of definite instructions from his government.

Lord Cecil, after accepting the President's proposal as a first step, said that if the situation was as serious as Dr. Sze decribed it the decision as to the next meeting must be left to the President and "ventured very respectfully" to appeal to his Japanese colleague to hasten instructions from his government. Mr. Yoshizawa replied that he was making every effort to obtain further information and would submit a more comprehensive report at the earliest possible moment. He understood Lord Cecil to have said that, if the statements made by the Chinese representative were correct, the Council could not hesitate to meet as soon as possible and even earlier than he (Yoshizawa) might ask. He hoped, however, that this interpretation was not correct.

Viscount Cecil said his meaning was that, in view of what the Chinese representative had said, the matter was extremely urgent, as Mr. Yoshizawa would undoubtedly agree, and he hoped the instructions which the Japanese representative was awaiting from his government would arrive at the earliest possible moment.

After further brief discussion in which Yoshizawa and Sze each attempted to have his own interpretation of the proposal accepted, the Council unanimously authorized the President to take the action he proposed and the meeting adjourned. The unanimous vote on this proposal was to prove of great importance in October when Yoshizawa tried to prevent the extending of the invitation to the United States to sit with the Council.

Within a few hours identic notes [46] were cabled to the Chinese and Japanese governments followed by one to the State Department at Washington outlining the action of the Council and giving the text of the notes to China and Japan. Thus the first official action of the Council looking toward a peaceful settlement of the dispute was taken the day following China's appeal. Viewing it as a first step the most captious critic of the League could not justly complain that the Council had been slow or faltering.

Two very pertinent comments on the day's proceedings are made by W. W. Willoughby. Referring to the Japanese warning to the Council to keep hands off, he says, "The assurances, repeatedly given by Japan, that she will do nothing to aggravate the situation in Manchuria and that she had no aggressive designs, need to be borne in mind for there can be little doubt but that, for the time being at least, the Council ascribed value to them and was thereby influenced in its action." [47] Of Mr. Yoshizawa's declaration, "The relations between the two peoples had become so acute that it was difficult for those who lived in Europe to appreciate them," [48] Willoughby writes:

This last statement brought forward a point of view upon which the Japanese continued to lay stress throughout the whole controversy, not only before the Council and Assembly of the League, but in the forum of public opinion throughout the world. Though not always explicitly stated, the argument upon this point seems to have been that because of this lack of understanding by other peoples, and especially by the Governments represented in the League, no attempt should be made either to pass moral judgment upon Japan or to declare the manner in which controversies between her and China should be settled. [49]

On the twenty-second, Mr. Stimson handed the Japanese Ambassador a memorandum to be delivered to his government. In this the Secretary of State expressed both surprise and concern over Japanese military operations in Manchuria. While stating the confidence the American Government felt as to Japan's intentions he made it plain that "the responsibility for determining the course of

[46] *Ibid.*, Annex 1334, Part II, p. 2454.
[47] W. W. Willoughby, *The Sino-Japanese Controversy and the League of Nations* (Baltimore, 1935), p. 50.
[48] *Official Journal*, December, 1931, p. 2271.   [49] Willoughby, *op. cit.*, pp. 53–54.

events" devolved largely upon Japan "for the reason that Japanese armed forces have seized and are exercising de facto control in South Manchuria." The note [50] closes with this word of warning:

What has occurred has already shaken the confidence of the public with regard to the stability of conditions in Manchuria, and it is believed that the crystallization of a situation suggesting the necessity for an indefinite continuance of military occupation will further undermine that confidence.

Although diplomatic in tone the memorandum is much stronger than was indicated at the time, and it is unfortunate that its contents were not made public at once. Had this been done the Japanese spokesmen could not have interpreted it to their press as they did, saying it showed a sympathetic attitude on the part of the United States.[51] Nor did the State Department press release for that day offset in any way the Japanese interpretation by saying merely that the Department attitude had not changed, that it still held that as the Japanese cabinet was trying to settle the matter amicably it should be given time to do so.

In this matter of the interpretation of the American attitude by the Japanese press there is an entirely different point of view from that expressed above: namely, that after September 22 the Japanese Government had no illusions as to where we stood, they knew and understood our position and therefore tried to keep us out of the League, that public opinion and the press in Japan mattered not in the least. Nevertheless, Mr. Stimson laid great stress on it and so have other writers, among them our last Ambassador to Japan, Joseph C. Grew.[52] At least, had public opinion been informed, even though it could not express itself and had little influence on events, the Japanese military group could not have played upon it as effectively as it did in the later stages of the case.

September 23 was perhaps the most fateful day of all. Although

[50] *Conditions in Manchuria*, pp. 4–5.
[51] *Trans-Pacific*, Oct. 1, 1931, has the following excerpt from *Jiji*, a Tokyo newspaper of fairly liberal policy: "In regard to the attitude of the United States Government toward the Manchurian incident, it is indicated by the memorandum which the Secretary of State, Colonel Henry L. Stimson, handed to Mr. Debuchi, the Japanese Ambassador in Washington. The document reveals that the United States Government is in sympathy with Japan in the present trouble."
[52] Joseph C. Grew, *Ten Years in Japan* (New York, 1944).

the Council did not meet again in public session until Friday, September 25, attempts to find a solution of the problem continued outside, particularly by the Committee of Five set up by the Council to work out a solution and put into effect provisions (1) and (2) of the Resolution of September 22. The personnel of this Committee— Lord Cecil, René Massigli, Dino Grandi, and Dr. Curtius, together with President Lerroux—caused considerable dissatisfaction among the smaller powers. Such committees were becoming the really effective means of discussing and handling controversies before the Council and the prospect of exclusion from them seemed not only humiliating but dangerous as it might lead to the complete dominance of the Council by its permanent members. On the other hand it could be argued that if worst came to worst and action had to be taken against one or the other of the parties to the conflict it would necessarily devolve upon these great powers to carry out that action, since the League had no forces of its own. And certainly, as the authors of *The League and Manchuria*[53] pointed out, the composition of the committee left little doubt as to the seriousness with which the Council regarded the situation.

The Committee of Five seems to have met almost continuously throughout the day. A full public session of the Council had been called for 6:45 P.M. but it had to be canceled because no decision had been reached on the matter of the Commission of Enquiry proposed by China. Consultations regarding this had begun on the twenty-second, after the morning session. It was to be a committee "on the spot," made up of the British and French military attachés who were then in Mukden, and consular representatives of Germany, Italy, and the United States; and it was spoken of as a "neutral" rather than a "League" commission in order to make it more palatable to certain sections of opinion in the United States. Lord Cecil and René Massigli pushed it, Curtius and Grandi followed suit. Everyone was for it except Yoshizawa and he had to consult Tokyo. As to American participation everything points to the conclusion that Hugh Wilson, our Minister to Switzerland, led the Secretary-

[53] *The League and Manchuria, the First Phase of the Chinese-Japanese Conflict, September 18–30* (Geneva Special Studies, Vol. II, No. 10, October, 1931).

General to believe that there was little if any doubt of Mr. Stimson's cooperation. No other conclusion seems likely in view of the fact that such a commission without the United States would have no hope of success from the start. But Mr. Wilson was mistaken. On the morning of the twenty-third, when Lerroux and others conferred with Yoshizawa, the Japanese representative was yielding, but in the afternoon he became defiant and obstinate. He had had word, it seems, from Washington that Stimson had seen Debuchi and had told him the United States would not approve such a move.[54] The same news had reached Tokyo also, and there, too, a stiffer attitude was taken.[55] Tokyo papers report a split in the cabinet and stress the fact that the United States disapproved of the League proposal. Some papers go further, declaring it evidence that this country approved the action taken in Manchuria and calling attention to Castle's known friendship for Japan.[56]

Mr. Stimson [57] tells the story of his part in the affair as follows:

[54] James T. Shotwell, *On the Rim of the Abyss* (New York, 1936), pp. 243–44.

[55] A news article in *Trans-Pacific* (weekly supplement of the Tokyo English-language newspaper, *The Japan Advertiser*) says in part:

"It was learned at the ministry of Foreign Affairs on September 25th, that the American Secretary of State, Mr. Henry L. Stimson, had told the Japanese Ambassador to Washington, Mr. Katsuji Debuchi, in the course of a conversation at the State Department, that the United States informed the League of Nations that it considered the League's suggestion to send a military commission of inquiry to Manchuria as inappropriate. [It was never proposed to send a "military" commission.]

"Ambassador Debuchi is reported to have expressed his appreciation of the American attitude and to have stated that the sending of a military commission as suggested by the League would not have been approved by Japan."

[56] A long editorial from Tokyo *Asahi*, a liberal paper, quoted in *Trans-Pacific*, October 8, contains the following interesting statements:

". . . Several reasons may be assigned for the action of the United States Government. In the first place, those directing the foreign policy of the United States know enough of the position of Japan in Manchuria to realize that no good will result by sending a commission of inquiry to Manchuria under the auspices of the League of Nations. By declining to approve the Council's proposal the United States Government indicated its belief that Japan was justified in moving troops into Manchuria and that her action not only did not threaten China's independence but did not violate the principles of the open door. . . .

"It would be interesting to learn the extent to which the sympathetic attitude of Secretary of State Stimson and Under-Secretary Castle toward Japan had to do with the United States' Government's decision to keep aloof from Manchuria.

"By trusting Japan to find a happy solution to the present military incident the United States has served the cause of peace in the Far East."

(Just as Munich provided "peace in our time"!)

[57] *Op. cit.*, pp. 42–44.

. . . Late in the evening [of September 22] came a cable reporting that the League was contemplating sending to Manchuria an investigating commission appointed by itself; that Japan objected but that the investigation would probably be made anyhow, if necessary under Chinese authority as the local sovereign in Manchuria. They wished to know whether we would join such a commission. The following morning, while I was considering the cable, it was reinforced by a message through our Minister to Switzerland over the telephone telling me of the proposal to send such a commission of investigation and also to send diplomatic notes to Japan and China on the subject of the outbreak. In the telephone message it was suggested that if we would permit an American representative to join in the discussion of these proposals at the table of the Council of the League or on its special committee appointed for consideration of this matter, the effect would be dramatic and beneficial.

I had no doubt as to the dramatic effect, but I was very gravely concerned as to the effect which that drama would have upon the people of Japan. By the telephone as well as a long cable sent the same day, I tried to make clear my views. I at once accepted the suggestion that we should support by a similar diplomatic note the League's proposed representation through the diplomatic channels to China and Japan. But I deprecated the proposal of sending by the League at that time an investigating commission to Manchuria *over and against the objection of Japan.*[58] I suggested that inasmuch as Oriental people were not so well acquainted as Occidentals with the method of judicial investigation and findings by third parties, but in my opinion were more inclined to settle their difficulties by direct negotiation between the parties involved, they should be permitted to try this method first. I told them that I felt there would be serious danger that, if the League sought to impose such an investigation upon Japan against her opposition, it would be popularly resented and would throw at once additional difficulties in the path of Shidehara's efforts at solution. I thought that this danger would be accentuated if the United States, which was not a member of the League and had no right to sit on the Council, should participate in the sending of such a commission. I urged them, in case they felt that the need of such a committee was now imperative, to follow the method which had become common in international matters of having such a commission appointed by the two nations themselves, China and Japan, with a membership from neutral nations, this method being one which was well understood and in general use in various treaties of conciliation.[59]

[58] The italics are Mr. Stimson's.
[59] In a footnote (p. 41) Mr. Stimson says: "I also pointed out that the Manchurian situation differed widely from the Greco-Bulgarian controversy in which such an

In summary I suggested that the most effective line of cooperation in the delicate situation prevailing in Manchuria would be for the American Government, through the diplomatic channels, to support the League in urging a settlement by the two countries themselves through direct negotiations; secondly, if this should not prove effective and outside action became necessary, that it should be taken through the machinery of the League, to which both countries were parties and which had already been invoked by China. Finally, if this should not be effective, we should all consider such action as might be possible under the Nine Power Treaty and the Pact of Paris.

By these cabled and telephoned messages, of which there is no record in the published documents, Mr. Stimson effectively put an end to the early sending of a neutral commission of enquiry to the scene of the conflict. By so doing he had supported Japan rather than China. It does not follow that the Council would have voted for a commission of enquiry had Mr. Stimson approved; but it is the opinion of competent observers, of men holding important posts in the Secretariat at that time, that it would have done so. When, on November 21 in Paris, Mr. Yoshizawa himself at long last proposed the sending of such a commission [60] Lord Cecil commented: "My Government and I myself have held this view from the very outset of these discussions. We should have been glad if some means of this kind could have been taken even in September last." [61] Mr. Yoshizawa, observers say, would have opposed it desperately, but the united strength of the Committee of Five plus the United States would have been too great for him and he would almost certainly have yielded.

Everyone who has been in Geneva for any length of time knows the *bise*, that cold northern wind which suddenly sweeps down from Alps in the sunniest of summer weather striking to the bone with a chill which the warmest of tweeds cannot keep out. So it was that day in September when the high hopes of the morning were blotted out by the black gloom which settled over League circles as it be-

---

investigating commission had been sent by the League. In that case the issue was over the determination of a Geographical line; while here the investigation would involve an enquiry into a large number of deep and complicated political differences."

[60] *Official Journal*, p. 2365.   [61] *Ibid.*, p. 2366.

came known that the United States would not approve, much less participate, in such a commission.[62]

It seems strange that, in relating these events of the twenty-third, Mr. Stimson does not mention the stand taken by China in the Council as early as the morning of the twenty-second—that China could not agree to direct negotiations with a country holding a large part of its territory in military occupation and having resorted to means other than diplomatic negotiations. If this information had not already reached him by cable, surely Mr. Wilson must have relayed it to him in the course of their telephone conversation. But in Washington there seems to have been little thought of China's desire in the matter. In fact that country is scarcely mentioned, Mr. Stimson's chief concern apparently being to avoid hurting the patriotic feelings of the Japanese. Was it because China was weak that it did not matter if direct negotiations were imposed upon her against her will? Writing in 1935 after the complete breakdown of all efforts of amicable settlement Mr. Stimson still thought he was justified in the course taken. He argues that the sending of such a commission of inquiry would have hastened the outbreak of nationalistic feeling which subsequently occurred and the downfall of the Minseito Cabinet which was then doing its best—a very poor best it proved to be—to check the army; that by remaining in office until December 10, Shidehara was eventually able to consent on behalf of Japan to the sending of the Lytton Commission, whereas if Japan had been overridden in the early stages the invaluable results of that Commission's report and work would have been lost.

Other reasons for the outbreak of nationalist feeling in Japan as well as possible results to the Shidehara Cabinet had the United States taken a different attitude have already been suggested. As to the fall of the cabinet, a study of articles written by Japanese observers for the *Trans-Pacific* and *Japan Advertiser* certainly indicates that this was due to internal problems, largely financial, much more than to the Manchurian crisis, although it is perhaps true, as one Far Eastern expert [63] has suggested, that had it been a pro-

[62] See Clarence Streit's account, New York *Times*, Sept. 18, 1932.
[63] Nathaniel Peffer, Professor of International Relations, Columbia University, in conference with the author, June, 1944.

military cabinet it would not have fallen, even though the internal difficulties were great. Also one might ask: Is it not possible that Shidehara and the Minseito Cabinet would have consented in the beginning to the Commission of Enquiry had it been urged strongly, but in friendly fashion, by both the League and the United States? And would not the report and work of the Lytton Commission, or of any other neutral commission, have proved far more effective if it could have been submitted to the League before Japan became so involved in Manchuria that there was no possibility of withdrawal without loss of face? American policy so delayed the sending of the commission that it went, not at once while the evidence was fresh and the area of occupation small, but months later when the situation had so deteriorated that there was no possibility of a peaceful settlement of the affair. Here again, despite Mr. Stimson's intent to support Foreign Minister Shidehara, the actual result was to strengthen the hands of the military.

The dampening effect of Mr. Stimson's message was somewhat offset by the warm tone of the formal note [64] to the Council, also sent through our Minister to Switzerland, in answer to the Council's communication of September 22. In this the Secretary of State indicated "wholehearted sympathy with the attitude of the League as expressed in the Council resolution." Notes, similar to those already sent by the Council, would be dispatched to China and Japan; cessation of hostilities and withdrawal from the dangerous situation had already been urged; and the United States would continue to work for the restoration of peace.

The response to this note which was made public after its reception on September 24 was electrifying. One might almost have thought the United States had consented to join the League, so enthusiastically was our promise of diplomatic support received. One of the best contemporary accounts of this is found in *The League and Manchuria:*

Early Thursday morning came one of the most far-reaching communications yet received by the League of Nations. Hardly had the Secretary-General reached his office when the American Minister

[64] *Conditions in Manchuria,* p. 5.

handed him a communication from Secretary of State Stimson to the President of the Council to the effect that the United States not only was "in whole-hearted sympathy" with the Council's action but would itself take similar action. Washington's response to the Council decision to keep it informed of developments in Geneva was more complete and more friendly than even the most optimistic had dared hope. The American Government took no middle course. . . . [There follows the text of the note.]

By this single short message the greatest gap in the mechanism for peace was dramatically closed. Not only did America not object to League action; not only was she not indifferent to it: on the contrary she approved it and supported it in the most positive terms. The two principal agencies working for peaceful settlement were, therefore, united, not divided; they would work together rather than apart.

This news, spreading rapidly through the Assembly, which was just coming together, was greeted with the utmost gratification. On all sides it was given an immense significance both for the particular case in question and for the future. For the first time the United States was cooperating with the Council in an effort to prevent war. Once before, in the Bolivia-Paraguay case, the Council had put to the United States the question of what action it would suggest in case war actually broke out, as seemed likely; the necessity of a reply, however, was obviated by an unexpectedly quick settlement of the dispute. In the Manchurian case, however, the United States had taken position firmly and positively; no doubt was left but that the American Government was with Council in fact if not in form.

What this may mean for the future organization of world peace is difficult to imagine. Delegates there were in Geneva who felt the precedent thus established was one of the most important in League development. No longer was America isolated, unattainable; clearly she had shown that, in case of world crisis, the Council might hope for her friendly collaboration. "This," as the London Times correspondent that day telegraphed, "brought the United States into closer cooperation with the League than at any other time." [65]

The American note was received early on the morning of the twenty-fourth; at five that afternoon the Committee of Five met to draft a reply and at seven the full Council was summoned in private meeting to approve it. It should be remembered that while the public was aware only of the formal communication from the

[65] *The League and Manchuria, the First Phase*, p. 18.

American Government the Council in framing its response had to consider also Mr. Stimson's cabled and telephone messages of the twenty-third. In an adroitly worded note the Council expressed the warmest appreciation and gratification of the attitude of the United States. "The Council," it continued, "has no preconceived method for solving the difficulties; it will keep the United States informed and hopes that Government will communicate with the Council. . . . It is by the continuance of common endeavour that a successful result is most likely to be achieved. The efforts which are now being made here will be continued by the Council in such form as the circumstances may require." [66]

This is obviously a direct bid for closer cooperation than the diplomatic support offered by Mr. Stimson's note, an attempt to keep the door open for the United States to participate directly in the Council's action in case the Secretary of State should change his views concerning the Committee of Enquiry or a consultative seat on the Council. As to the latter there seems to have been some idea of extending an outright invitation to the United States but this could not be risked after the substance of Mr. Wilson's transatlantic conversation was made known to the members. The Council therefore contented itself with letting the American government know that its collaboration was so desirable that the League could conform its action to any form the United States might think preferable—it had no "preconceived method" of its own on which it insisted.

That collaboration might be difficult was recognized. The excerpt from *The League and Manchuria* quoted above speaks of the closing of the gap in the mechanism of peace. But this was exactly what had not occurred. With the best will in the world to attain a peaceful solution—and there is no reason to doubt the sincerity of either Washington or Geneva in this respect—there were serious obstacles to success even if the Council and Washington had seen eye to eye as to how best to handle the situation. No technique of working together had been built up, and the United States had for too long held itself rather disdainfully aloof from League action; the isolationist sentiment fostered by Mr. Stimson's own political party

[66] *Conditions in Manchuria*, pp. 7–8; also *Official Journal*, Annex 1334, pp. 2455–56.

precluded the possibility of working out such a technique overnight. The gap remained, no one knowing quite how to close it; and it was precisely through this gap that Japan was able to worm her way not only to the complete separation of Manchuria from China and her own withdrawal from the League but to her formal declaration of a New Order in East Asia and the ensuing war in the Far East.

Mr. Stimson's promise of diplomatic support of the Council's efforts was carried out on the twenty-fourth by identic notes to the Chinese and Japanese governments.

September 24, 1931

The Government and people of the United States have observed with regret and with great concern events of the past few days in Manchuria. In view of the sincere desire of the people of this country that principles and methods of peace shall prevail in international relations, and of the existence of treaties, to several of which the United States is a party, the provisions of which are intended to regulate the adjustment of controversies between nations without resort to force, the American Government feels warranted in expressing to the Chinese and Japanese Governments its hope that they will cause their military forces to refrain from any further hostilities, will so dispose respectively of their armed forces as to satisfy the requirements of international law and international agreements, and will refrain from activities which may prejudice the attainment by amicable methods of an adjustment of their differences.[67]

When these notes were received, China and Japan had already dispatched their answers to the Council; what Mr. Stimson said or failed to say was of no effect.

SEPTEMBER 25 TO 30.—Late in the evening of the twenty-fourth, Mr. Yoshizawa, according to his statement to the press, had received no instructions from his government, no answer to his urgent request for a reply regarding the proposed neutral Commission of Inquiry. But on the morning of the twenty-fifth there was delivered to President Lerroux both the Japanese reply to the Council's note of September 22 and the first official public statement of that government regarding the situation in Manchuria. The Chinese reply to the note of the twenty-second had been received the preceding day; there was therefore no reason for further delay

[67] *Conditions in Manchuria*, p. 8.

and the Council was summoned to meet that afternoon at five-fifteen.

The President opened the discussion with an expression of appreciation for the promptness with which both governments had answered, adding that he felt the Council had every reason to be satisfied with the assurance of the Japanese Government that it "had withdrawn the greater part of its forces to the railway zone and that they were concentrated there." [68]

Mr. Yoshizawa asked that in view of their importance the two documents submitted by his government be read. The first,[69] in reply to the Council notes of September 22, indicates a qualified acceptance of the suggestions contained therein. In carefully worded phrases it states the official position that Japanese troops acted only in self-defense and for the protection of the railway and the safety of Japanese subjects; that they had already been withdrawn in part to the railway zones and this withdrawal would be continued as the situation improved. It repeats the Japanese determination to secure a settlement through direct negotiations with China. The official statement,[70] issued in Tokyo on the twenty-fourth following an extraordinary session of the cabinet, takes the same position as to the reasons for military action in Manchuria and the withdrawal of troops. Japan, it asserts, has no territorial designs in Manchuria but desires only to make it a safe place for Japanese nationals and Japanese capital.

It is the proper duty of a government to protect the rights and interests legitimately enjoyed by the nation or individuals. . . . The Japanese Government, true to established policy, is prepared to cooperate with the Chinese Government in order to prevent the present incident from developing into a disastrous situation between the two countries and to work out such constructive plans as will once for all eradicate causes for further friction. The Japanese Government would be more than gratified if the present difficulty could be brought to a solution which will give a new turn to mutual relations of the two countries.

In neither communication is there the slightest recognition of the Council's competence to proceed to a settlement. In fact just the opposite view was taken in Tokyo—that the Council had no right

[68] *Official Journal*, p. 2279.   [69] *Ibid.*, pp. 2279–80.
[70] *Ibid.*, pp. 2280–81, and Annex 1334, X4, pp. 2477–78.

to undertake a settlement unless both parties requested it and Japan had no intention of so doing.[71]

There followed a long and carefully prepared statement [72] from Mr. Yoshizawa in which he declared that the documents just read confirmed in every respect the statements he had made on his own responsibility at the previous meetings and that they cleared the atmosphere which had been "obscured by alarming and exaggerated reports." He closed with these words:

I need not dwell on the Council's mission nor on the action which the League should take in the event of difficulties between its Members. Its essential mission is to bring about a pacific settlement of the dispute. The method may vary according to the circumstances, but one point is clear —namely, that it is necessary to respect the wishes of the parties. If the latter, or one of them, clearly express their views as to the choice of procedure, it seems to me that it is the duty of the Council—which is, moreover, confirmed by practice—to respect their desires and to allow the parties in conflict the time necessary to achieve the proposed object, which is the settlement of the problem. In the present case it seems to me that the Council, in view of its nature, would do well not to intervene prematurely, as by so doing it might run the risk of adversely affecting the situation which already shows signs of improvement. I would repeat that my Government is prepared immediately to enter into negotiations with the Chinese Government with a view to a satisfactory settlement of the incident.

Like Mr. Stimson Mr. Yoshizawa overlooked the fact that China also had clearly expressed her choice of procedure—that a neutral commission be sent to inquire into the facts.

When Mr. Yoshizawa had finished speaking Dr. Sze requested that the Chinese reply [73] to the Council note of September 22 be read. The Nanking government accepted the Council's suggestions unreservedly, promised China would do nothing to hinder their being carried out, but at the same time made it plain the suggestions were considered as a first step only. As to the withdrawal of Japanese troops the note requested prompt action as "the situation is growing in gravity with every hour and the effective application of the Council's decision brooks absolutely no delay." Full protection of life and

[71] *Trans-Pacific*, Oct. 1, 1931, p. 11.   [72] *Official Journal*, p. 2281.
[73] *Ibid.*, p. 2282, and Annex 1334, III, pp. 2484–85.

property was assured by the Chinese Government as soon as it regained control of the areas to be evacuated by the Japanese. Dr. Sze [74] emphasized these facts and again proposed that, in conformity with established precedents, a neutral commission should be appointed by the Council to supervise the withdrawal. Commenting on Mr. Yoshizawa's prepared statement Dr. Sze gave voice to apprehensions which in the light of recent world events have a Cassandra-like note of prophecy:

. . . He [the Japanese representative] has stated . . . "There still remain some detachments in Mukden and Kirin, and a small number of men in a few other places. . . ."

This is a very interesting statement and I wonder whether the Japanese representative would tell us what he considers "a small number of men" and what are the "few other places."

He has said that the measures taken were necessary for the protection of Japanese lives and property. If you will permit me to say so it is a dangerous principle to assert that, in order to protect nationals and their property in a foreign country, a large number of troops may occupy so many places, destroy so much property and kill so many innocent people. In every country in the world there are nationals of other countries. Is this principle going to be the new principle for the world? This question deserves the closest attention, not only of the Members of the Council, but of the other nations. [75]

A reference to Article 15 of the Covenant brought from Viscount Cecil a sharp rejoinder which is ample evidence of the change in attitude previously referred to. It not only indicates a withdrawal of support from China but has a note of sympathy with Japan quite different from the antagonism apparent in the curious interchange between Cecil and Yoshizawa at the close of the session on September 22. [76]

In the course of his remarks Dr. Sze had said:

It appears to my Government that, in conformity with precedent, the next and immediate step on the part of the Council should be to point out to the Government of Japan that, unless there is an immediate withdrawal, Japan will place herself in opposition to the categorical obligation assumed by her under the first paragraph of Article 15 of the Covenant, to submit to the Council disputes which are likely to lead to a rup-

[74] *Ibid.*, pp. 2282–84.　　　[75] *Ibid.*, p. 2284.　　　[76] *Ibid.*, p. 2273.

ture and which are not submitted to arbitration or judicial settlement, and it need hardly be observed that, if Article 15 is brought into operation, the procedure to be taken by the parties to the dispute and by the Council or the Assembly, if the question is referred to it, is no longer a matter of discretion, but is stated definitely and with particularity.[77]

Viscount Cecil's statement as given in the *Official Journal* follows:

Viscount Cecil said he would like to indicate briefly how he understood the actual position in which the Council was placed.

As he understood it, the matter had been brought before the Council under Article 11 of the Covenant, and therefore he did not understand the reference of the Chinese representative to Article 15, which could be invoked, as the Chinese representative was aware, by the procedure indicated therein, but which had not been invoked in the present case. The duty of the Council as Lord Cecil had always understood it and as was expressed clearly in Article 11, was to "take any action that may be deemed wise and effectual to safeguard the peace of nations." That was the Council's duty. It had not to settle the dispute or pass any judgment on the action of the parties, or, indeed, to do anything but safeguard the peace of nations. It was only when peace had been safeguarded, for that was primarily the duty of the Council, that any question as to settlement of the actual dispute could arise.

Lord Cecil agreed with his Japanese colleague that, primarily, the question of the dispute was a matter for the parties and not for the Council to deal with, unless it came before the latter under Article 15, or unless the parties had signed some general arbitration treaty, or what was called the General Act; in that case they were bound by their contractual agreement. But at the present stage the business of the Council, acting under Article 11, was to safeguard the peace of nations. That, at any rate, was his reason for accepting the proceedings at the previous Council meeting, when it urged both parties to refrain from action which would aggravate the dispute and to withdraw, as soon as possible, any troops that had penetrated into the territory of the other, apart from their treaty rights. Such seemed to him to be the duty of the Council, which would have failed in its duty if it had not taken that course.

It was with the greatest pleasure that he had recognized from the statement made by his Japanese colleague that, in point of fact, even before receiving the Council's communication, the Japanese troops were being withdrawn. The Japanese representative would contradict him if he said anything inaccurate, but Lord Cecil understood that that was his statement, and so far as he knew, the Chinese representative did not dis-

[77] *Ibid.*, p. 2283.

pute the fact. The Chinese representative said there were still troops occupying the territory of China which the Japanese Government was not entitled to under treaty obligations, and it was clear that the Council would desire—and the Japanese Government too, he hoped—that those troops should be withdrawn as rapidly as possible. That was the obvious precaution which the Council ought to take to preserve the peace of nations.

Both sides admitted that the process of withdrawal was in progress, and there was every reason to hope that the duty of the Council to safeguard the peace of nations might in a short time be regarded as having been fully accomplished. If the Council entertained any doubts on the question, it would have to consider what its duty was under those circumstances.

He had submitted these observations merely to make quite clear what he took to be the duty of the Council in the matter, and what he had always believed to be the general understanding on that point.[78]

President Lerroux then closed the meeting with a brief summary of the main points of the Chinese and Japanese statements and an appeal in the name of the Council to the Japanese to withdraw their troops to the railway zone as soon as possible. In the meantime in view of the importance of the statements made by the two parties he proposed postponing the discussion in order that the members might have time to study them.

This fourth public meeting of the Council did not meet with the same general approval as the previous meetings. It was felt by many that the Council had come out a bad second-best in the discussions and that Japan had successfully defied both the League and the United States. Especially harsh was the criticism of Lord Cecil. The Secretariat view, however, was that, judged by Japanese standards, the reply of that government was really a great concession, that Lord Cecil and the rest of the Council went to extremes in an effort to save Japan's face, even at the sacrifice of their own, hoping thereby to secure a continued withdrawal of Japanese troops, and finally, that they were following the policy, urged upon them by Mr. Stimson, of conciliating Japan. Certainly there developed for a few days in Geneva the hope that the confidence reposed in Japan would influence that government to begin immediately and complete within

[78] *Ibid.*, pp. 2284-85.

a short time the withdrawal of the remaining troops. A statement by Viscount Ishii [79] in Tokyo gave grounds for this hope, which was strengthened by the report that following the meeting on the twenty-fifth the Japanese delegation urged their government to take such action, since "Japan's honor and place among the civilized powers depended on its leaning backward now to carry out Kenkichi Yoshizawa's promises of a quick withdrawal." [80] That such action by the government would be received sympathetically at home is evidenced by the editorial in the Tokyo Asahi, previously referred to, in which a discussion of the American note of September 24 closes with these words:

By trusting Japan to find a happy solution to the present military incident the United States has served the cause of peace in the Far East. *It is to be hoped now that we will live up to the promises of the Japanese Government contained in its reply to the note of the United States.*[81]

Washington was as confident as Geneva, according to a special dispatch to the New York *Times:*

A stronger note of optimism for an amicable solution of the Manchurian clash between Japan and China was evident here today. The State Department said developments of the past two days were of a hopeful character and, with Japan evidently withdrawing her troops to the railroad zone and bent upon a direct solution of outstanding points with China, there was no disposition to force matters by any more moves on the part of the United States Government for the present.

That the administration would mark time in the situation was indicated when Secretary Stimson left this afternoon to spend the week-end at his New York home. Unofficial reports from Geneva that the League of Nations had abandoned the suggestion of appointing an international commission to act in Manchuria and was content to leave the situation for direct adjustment by China and Japan were accepted as pointing to an agreement on policy with this country.

[79] Viscount Ishii, who had been a strong supporter of the League, had expressed great indignation over the proposal to send a neutral commission to Manchuria, as reflecting upon Japan's integrity. He implied that all that was necessary was for the Council to have faith in Japanese assurances and the troops would be speedily withdrawn. Full accounts of this speech were carried in the New York *Times* of Sept. 26, and in *Trans-Pacific*, Oct. 1.

[80] Clarence Streit, New York *Times*, Sept. 27 and 28.

[81] These are the concluding words of the excerpt quoted in note 56, above. The italics are mine. See also *Trans-Pacific*, Oct. 8, 1931.

Katsuji Debuchi, the Japanese Ambassador, gave to Secretary Stimson today the text of the statement issued by his government yesterday. The tone of this document was regarded as suggesting that Japan would withdraw her troops to the South Manchurian railroad zone and that she was trying to straighten out the situation. The statement was looked upon as indicating a peaceful solution of the crisis.[82]

But in Nanking a very different view was taken. Hallett Abend in a dispatch to the New York *Times* quotes a Nanking cabinet spokesman as follows:

In view of the mounting number of acts of open aggression by the Japanese in Manchuria which have startled the world in the last few days, government leaders here are at a loss to understand the attitude of the United States and the powers vitally concerned with peace in the Far East. The territorial integrity of China, the safeguarding of which for decades has been one of the cardinal principles of American policy in the Orient, appears seriously menaced, and the Chinese Government is amazed at what seems to be Washington's policy of temporizing instead of sharply calling upon Japan for an explanation of her actions and a clear definition of her present intentions.

In some quarters the conjecture is made that the American State Department is handling the matter with kid gloves, believing that for the present the adoption of a stronger attitude would embarrass the civilian faction of the Tokyo Government, which is reported to be opposed to the high-handed policies of the Japanese military and naval cliques. . . .

China, which knows Japan as a man knows his next door neighbor, is convinced that every day which passes without adequate expression of foreign condemnation of the rape of Manchuria serves only to strengthen the grip which Japan's militarists have upon the Tokyo Government, making more difficult the accession to real power of the group of civilians who have been leading Japan toward an enlightened liberalism.

China is convinced that the longer the military continue bolting with the bit between their teeth the more they will succeed in arousing the passions and the warlike spirit of the Japanese people, and every day that the present tension is prolonged the more difficult is the Chinese Government's self-appointed task of restraining Chinese people from retaliatory measures.

If Japanese aggression continues unchecked there is almost certain to arise some serious clash or incident which, it is believed, is exactly what the Japanese responsible for the present situation desire to promote.[83]

[82] New York *Times*, Sept. 26, 1931.   [83] *Ibid.*

Far from being hopeful, the situation at the close of September 25 appears now to have been deadlocked, with Japan insisting on direct negotiations and refusing a neutral Commission of Enquiry, while China continued to demand that such a commission supervise the withdrawal of Japanese troops and refused to consider direct negotiations so long as these remained outside the treaty zone. This deadlock continued through the next public meeting of the Council on Monday, September 28, although China then made a valiant if unsuccessful attempt to compromise with Japan. It will be remembered that Mr. Stimson, on September 22, while advising against the sending of a neutral investigating commission urged the Council, "in case they felt that the need of such a commission was now imperative, to follow the method which had become common in international matters of having such a commission appointed by the two nations themselves, China and Japan, *with a membership from neutral nations*, this method being one which was well understood and in general use in treaties of conciliation." [84]

Whether any pressure was brought to bear upon the Chinese over the week end, whether they made up their own minds following Friday's meeting that they would have to make some concessions, or whether from the beginning they had been considering Mr. Stimson's suggestion and thought it feasible, we do not know. However, Dr. Sze's proposal bears such strong resemblance to that of the American Secretary of State that we are inclined to believe not only was there a direct connection between the two but the Chinese delegation, in following Mr. Stimson's advice, was trying to win the support of this country and regain some of the ground lost to Japan as a result of Lord Cecil's stand on Friday.

Through all of Monday's discussion ran the thread of the debate over the Chinese proposal. Following up Mr. Yoshizawa's assurance that Japan desired to complete the withdrawal of troops as soon as possible Dr. Sze said they were all agreed as to the desirability of such action but the question remained as to how this was to be carried out. The Chinese view was well known.

It was that a neutral Commission of Enquiry should be sent, and that Japan should accept that, as she had now accepted the Chinese assurance

[84] Stimson, *op. cit.*, pp. 43–44. Italics mine.

to protect Japanese life and property. But as he [Sze] was anxious to be conciliatory and to meet the representative from Japan more than half-way he proposed that the Council should help the parties to reach an agreement as to the arrangements on the spot, which would make it possible to fix an early date for the completion of the withdrawal of troops and render it unnecessary for the Council to send a Commission of Enquiry from Geneva. . . .

Mr. Yoshizawa replied that the most important points raised by the Chinese representatives seemed to be the immediate withdrawal of the troops within the railway zone, and the commission of observers. He was convinced that he had fully explained, not only in his statement that day, but also last Friday, the reason for which the Japanese Government was unable to agree to those two suggestions. . . .

. . . With regard to observers, [Mr. Sze] had said that he would prefer that a commission of neutral observers should be sent to the spot, but, in order to be conciliatory, he had suggested that the Council should help the parties to come to an agreement as to arrangements on the spot which would make it possible to fix an early date for the completion of the withdrawal, thereby rendering unnecessary the sending of a Commission of Enquiry.

Mr. Yoshizawa . . . was prepared to telegraph at once to Tokio Mr. Sze's second suggestion for the organization of a Sino-Japanese commission on the spot with a view to facilitating the evacuation.

Mr. Sze said that the Council, having received the appeal from China and China having entrusted her case to the Council, he expected that the commission would report to the Council in order that the latter might be informed of the speedy and complete withdrawal of the troops. . . .

Mr. Yoshizawa . . . desired, however, to ask whether Mr. Sze had in mind a commission composed only of Japanese and Chinese or a commission including members of other nationalities as well.

Mr. Sze replied that, in view of the fact that the Japanese representative had, on previous occasions and again at the present meeting, questioned the accuracy of reports, and that there were matters on which the representatives of the two countries did not agree, it was possible that the same thing might happen—although Mr. Sze hoped it would not—in arranging for the withdrawal of troops. In those circumstances and as the Council was assisting the two parties, Mr. Sze considered that it should appoint a neutral representative or representatives who might be able to help in settling any differences and also in removing any possibility of a misunderstanding. . . .

Mr. Yoshizawa replied that in his first statement he had fully explained his Government's position with regard to evacuation and the commission of observers. He had said at the end of his statement: "In these circumstances all measures other than those mentioned above are unnecessary." He was therefore unable to agree to the Chinese representative's suggestion with reference to the sending of the commission to Manchuria, if that commission was to be composed on the lines indicated by Mr. Sze in his last remarks.

Mr. Sze pointed out that he had never used the words "a Commission of Observers." He had said that the Council would help the parties to arrange a conciliation. He had not suggested a commission to proceed from Geneva, because there were neutrals on the spot who would help the two parties to arrive at an amicable settlement. As the Japanese representative had said that Japan was anxious to live in the most friendly relations with China, he would most certainly welcome someone to help in the removal of any possible misunderstanding that might have arisen.

Viscount Cecil thought the suggestion made by the Chinese representative an interesting one, and hoped that his Japanese colleague would be able to give it further consideration.

If he understood the Chinese suggestion rightly, it was that there should be some kind of committee or meeting formed in Manchuria, consisting essentially of Chinese and Japanese representatives. The Chinese representative had also suggested that the League might do something to help the two parties to come to an agreement. If Mr. Yoshizawa thought that suggestion of use, the Council might begin by bringing the Chinese and Japanese together, to see if they could arrive at an agreement.

As Lord Cecil had said at the last meeting, the chief business of the League was to promote an agreement between the parties after they had succeeded—if they did succeed—in avoiding all danger of the dispute degenerating into a war. In saying that, Lord Cecil had not meant to suggest that the League was not interested in seeing such an agreement being made. On the contrary. Since the League's business was to bring about peace and agreement, it was intensely interested in an agreement being reached between the two parties, but according to all the previous practice of the League, it had always been left to the parties to come to an agreement if they could do so. He hoped that his Japanese colleague would consider carefully whether a meeting of Chinese and Japanese might not be of service in arranging at least evacuation and other matters of that kind. If that meeting should prove fruitless, the Council would then have to consider if anything else could be done by it to bring about an agreement.

In conclusion, Lord Cecil suggested that, in order to avoid misunderstanding, the Chinese representative might put his proposal in writing.

Mr. Sze would gladly conform to the request to put his suggestion in writing [Annex 1334, Section VIII]. He would, however, point out that he had said that the Council could help the parties to come to an agreement by arrangements on the spot. He had not said that China or Japan alone could arrange matters, but that the Council could arrange them and that the Council might see fit to select its representative on the spot.

Viscount Cecil thought that in that case the Council would be unable to carry the matter further at the present stage.

Mr. Yoshizawa repeated that he was quite ready to submit Lord Cecil's suggestion for consideration by his Government, but, if that suggestion was to be supplemented by the further suggestion made by the Chinese representative, he would be unable to do so. He appreciated the motives with which Lord Cecil had made his suggestion. Japan had no intention of making war upon China.

Mr. Yoshizawa added that the Japanese Government was endeavouring to bring about a happy solution of the affair at the earliest possible date and for that reason he welcomed any suggestion which would pave the way to it.

He interpreted Lord Cecil's suggestion to mean that the Chinese and Japanese would endeavour to come to an agreement without help from outsiders. If that interpretation were correct, he would not fail to transmit the suggestion to his Government.

Mr. Sze said that there seemed to be some misapprehension on the part of the representative of Japan. He, Mr. Sze, had made a proposal which Lord Cecil had sought to restate in his own words, and this version by Lord Cecil Mr. Sze had corrected.

Viscount Cecil regretted that there should be any possible misunderstanding in the matter. He had thought in the first place that his Chinese colleague's suggestion applied to the question of the method, time, etc., of the evacuation, and nothing else.

It was true that Mr. Sze had added that he thought the League could help the parties to come to an agreement. The only difference was that it was now suggested that the Chinese and Japanese should meet and try to come to an agreement. If they did not do so, the Council would be no worse off than it was at present, and it could then say what further steps could be taken. Lord Cecil merely wished to make it quite clear that he was referring solely to the question of evacuation, and that he was not dealing with other questions at the moment. It would, however, be difficult to carry the matter further at the present meeting.

The President did not think that there was any advantage in discussing the matter further at that meeting. The statements which had been made would need to be carefully studied by the members of the Council. He would summon another meeting shortly, but, as the Assembly was closing on the following day, the Council would no doubt agree that he should explain the situation to it. He therefore proposed to ask permission of the President of the Assembly to speak on the following day in order to give an impartial report on the question, and on the manner in which the Council had so far carried out its duties under Article 11 of the Covenant.[85]

If Lord Cecil's words of September 25, tacitly agreed to by the rest of the Council, had for their object the persuasion of Japan to a more moderate course they fell far short of achievement. For Japan was not thus to be moved on the two immediate issues of evacuation and a neutral commission. Certainly Dr. Sze's compromise was clearly stated in the beginning when he proposed "that the Council should help the parties to reach an agreement as to arrangements on the spot," and later when he said the Council "should appoint a neutral representative or representatives." And yet we find Mr. Yoshizawa referring first to a "Sino-Japanese commission," then to a "Commission of Observers," trying again and again to give to the Chinese proposal an interpretation that was obviously not there. Again Lord Cecil seemed to be playing into the hands of Japan and to an even greater extent than on Friday. Had a statesman of less personal integrity and of a lesser devotion to the League been involved in this discussion one could easily read into the minutes of Monday's Council meeting a deliberate attempt to twist the meaning of Dr. Sze's suggestion and to trap him into consenting to some form of direct negotiations with Japan. And such might have been the result except for the alertness with which the Chinese representative followed the discussion and challenged every misinterpretation of his words.

It may be that the apparent change in Lord Cecil's position was in part a reflection of conservative opinion in Great Britain as expressed in a leading article of the London *Times* of September 26:

It is no exaggeration to say that the American Government, though not a member of the League, has been in closer collaboration with it during the last few days than at any previous time. In one respect, indeed, it has handled a difficult and obscure situation more skillfully than the Council

[85] *Official Journal,* pp. 2289-93. Reproduced here are only those sections of the debate having to do with the Chinese compromise proposal.

was at first disposed to do. The manner of Mr. Stimson's intervention was as tactful as was the text of his communication to the Japanese and Chinese Governments. His refusal to support the proposal mooted at the meeting of the League Council for the dispatch of a Military Commission of Inquiry to Manchuria showed a sagacious appreciation of the dangers inseparable from such a step. Any action which gave the proud and sensitive islanders the impression, however unfounded, that their government was regarded with distrust by other Powers must have increased the embarrassments at Tokio and might have defeated the good intentions at Geneva.

Observers in Geneva, however, held a different view, and the opinion was freely expressed [86] that in following the advice of the United States as to the sending of a neutral commission the League was abdicating its duty, that if a Great Power had not been involved in the case the Council would have taken immediate steps to find out for itself exactly what was happening. Whatever may have been the motives, whose the blame, however much opinion might differ as to courses of action, the fact remains that at the close of Monday's session the deadlock continued; China still insisted on some sort of neutral aid in arrangements for evacuation and Japan persisted in her demand for direct negotiations between the two parties alone.

No public comment on this fifth public session of the Council was made by the State Department in Washington, the day's statement to the press dealing largely with the Chinese and Japanese replies to Secretary Stimson's identic notes of the twenty-fourth.[87] The Chinese note,[88] after expressing the gratification of the government and people at the interest of the United States in the maintenance of peace between China and Japan, gives some further details of Japanese aggression in Manchuria and concludes with these words:

The Chinese Government can conceive no other way to satisfy the requirements of international law and international agreements, when international law and international agreements have already been trampled under foot, than for Japan to withdraw her troops immediately and completely from the occupied areas and to give full redress to the aggrieved party, the Chinese Government and the Chinese people.

[86] *The League and Manchuria, the First Phase,* p. 29.   [87] P. 54, above.
[88] *Conditions in Manchuria,* pp. 9–10.

It is the earnest hope of the Chinese Government that most effective means will be promptly taken for maintaining the dignity and inviolability of the international treaties above referred to, so that all efforts heretofore made by the various powers, especially the United States, for the preservation of peace, might not be in vain.

The Japanese reply after acknowledging the receipt of the American note continues:

The Japanese Government is deeply sensible of the friendly concern and the fairness of views with which the American Government has observed the recent course of events in Manchuria. In common with the hope expressed by the American Government, it has already caused the Japanese military forces in Manchuria to refrain from any further acts of hostility, unless their own safety, as well as the security of the South Manchuria Railway and of Japanese lives and property within that railway zone is jeopardized by the aggression of Chinese troops or armed bands. Every care has been, and will continue to be exercised by the Japanese forces to observe all the requirements of international law and international agreements, and to avoid any action that is calculated to prejudice an amicable settlement of the differences between Japan and China.

The Japanese Government is confident that by frank and unimpassioned discussion between the two parties in conflict, in the light of their true and lasting interests, an adjustment will be found to set at rest the existing tension in Manchuria.[89]

Regarding these replies Mr. Stimson has written:

In its replies to these notes [90] the Japanese Government asserted that its troops had acted only to the extent necessary to insure their own safety, the protection of the railway and the safety of Japanese nationals. They announced that they had already withdrawn the greater portion of their forces back into the railway zone, leaving only a few small bodies quartered in several places outside, and that their forces were being withdrawn to the fullest extent consonant with the safety of their nationals and the safety of their railroad. They also asserted their profound desire of reaching a peaceful settlement of the problem "as rapidly as possible by the negotiations between the two countries."

[89] *Ibid.*, pp. 10–11.
[90] Mr. Stimson's use of the plural here must include the memorandum of September 22 as well as the formal note of the 24th; as to "replies," there seems to be only one, that to the note of September 24, above. There was no reply to the memorandum and a Japanese statement of the time said none was necessary.

On the other hand, the Chinese Government in its reply notes of the 22nd and 24th, respectively,[91] disclaimed all responsibility for the outbreak; asserted that it had been entirely caused by Japanese aggression and that their own troops had not even offered resistance to the attacks of the Japanese; recited that the acts of aggression were continuing; pledged their readiness to abstain from any aggravation of the situation and assumed full responsibility for the protection of life and property as soon as the occupied areas should be evacuated by the Japanese troops.[92]

Again Mr. Stimson failed to take the people of the United States into his confidence. Of the contents of the notes the public knew nothing, only the bare fact that notes had been sent and answers received, as is evidenced by the following dispatch from the New York *Times* of September 29:

Japan and China replied today to Secretary Stimson's identic notes of last week appealing for a peaceful adjustment of the Manchurian crisis in communications expressing appreciation for the friendly interest of the United States.

Baron Shidehara, the Japanese Foreign Minister, delivered the Japanese note to Edwin L. Neville, the American Chargé d'Affaires, in Tokyo and Ambassador Debuchi delivered a copy to the State Department here.

The Chinese note was delivered here by Dr. Yung Kwai, the Chinese Chargé d'Affaires. Supplementing the note, the Chinese Legation made public a statement describing alleged bombing by Japanese of trains, on one of which J. D. Thompson, British manager of the Peiping Mukden Railway was a passenger, with numerous casualties.

Ambassador Debuchi spent an hour with Secretary Stimson and Under-Secretary Castle and gave them a detailed report of conditions in Manchuria. It was understood he reported that the withdrawal of Japanese troops to the railroad zone was progressing although it was not yet completed.

Dr. Yung Kwai spent some time with Mr. Castle discussing the situation from the Chinese standpoint.

It was said, as a result of these conversations and the two notes, that the United States saw no reason for further action in the situation at this

[91] This must refer to the Chinese note of appeal under the Kellogg Pact, dated September 21, and to their note of the 28th in answer to Stimson's of the 24th. So far as Senate Document No. 55 shows, the only communication to China up to September 28, is that of the 24th.
[92] Stimson, *op. cit.,* pp. 47–48.

time. It is recognized that the reaction in China, as evidenced by the attack by students on C. T. Wang, the Foreign Minister, ·is serious but there is encouragement in the fact that the rioting has occurred far away from the section under Japanese military occupation.

Officials are hopeful that in a few days the situation will quiet down and that then progress can be made on an adjustment of the Manchurian question through diplomatic channels.

Of a far more important event of the twenty-eighth no mention at all was made to the press. Sometime before this date, Mr. Stimson, feeling that his sources of information as to the exact situation in Manchuria were insufficient, had informed Baron Shidehara that he wished to send two of our representatives in the Far East to make investigations on the spot and had requested that they be given every facility to carry out their inquiry. Baron Shidehara assured Mr. Stimson of the fullest cooperation on the part of the Japanese Government, and on September 28 Mr. Stimson cabled secret instructions to the men selected, E. Laurence Salisbury, Second Secretary of the embassy in Tokyo, and George C. Hanson, Consul General in Harbin, both "men of long experience in the Far East, of tested capacity and thoroughly trusted by us." [93]

The text of their instructions is not included in the documents submitted to the Senate in January, 1932, but Mr. Stimson gives the substance of them in his *Far Eastern Crisis:*

They were to visit the various points where there had been fighting or where the Japanese troops had advanced beyond their treaty boundaries. They were to report their judgment as to the justification for these troop movements; their scope and extent and the reasons alleged for them. They were to gather evidence as to whether the proposed occupation was really temporary and whether the troops were to be withdrawn after the danger passed. They were to report on the form of civil administration, if any, set up by the Japanese in the Chinese cities and to report all interference by the Japanese military with the Chinese civil administration, particularly in respect to the native and international sections of Mukden and as to whether the civil administration had been in any respect restored in that city so that it could act with independence. They were also to report as to the attitude of the Chinese population in Manchuria towards the Japanese and whether it was such as to offer a

[93] *Ibid.,* p. 45.

genuine excuse for the non-withdrawal of the Japanese troops. In summary they were to report how far the Japanese occupation in Manchuria had been extended and whether there was any justification for the extension; also whether there was any intention manifested to restore the status quo-ante.[94]

From this it would seem that Mr. Stimson was beginning to have some doubts as to the Japanese intentions. Of the results obtained Mr. Stimson says:

Hanson and Salisbury promptly took up their work and within a very short time I was beginning to receive from them on the ground a series of reports upon the situation which was of the utmost value in crystallizing my own judgment as to what had occurred, and what was likely to be the outcome of events soon to be set in rapid motion.[95]

The Council met in public session on September 29 but the Chinese appeal was not on the agenda. A number of private conferences were held [96] in an effort to break the existing deadlock, and late in the day the Committee of Five met to prepare a draft resolution for presentation to the full Council the next day. The Chinese delegation meanwhile, following Lord Cecil's suggestion,[97] had put their compromise proposal into writing and this was circulated to the Council members on the morning of the thirtieth.[98] The text follows:

WHEREAS the Chinese Government still believes that the best method that may be devised by the Council for securing the prompt and complete withdrawal of the Japanese troops and police and the full reestablishment of the status quo ante, is the sending of a neutral commission to Manchuria, and,

WHEREAS the Chinese representative is desirous of being as conciliatory as possible and of meeting half-way the wishes of the Japanese Government:

Therefore, the following proposal is made:

That the Council shall help the parties to come to an agreement as to arrangements on the spot which will make it possible to fix an early date for the completion of the withdrawal of all troops, police and aerial forces, thereby making it unnecessary to send a Commission of Enquiry

---

[94] *Ibid.,* pp. 45–46.   [95] *Ibid.* For the remainder of this story see Chaps. III and VII.
[96] Willoughby, *op. cit.,* pp. 70–71; also *The League and Manchuria, the First Phase,* p. 32.
[97] See p. 64, above.   [98] *Official Journal,* Annex 1334, VIII, 2457.

in connection with the complete restoration of the status quo ante.

That the Council in making the arrangements referred to shall appoint neutral persons on the spot to represent it, who shall participate in all arrangements made and report currently to the Council.

Meeting in final session at 4:00 P.M. of the thirtieth, the Council first cleared up all other matters on its agenda, adjourned for a short recess, and then resumed at 5:45 for the discussion of the Chinese appeal. Before introducing the draft resolution, President Lerroux read a prepared statement emphasizing the essential point of the problem, the withdrawal of troops to the railway zone. He said in part:

. . . Under that article of the Covenant under which an appeal has been made to the Council, the duty of the League is "to take such action as may be deemed wise and effectual to safeguard the peace of nations," and the Council, anxious to carry out its duty in the matter now before it, has singled out one object as being of immediate and paramount importance—namely, the withdrawl of troops to the railway zone. Nevertheless, it could not but admit that, in the special circumstances, a certain time had to be allowed for the withdrawal, particularly in order to ensure the safety of Japanese life and property.

Both the parties have concurred with the other Members of the Council in recognizing, without prejudice to their views as to the method of settlement of questions outstanding between them, the essential importance of the withdrawal of the troops in accordance with the above conditions, and the parties have each taken steps to that end.

In these circumstances, I am inclined to think that no useful purpose would be served by continuing our discussions at the present moment. A certain amount of time, which the Council, together with the parties, will desire to be as short as possible, is still required for the complete withdrawal of troops to the railway zone.

In my opinion, the Council, which must watch closely the development of the situation, will in present circumstances best serve the interests of peace and good understanding by adjourning for a short time, and I therefore beg to propose the resolution which is before you.[99]

He then read the following draft resolution:

The Council:

1. Notes the replies of the Chinese and Japanese Governments to the urgent appeal addressed to them by its President and the steps that have already been taken in response to that appeal;

[99] *Official Journal*, p. 2307.

2. Recognizes the importance of the Japanese Government's statement that it has no territorial designs in Manchuria;

3. Notes the Japanese representative's statement that his Government will continue, as rapidly as possible, the withdrawal of its troops, which has already been begun, into the railway zone in proportion as the safety of the lives and property of Japanese nationals is effectively assured and that it hopes to carry out this intention in full as speedily as may be;

4. Notes the Chinese representative's statement that his Government will assume responsibility for the safety of the lives and property of Japanese nationals outside that zone as the withdrawal of the Japanese troops continues and the Chinese local authorities and police forces are re-established;

5. Being convinced that both Governments are anxious to avoid taking any action which might disturb the peace and good understanding between the two nations, notes that the Chinese and Japanese representatives have given assurances that their respective Governments will take all necessary steps to prevent any extension of the scope of the incident or any aggravation of the situation;

6. Requests both parties to do all in their power to hasten the restoration of normal relations between them and for that purpose to continue and speedily complete the execution of the above-mentioned undertakings;

7. Requests both parties to furnish the Council at frequent intervals with full information as to the development of the situation;

8. Decides, in the absence of any unforeseen occurrence which might render an immediate meeting essential, to meet again at Geneva on Wednesday, October 14th, 1931, to consider the situation as it then stands;

9. Authorizes its President to cancel the meeting of the Council fixed for October 14th should he decide, after consulting his colleagues, and more particularly the representatives of the two parties, that, in view of such information as he may have received from the two parties or from other members of the Council as to the development of the situation, the meeting is no longer necessary.[100]

Mr. Yoshizawa immediately accepted the resolution without qualification or interpretation of any sort. He then suggested that instead of taking special measures to obtain information on the spot, "a question to which several of his colleagues apparently attached

[100] *Ibid.*, pp. 2307–8.

great importance," each member of the Council should send to the Secretary-General any information his government had received and thought desirable to communicate to the other Members.

Commenting first on the fact that the Japanese representative now recognized the need for neutral information and on the Council's request for information, Dr. Sze accepted the resolution according to the following interpretation:

. . . By these means, and in the light of the Japanese representative's statement, Mr. Sze hoped that, as a first step towards the restoration of normal relations between the two countries, the unfortunate situation with which the Council was now dealing would speedily come to an end. In this connection, he noted with satisfaction that, by the terms of the proposed resolution, the Council was conscious of its responsibility for helping both parties to secure the complete and prompt withdrawal of the armed forces of Japan and the full re-establishment of the status quo ante, and would remain in session until that responsibility was fully discharged. That, indeed, was made clear in the appeal which the Council had addressed to the parties on September 22nd, when it had authorized its President, in consultation with the parties, to endeavour to find adequate means of enabling the withdrawal of troops to take place forthwith without endangering the safety of life or property.

The Chinese representative recognized that, if by October 14th the complete withdrawal and the re-establishment of the status quo ante had been effected, the measures at present being employed would have proved adequate; but if, contrary to the strongly expressed hope of his Japanese colleague—a hope that was shared by the Council and the Chinese Government—this happy result was not achieved by that date, the Council would, of course, have to examine what other measures might be required in the circumstances.

Upon that head, Mr. Sze had made two proposals: first, a Committee of Enquiry; and secondly, local arrangements. The Council would no doubt give them due consideration on October 14th in the course of its general survey of the situation, but he must repeat that he fervently hoped and believed—as did all his colleagues on the Council—that by that date no such action would prove necessary.

With reference to the President's statement, the Chinese representative had not failed to recognize that the complete withdrawal of the armed forces of Japan and the full re-establishment of the status quo ante, while a distinct and separate matter, constituted but a single and preliminary step in the adjustment of the controversy which the Government of China had submitted to the Council. He therefore deemed it proper to say that, when the complete and full re-establishment of the status quo ante had been effected, the Government of China reserved all its rights under the Covenant and would continue to look to the Council for aid in determining the several responsibilities of the two parties for the events which had occurred since the night of September 18th, and the fixing of the reparation justly due. It was with the foregoing understanding that the Chinese representative accepted the resolution.[101]

Mr. Yoshizawa said he was unable to accept Dr. Sze's interpretation. He only accepted the draft resolution as it stood.

Without further discussion the draft resolution was unanimously adopted. Announcing this adoption the President said he thought there was no need to go into matters of interpretation at this time; the rights of both parties obviously remained intact and either would be entitled to submit his point of view to the Council later. He then adjourned the session to October 14.

By its unanimous adoption this resolution of September 30 became immediately binding upon both parties; by its acceptance Japan was committed to the speedy withdrawal of her troops into the railway zone, China to the protection of Japanese lives and property in the territory so evacuated; both governments were bound by their promises not to aggravate the situation and were requested by the Council to hasten the restoration of normal relations between them. That the Chinese representative was not satisfied with the resolution is shown by his lengthy interpretation of it. Dr. Sze objected to the fact that there was no provision either for a Commission of Enquiry or for the appointment of neutral representatives on the spot with instructions to report to the Council on the situation as they found it. In the conferences preceding the final session he attempted to have at least the latter inserted in the resolution and also to have a date fixed for the final withdrawal of troops to the railway zone. But the Japanese representative was successful in having both of these vital points eliminated from the draft resolution. Without arrangements for some kind of neutral supervision the phrase in Section 3 of the resolution, "in proportion as the safety of the lives and property of Japanese nationals is assured," gave the army command in Manchuria all the leeway it needed to

[101] *Ibid.*, p. 2308.

continue the military occupation indefinitely, and so it was interpreted in Tokyo and in Mukden.[102] As to the reasons why these loopholes were left, it seems that the Japanese delegation had let it be understood that if no definite date were set the withdrawal would be completed within two weeks; it was also understood that the United States opposed the fixing of a date as well as the sending of a Commission of Enquiry [103] and for much the same reasons: that the Japanese militarists would be offended, their opposition stiffened, and Shidehara's position thereby made more difficult.[104] It was recognized also that it would be difficult if not impossible for the Council to determine from Geneva just how long the evacuation and restoration of order would take.[105] They compromised therefore by adjourning for two weeks with the implication that the withdrawal should be completed by that time if at all possible.

Despite the weakness caused by these two omissions the Resolution of September 30 represents nevertheless a momentous step on the part of the Council of the League of Nations. For the first time in League history a case involving one of the Great Powers in a great issue had come formally before them. Not only was the case an exceedingly complicated one, but the general international situation added to the difficulties of a successful solution. Yet the Council had not attempted to evade its responsibility. It had, at the close of the first day's discussion, addressed a formal appeal to both parties to refrain from aggravating the situation pending a peaceful settlement of the dispute; it had asked for and received from the United States an assurance of diplomatic support and at the end of ten days of anxious deliberation it had unanimously adopted a resolution which placed upon Japan, the Great Power involved, the burden of responsibility for the future development of the situation. Moreover the Japanese delegation had tacitly accepted this responsibility, for, while Mr. Yoshizawa expressly repudiated Dr. Sze's interpretation of the resolution, at no time did he take exception to President Ler-

---

[102] *Trans-Pacific*, Oct. 8 and 15.   [103] Willoughby, *op. cit.*, pp. 74–76.
[104] For discussion of Yoshizawa's relation to Shidehara, see Chap. IV.
[105] Whether by accident or design the fact that the Chinese proposal of neutral representatives would have taken care of this seems to have been completely ignored.

roux's declaration that the Council "has singled out one object as being of immediate and paramount importance, namely the withdrawal of troops to the railway zone."

And so we turn to Washington, as Geneva and Tokyo turned on the first of October, 1931. Mr. Stimson in his note of September 24 had assured the Council that the Government of the United States was in wholehearted sympathy with the attitude of the League as expressed in the Council's resolution of September 22, and there was no appreciable change in that attitude as expressed in the resolution of September 30; he had promised that he would continue to work for the restoration of peace; he had advised the Council not to send a neutral commission to the scene of the conflict and the Council had followed his advice.[106] Now, in the Resolution of September 30, the Council had taken a step which it earnestly hoped would lead to a peaceful settlement. How would Mr. Stimson carry out his promise of support? What action would he take?

We read the New York *Times* of October 1, 1931, and find the League action of the previous day given first place. We turn to the dispatch from Washington to see what the State Department has to say. There is no mention of it. But after all, even considering the difference of time between Geneva and Washington, it is too soon for a considered comment on such a vital matter. So we wait for the paper of October 2. Still no comment, although the Washington letter says, "Colonel Stimson also received today Katsuji Debuchi, the Japanese Ambassador to the United States, while Dr. Yung Kwai, the Chinese Chargé d'Affaires, conferred with State Department officials." [107] And again on October 3, no comment, on October 4 the same, and so on until October 8, when Chinchow, a Chinese city far

---

[106] The fact that they may also have been following their own inclinations in the matter does not alter this.

[107] So far as it has been possible to check, it seems certain that up to this time, Oct. 1, 1931, Mr. Stimson had not talked personally with Yung Kwai, although he had had several conferences with Ambassador Debuchi. This would seem to be a strange situation. Even though State Department etiquette may ordinarily provide that a mere Chargé be received by a head of a division—in this case Dr. Stanley Hornbeck—one would think that in such a crisis, formalities would be set aside. Certainly Baron Shidehara received our Chargé in the absence of Ambassador Forbes from Tokyo. But not until after the bombing of Chinchow on October 8 is there any mention of Mr. Stimson seeing Dr. Yung. See Chap. III, p. 85, below.

removed from the original scene of conflict, is bombed by the Japanese and a new crisis is at hand. Did Mr. Stimson actually do nothing at this critical time? Senate Document No. 55, *Conditions in Manchuria*, contains no information on this point; the press releases make no mention of any action by the State Department; nor, in his *Far Eastern Crisis*, does Mr. Stimson have anything to say on the subject of supporting the League action at this juncture. We do know, however, that Mr. Stimson saw Ambassador Debuchi on October 1, though of what they said there is no record yet published. And tucked away in a news report in the *Trans-Pacific* of October 15 [108] we find a statement that the American Chargé d'Affaires called on Baron Shidehara to deliver orally a message from Mr. Stimson, similar to the League of Nations note, reminding Japan not to aggravate the situation. This message, being oral, did not require a reply, said the Foreign Office spokesman.

After a lapse of five years, in which time his thoughts may well have been colored by events and his own changing views, Mr. Stimson thus expressed his conclusion as to the resolution and the resulting situation:

The important thing about this resolution was the commitments assumed by the Japanese representative. That action and the consequent unanimity made the resolution legally binding upon all parties. We were to that extent much cheered and encouraged. It seemed as though the outbreak might be in a fair way to be terminated and the status quo ante restored. It looked as though Baron Shidehara might succeed in maintaining his authority and former policy and that, while there might and undoubtedly would be difficult questions to solve before normal relations could be resumed, they might be nevertheless solved without further hostilities and in a way satisfactory to both nations. I was personally encouraged by Baron Shidehara's prompt readiness to give my investigators access to the locality, a permission which had been acquiesced in by the military authorities.

There was, however, still cause for anxiety. Baron Shidehara had been compelled to adopt in his notes a position on behalf of his government which strained our credulity; his excuses for Japanese action did not sufficiently tally with the facts even as they were thus far disclosed. Making all possible allowance for provocation by the Chinese, we knew

[108] *Trans-Pacific*, Oct. 15, p. 9.

of nothing which would justify as a necessary protection of life and property the actual steps taken by the Japanese army. It had acted with a promptness and vigor which indicated careful planning. It was now in possession of all of Southern Manchuria. It was hardly to be expected that it would be dislodged from that advantageous position until it had obtained its "pound of flesh" as a quid pro quo, and certain features already disclosed in the correspondence indicated that the Japanese government itself might ratify and assume such a position behind the army.

While we should welcome a negotiated settlement between the two parties concerned, the kind of negotiation which we had in mind was quite different from one in which one of the negotiators was backing up its arguments with an armed force holding the other by the throat. Such a negotiation could not be reconciled with the terms of the great treaties to which we were all parties. I think, however, it is accurate to say that few if any observers then expected that the Japanese forces and government would develop such a complete disregard of treaty obligations or world opinion as was exhibited within a few months.[109]

Despite the qualification expressed in the last sentence it is clear that Mr. Stimson had his doubts, and this makes it all the harder to comprehend his complete silence after September 30. It goes without saying that he could not have been as outspoken as in the excerpts quoted above, without infuriating the Japanese, the civilian as well as the military group, but he could have taken official notice of the resolution. If, instead of withholding all comment, he had taken the public into his confidence, if, instead of an oral message to Baron Shidehara which required no reply, he had followed up the League resolution with a formal communication along similar lines as must have been expected in Geneva, the situation might have been different. Had he done these two things, and had the interviews given out at the State Department not been so consistently optimistic in their assurances that Japan was to be trusted and that all was well, American public opinion, ever more favorable to China than to Japan, would probably have supported him in a sterner attitude and a bolder tone. And the Japanese press, anxiously watching the reaction of this country, could not have claimed that our sympathies were with them.

There will, of course, be criticism of such an interpretation of

[109] Stimson, *op. cit.,* pp. 49–50.

the possible results of cooperation between the United States and the League: (1) by those who believe that, even in 1931, the League was powerless, that it was never Geneva but Downing Street and the Quai d'Orsay which determined courses of action; (2) by those who insist that pressure on Japan in September and October of 1931 could have resulted only in war. Assuming that both of these are right (and I do not agree that they are) where is the difference in the long run? Great Britain and France were members of the League, permanent members of the Council. Would American collaboration with them, resulting in the combined pressure of these three Great Powers, all of whom had been associated with Japan in the first World War and all of whom had important interests in the Far East, have been less effective because it was exerted through the machinery of the League? If the thing that was vital was the closing of the gap between the United States and Great Britain, did it matter whether that gap was closed inside or outside the framework of the League?

Regardless of differences of opinion on these points the fact remains that it was here we let a war grow; it was here in these September days, through lack of close collaboration, in holding back when we should have pushed on, that we lost our first great battle for world peace; here we dawdled, here we made our mistakes. We would not face the issue in 1931 and so we fought a war in 1941.

III

FIRST INTERLUDE

October 1 to 12

THE INTERLUDE between the September and October meetings of the Council was a critical one. The failure to seize the psychological moment on September 23 was serious but not necessarily fatal. Although the chances of obtaining a peaceful settlement of the conflict were greatly lessened by that failure, such a settlement, if accompanied by compromises on all sides, was still a possibility. Needless to say, no settlement could have been accepted by Japan which failed to save her face in the eyes of the world and of her own people. Such an opportunity had been offered her more than once in the course of the September meetings; the resolution of the thirtieth was the culmination of efforts in this direction. While only a handful of optimists in Geneva and elsewhere believed that Japan would take seriously the implication that her withdrawal to the railway zone was to be completed by October 14, there were many who hoped there would be sufficient progress by that time to show Japan's good intentions and to make further action by the Council unnecessary. Skeptics there were who felt that the League had failed completely and that each nation must henceforth look entirely to itself for the protection of its interest.[1] Unfortunately the events of the next two weeks proved the skeptics to have been more nearly right. So long as the Council was in session, the radical military group in Japan had exercised a certain amount of self-restraint but immediately that influence was removed the situation deteriorated rapidly.[2] Japanese army officers in Manchuria took matters in their

[1] Outstanding German newspapers were included in this group, among them the *Deutsche Allgemeine Zeitung* (Oct. 2, 1931), and the *Deutsche Tageszeitung* (Oct. 5). *The Paris Journal* (Oct. 2) pointed out: "The Japanese have not let themselves be manoeuvred out of position. They have rejected any compromise."

Other editorial writers pointed to the dangers of the situation and the importance of strengthening and using the existing machinery of the League for settling disputes.

[2] W. W. Willoughby, *The Sino-Japanese Controversy and the League of Nations* (Baltimore, 1935), p. 79.

own hands and the civilian element in the Cabinet was either unable or unwilling to do anything about it. Step by step Wakatsuki and Shidehara yielded to the military and increased the scope of their terms for a settlement.

The events of this fortnight fall into three major divisions:

(1) the expansion of the "Mukden incident" into a crisis involving the whole of Manchuria,

(2) the development of policy in Washington, and

(3) preparation for the October Council meetings.

Because we are especially concerned with the impact of American policy on the League and Japan, that phase of events is examined in greater detail than the others. It is, however, impossible to separate them entirely.

After the outbreak of war in September, 1939, the public became distrustful of periods of seeming inactivity, as these all too often proved to be forerunners of spectacular events in some new and unexpected region; but in 1931 the comparative quiet of the first week in October was looked upon as a good omen. In vain did the telegrams, with which Nanking continued to deluge Washington and Geneva,[3] warn that Japan was up to no good; both the State Department and the League Secretariat assumed, in public at least, that Japan was carrying out its obligations under the Council Resolution. To both, therefore, came a rude awakening on October 8 when the news of the bombing of Chinchow burst upon a world as yet unaccustomed to the wholesale destruction of cities and civilians from the air. Shocked by the brutality of the act, they nevertheless failed to grasp its full significance. Here was a real crossroads, not only in Manchuria and in the life of the League, but in that internal struggle for control of the Japanese government on which Mr. Stimson rightly placed so much stress; and, as has happened so many times since 1931, it was the party of violence and force which chose the fastest and most direct route to its goal.

Just as Hitler's occupation of the non-German lands of Czechoslovakia marks the point where the most determined appeasers could no longer justify his actions on racial and national grounds, so in the bombing of Chinchow the Japanese course definitely crossed the

[3] *Official Journal*, Annex 1334, pp. 2457–76.

boundary of self-defense and maintenance of treaty rights and showed itself to be one of aggression. Chinchow, a railway center on the Peiping-Mukden line, more than one hundred miles southwest of Mukden and at no point closer than fifty miles to the South Manchurian Railway,[4] had been chosen as the seat of the provincial government by Chang Hsueh-liang after the occupation of Mukden. On October 6 General Honjo announced that the authority of the young Marshal, "that stinking, rapacious youth," [5] would no longer be recognized by Japan. The Foreign Office in Tokyo immediately declared that the announcement had been made without official instructions, yet within forty-eight hours Chinchow was bombed. The Japanese army claimed to have been forced to new military operations against their will by Chinese provocations [6]—by anti-Japanese demonstrations, by growing banditry and the activities of disbanded soldiers—and alleged also that Chang was preparing an army to be used against the Japanese in Manchuria. According to their account the bombing was directed against the military barracks and the Communications University where the offices of the civil government had been set up. By 1941 the bombing of a civil administration by military forces had come to be an accepted part of total war as carried on by the Axis, but in 1931 this was far from the case and the Lytton Commission declared that it could not be justified, adding that there was "doubt whether the area bombed was in fact as restricted as the Japanese alleged." [7]

But all this was later. As at Mukden the army in Manchuria had seized the initiative, and the Foreign Office and the Premier seem to have been as greatly surprised as the rest of the world. Even so experienced an observer as Hugh Byas felt that a major cabinet crisis was at hand. To the New York *Times* he wrote:

If the news received from Mukden tonight of the army's latest move is correct it indicates a grave extension of the occupied area and apparently so serious a deviation from Japan's declared policy that the fall of the government can hardly be avoided.[8]

[4] Map 3, *Lytton Report.*
[5] It was thus that the Japanese general characterized Chang in the leaflets dropped on Chinchow. See *Official Journal*, p. 2475.
[6] *Lytton Report*, p. 72.   [7] *Ibid.*
[8] Hugh Byas, in the New York *Times*, Oct. 9, 1931.

The crisis, however, did not develop. The Cabinet met and discussed the Chinchow affair only briefly. The action was deplored but not repudiated. No resignations were asked, none offered, nor was there any suggestion of reprimanding General Honjo. Admitting that its hand had been forced, the Cabinet expressed itself as disposed to agree with the army's avowed purpose to abolish completely the government and authority of Chang Hsueh-liang.[9] This agreement was confirmed shortly after by the formal statement of October 12.[10]

While one cannot say with certainty that strong and immediate support of the September Resolution by the United States would have changed the course of events, there is, at least, the possibility that had Japan actually been confronted with even this much evidence of unified world opinion and effort she would have proceeded differently.[11] But that evidence was lacking. Geneva waited in vain for word that Washington had followed suit.[12] Disheartening to say the least! And not the least perplexing of the many questions raised by this whole affair is that of Mr. Stimson's psychology, which led him to make the same kind of mistake in October as he had made in September. Just as on September 23 he had balked the League's proposal of a neutral commission and had then rushed into the breach with a warm note to the Council promising wholehearted support, so now in October he withheld on the one hand what he promised on the other. For more than a week after September 30, so far as the world or the Council knew, Mr. Stimson made no move in support of the Resolution.[13] Yet on October 5 he cabled Sir Eric Drummond not only assuring him of our continued support and outlining the form which collaboration should take but urging the Council to use all the authority within its competence against Japan. Later Sir Eric asked and received Mr. Stimson's permission to circulate the note among the Council members and this was done on October 12.[14] The

---

[9] *Ibid.* [10] See p. 90, below.
[11] There is no evidence that public opinion in Japan was so aroused that compromise would have been impossible at this time.
[12] Chap. II, above. [13] *Ibid.*
[14] *Conditions in Manchuria*, p. 14; also Stimson, *Far Eastern Crisis* (New York, 1936), p. 51. Considerable confusion exists as to the date of this note. In the references cited above it is dated October 5; in the State Department press release of

authors of The League and Manchuria call it a "strange coincidence" [15] that the note was made public on the same day as the Japanese note, with its portentous statement regarding "fundamental points." [16] Rather it seems likely that the Secretary General was using the American message to offset that of Japan and to strengthen the opposition to that country on the eve of the Council meeting, and that he had withheld its earlier publication as it would have been without value so long as the State Department took no action in support of the September Resolution.[17]

But now Chinchow had been bombed and with that event had vanished every hope of a peaceful settlement. Completely shattered was Mr. Stimson's confidence in the assurances which fell so glibly from the smiling lips of Ambassador Debuchi.[18] A note of concern replaces for a time the easy optimism of the State Department's earlier utterances and for the first time the seriousness of the situation is admitted.[19]

The next few days were busy ones for Mr. Stimson and his advisors. On October 8, after receiving the news of the bombing of Chinchow the Secretary had a long conference with Dr. Yung at which, apparently for the first time, the Chargé had the opportunity to outline directly to Mr. Stimson the Chinese point of view. On October 9, Mr. Stimson made a full report of the situation to the Cabinet at its regular weekly meeting. It is fairly safe to assume that this was the first time the matter had been taken up with the Cabinet in as much as there is no earlier mention of such a discussion either in statements

October 10 it is referred to as of October 9, the same date being given in the recent State Department publication *War and Peace;* in the *Official Journal* (Annex 1334, p. 2485) it is dated October 12. There can be little question, however, that in Geneva it was looked upon as urging the Council to action after Chinchow, rather than as in support of the September resolution.

[15] *The League and Manchuria, the Second Phase of the Chinese-Japanese Conflict* (Geneva Special Studies, Vol. II, No. 11, November, 1931), p. 3.
[16] See pp. 91–92, below.
[17] This interpretation is open to question. A competent observer has remarked that Sir Eric Drummond would publish anything he could get from the United States as soon as he could get it.
[18] In justice to both Mr. Stimson and Ambassador Debuchi it should be said that Mr. Stimson probably believed the Ambassador because the latter believed he was speaking the truth when he said the Foreign Office could and would control the situation. He seems to have been thoroughly loyal to Baron Shidehara and his awakening must have been fully as painful as Mr. Stimson's.
[19] New York *Times,* Oct. 9 and 10.

to the press or in the Far Eastern Crisis.[20] And on October 10, again apparently for the first time, Mr. Stimson discussed the matter with President Hoover. As to this last point it is probable that, although he had not conferred with Mr. Hoover personally, he was kept informed of the President's views through Under Secretary Castle, and in this way Mr. Hoover exercised from the outset not only a restraining influence on our policy of collaboration with the League but the finally decisive influence against any action threatening "complications." The fact remains that at a very serious juncture in our foreign relations the Secretary of State appears to have been dependent on secondhand reports from two highly important sources. Mr. Castle could relay the President's views on intervention and collaboration to Mr. Stimson, he could tell the President what Mr. Stimson thought about the matter, but feeling as he did about China, Japan, and the League, he could not or would not present the situation in a light which would induce the President to take a vigorous position in support of the League's effort to stop Japan. As to Dr. Yung, Chargé d'Affaires of a minor legation he may have been, but, in the absence of the Chinese Minister, he was his country's representative; there was no one else from whom Mr. Stimson could obtain the requisite information at first hand.

That the Secretary of State should have delayed for three weeks discussing with the President a matter of foreign policy so vital to the interests of this country may seem strange, but the serious financial crisis which coincided with the Mukden incident must not be forgotten. That this had occupied Mr. Hoover's attention so completely that he had given little if any thought to Manchuria is quite understandable even though unfortunate. Now, however, "domestic matters were momentarily quiet" and Mr. Stimson "found the President keen and interested" [21] in the problem. The Cabinet meeting of the previous day had made the general situation clear and the time was devoted to the question of how best to cooperate with the League. Mr. Stimson urged the President to agree to the Council

---

[20] This point, also, is open to question but it is implied by Mr. Stimson's failure to mention earlier conferences and by the character of his remarks concerning this one. See Stimson, *op. cit.*, pp. 60–62; see also New York *Times*, October 10.
[21] Stimson, *op. cit.*, pp. 60–62.

request that we sit jointly with them in some discussion of the controversy in order that a demonstration of solidarity of opinion be furnished the world and Japan. To this the President consented provided the discussion was centered on the Kellogg Pact.

On this same day Mr. Stimson addressed a rather mild diplomatic note [22] to each of the countries concerned. The bombing of Chinchow was not specifically mentioned, merely referred to as "the events of the last forty-eight hours." The next day, however, dissatisfied with the explanation of Ambassador Debuchi, he followed this with a stern admonition to Japan alone, in which he declared that the bombing of Chinchow could not be minimized, that he was at a loss to see what right Japanese planes had to fly over a town more than fifty miles distant from the railway zone, and that their explanations of the attack were quite at variance with Japanese commitments under the resolutions of September 30. The note concludes:

The Secretary of State is thus constrained to regard the bombing of Chinchow as of very serious importance and he would welcome any further information from the Minister for Foreign Affairs which would throw light on this. [23]

These events naturally intensified the preparations being made by the Chinese and Japanese delegations for the reconvening of the Council. Following the adjournment on September 30, Nanking had acted upon the assumption that the recommendations contained in the Resolution would be carried out. [24] Arrangements were made for the appointment of Chinese military officials and the disposition of troops by Marshal Chang Hsueh-liang to take over the occupied areas and maintain order as the Japanese withdrew. Both the League and Japan were notified of this. Japan, on the other hand, continued the practice of shifting her armed forces from one point to another, giving the appearance of movement but without any material withdrawal or reduction in numbers. [25] Very shortly she began to give reasons for not withdrawing: the process must necessarily be slow

[22] *Conditions in Manchuria*, pp. 15–16.   [23] *Ibid.*, pp. 16–17.
[24] This is not meant to imply that they believed the Japanese would withdraw. Far from it. But they took no chance that the blame for failure should be placed upon them (China).
[25] *Official Journal*, Annex 1334, British and German official information, pp. 2486–87.

in order to protect the lives and property of Japanese nationals; there was no Chinese civilian administration with adequate police power to take over the occupied areas, and so on.

On October 3 the Chinese Government addressed a note to the United States through Nelson T. Johnson, our Minister at Peiping, requesting that this government along with members of the Council, send representatives to Manchuria, "to collect information on the progress of evacuation and all the relevant circumstances for the information of the Council." [26] In his reply of October 5 [27] Mr. Johnson, acting under instructions from the State Department, informed Nanking officially and in writing of the Salisbury-Hanson Mission, [28] and pointed out that the Acting-Minister for Foreign Affairs had been notified of this two days earlier—on October 3. He concludes with these words:

The American Government had thus anticipated the Chinese Government's request and it is confident that the Chinese Government will regard this action on its part as another evidence of its desire to make its due contribution in the common effort which is being made to insure reliance on peaceful methods for the settling of this dispute which clearly is a matter of concern to the whole world. [29]

In this incident we have another interesting and significant sidelight on the State Department's attitude toward keeping the American people informed. Messrs. Salisbury and Hanson received their instructions on September 28, the Chinese note was sent on October 3, and our Minister's reply on October 5. On October 6 the New York *Times* carried the following dispatch under a Washington date line of October 5:

The State Department today received a note from the Nanking Government requesting the appointment of an American commission to investigate the Manchurian situation prior to October 14. . . . Every indication here is that the United States will not act on the suggestion.

Not only is it held that it would be virtually impossible for a commission to reach the scene and investigate prior to the Council's meeting but

[26] *Conditions in Manchuria*, p. 12.   [27] *Ibid.*, p. 13.   [28] Chap. II.
[29] Other governments were taking similar steps as evidenced by the British and German telegrams previously referred to and by a Peiping dispatch to the New York *Times* (Oct. 5) stating that the Spanish Consul-General in Shanghai had been instructed to proceed to Manchuria to investigate the situation there.

there is no desire here to make any move which might aggravate the situation.

The United States has the promise of Japan that she is withdrawing from the danger zones in Manchuria and information received here is that the withdrawal is proceeding steadily,[30] although slowly, due to the delicate situation.

The text of the Nanking note was not made public. It was explained that China had not agreed to its publication. Secretary Stimson will give consideration to the appeal and discuss it with Far Eastern experts in the State Department. A reply will probably then be sent.[31]

And on October 8 the following appeared:

The State Department has sent Lawrence E. Salisbury, second secretary of the United States Embassy in Tokyo, and George C. Hanson, Consul-General in Harbin, to South Manchuria as observers, in order that they may report fully upon the Sino-Japanese situation there. Therefore, it is considered unnecessary to dispatch an investigating committee to South Manchuria as requested by China.

Orders sending the two officials to South Manchuria were issued on September 28th and the two men arrived in Mukden on Monday, but no announcement of their mission was made until the dispatch of a note to China replying to the request of the Nanking Government for an investigation forced a disclosure to-day.

The announcement was withheld, it was explained, because of the possibility that the Salisbury-Hanson mission might be misunderstood. It was emphasized that the two officials would serve only as "reporters." They had been sent to South Manchuria, it was said, because Secretary Stimson felt his own sources of information there were inadequate and he desired to know the facts of the situation from American officials.[32]

As both the Chinese and Japanese governments had been consulted and had agreed to give the American officials every possible aid in determining the facts why should the information have been withheld at home? If the Department felt it could not release the news until their arrival in Mukden—this was apparently on October 5—why did they not maintain silence until the complete facts could be given? What purpose was served by issuing such conflicting statements as the foregoing? An inquisitive mind might also ask

---

[30] Evidence to the contrary is given by the British and German telegrams, *Official Journal*, Annex 1334, pp. 2486–87.
[31] New York *Times*, Oct. 6.   [32] *Ibid.*, Oct. 8.

whether the Chinese note of October 3 was written before or after Mr. Johnson relayed the information that Messrs. Salisbury and Hanson had been instructed to go to Mukden. Since the Chinese government knew the plan was under consideration, the note, if written earlier, may have been intended to hasten its fulfillment. If written afterwards it seems likely that the note was designed to force the hand of the State Department to make public the action taken, implying as it did that Mr. Stimson was not entirely satisfied with the Japanese explanations of what was going on in Manchuria.

Returning to the story of preparations for the Council meeting we find that two communications from the Japanese to the Chinese government were circulated by the former to members of the Council on October 10 and 11.[33] Both are dated October 9, but seem to have been written before the bombing of Chinchow. Both state the Japanese case for self-defense, accuse China of anti-Japanese activities, and insist on direct negotiations between the two countries. The second of these, in answer to a Chinese note of October 5,[34] mentions for the first time the "fundamental points" which were to play such an important part in the discussions of October 23 and 24:

(3) Japanese Government considers most urgent task of moment is collaboration of our two Governments with a view to calming excited national feelings, by rapidly establishing *through direct negotiations on fundamental points* capable of constituting a basis of allowing a resumption of normal relations.

(4) Japanese Government is ready to negotiate immediately with responsible representatives of Chinese Government in order to establish *fundamental points* referred to.[35]

On October 9, Dr. Sze in behalf of his government asked that the Council be summoned forthwith, while a telegram of the same date from Nanking [36] urged that vigorous measures be taken to conserve peace and that a League commission be sent to Chinchow to investigate and report to the Council.[37] The American Minister to China was informed of this with the request that the United States partici-

---

[33] *Official Journal*, Annex 1334, X, Nos. 12 and 13, pp. 2482, 2483.
[34] The Chinese note of October 5 was not communicated to the Secretariat—see *ibid.*, p. 2483, footnote.
[35] *Ibid.*, p. 2483. Italics mine.   [36] *Ibid.*, XI, p. 2483.   [37] *Ibid.*, IX, p. 2473.

pate.[38] President Lerroux lost no time in convening the Council on October 13,[39] a day earlier than originally planned. He also appealed to the Chinese and Japanese governments to refrain from any action which might aggravate the situation.[40]

The Japanese reply [41] to this appeal is most significant, not only because of its reference to the "fundamental points" of settlement but because for the first time the official Japanese position is fully set forth; not piecemeal answers to particular questions as in September, not the unauthorized views of the military clique, but the considered statement of the entire Cabinet headed by Premier Wakatsuki and Foreign Minister Shidehara in whom such confidence had been placed by Mr. Stimson and the Council. A highly important document this; yet, in the flurry of preparation for the Council meeting the next day, of circulating information sent to the Secretariat by Council members from their representatives on the spot, it seems to have been hastily read and not at all digested. Even a hurried reading should have made clear the utter lack of any disposition on the part of the Japanese Cabinet to persuade the army in Manchuria to recede from its position. The gist of the statement is as follows: a friendly solution can be obtained only by means of direct negotiation between the two countries; a new state of affairs, created by various types of Chinese provocation, now exists in Manchuria, but military operations incident to this have ceased; the sending of naval vessels to the Yangtse [42] is for the purpose of protecting Japanese nationals and "does not exceed the usual action taken by the Powers under similar circumstances"; withdrawal of Japanese armed forces to the railway zone is hampered by the fact that Chinese authorities are not capable of guaranteeing protection to lives and property of Japanese nationals in Manchuria or elsewhere; "it is essential to agree upon certain main principles to form a foundation for the maintenance of normal relations between the two countries" and the "Japanese Government is prepared to open negotiations with the responsible representatives of China on these fundamental points."

Circulated to the Council members on October 12, read in the

[38] *Conditions in Manchuria*, p. 15.　　[39] *Official Journal*, Annex 1334, XII, p. 2483.
[40] *Ibid.*, XIII, p. 2484.　　[41] *Ibid.*, XIV, pp. 2484–85.
[42] This incident seems beyond the scope of this study so has not been discussed.

afternoon meeting of October 13 at the request of Mr. Yoshizawa, its portent seems to have escaped general notice until October 23.[43] Much time and effort might have been saved had Lord Cecil seized on this ten days earlier, if his demand for clarification of these "fundamental points" had been made on October 13 at the beginning of the session instead of on October 23 when tempers were frayed, nerves taut from days of fruitless negotiations. Then, with Mr. Stimson's note and its strong encouragement to action fresh in their minds, with public opinion in all countries aroused by the bombing of Chinchow, immediate pressure on Yoshizawa and on Tokyo might have brought results, provided, of course, that the pressure had been sufficiently strong for Tokyo militarists to realize that yielding was necessary.

[43] *Official Journal*, Minutes, p. 2349.

IV

PRENTISS GILBERT SITS WITH THE COUNCIL

OCTOBER 13 TO 24.—When the Council reconvened on October 13 it was recognized that the situation had changed for the worse. No longer was there any hope of localizing the conflict and reaching a solution based solely on the Mukden incident; instead, they were faced with the whole Manchurian problem, indeed with the entire question of Sino-Japanese relations. And this had come to pass largely through permitting Japan to play her own game unhindered.

Japanese tactics throughout the whole time the case was under consideration deserve careful study, not because they were new or strange but because they were typical, part and parcel with all of Japan's efforts to dominate China by diplomacy or by force, and a portent of things to come in her relations with the Western powers having interests in the Pacific. In substance these tactics were simple; to cloud the issues and confuse the minds of the delegates, many of whom knew little or nothing of the Fast East; [1] to delay a decision by every possible means so that time was given to the army to entrench itself in Manchuria and to arouse national feeling in Japan so there could be no drawing back; to use the Mukden incident, whatever its origin, as a springboard from which to effect a settlement of their relations with China while the army was still in control of Chinese territory; and, by no means last, to so divide the opposition as to make it ineffective—in particular to prevent a rapprochement between the United States and the League, or the United States and Great Britain. It had been comparatively easy to obscure the issues during the September meetings: the good record of Shide-

---

[1] This was before the Far Eastern experts were brought in. Hugh Wilson characterizes the early debates in the Council as of an "Alice-in-Wonderland" type. This, he says, changed very rapidly as the members recognized "the overwhelming challenge" of the Manchurian incident. "Members began to study deeply and, above all, to summon their Far Eastern experts from the foreign office." Hugh R. Wilson, *Diplomat between Wars* (New York, 1941), pp. 261–62.

hara in international affairs, as opposed to recent cases of Chinese banditry and antiforeign sentiment, was used with telling effect; while most of the delegates must have found it very difficult to follow the complicated discussion of September 22 [2] on the question of direct negotiations. Efforts to delay proceedings are also very apparent during this time—for example, the frequent demands for adjournment, the repeated requests for time to consult Tokyo and the protracted time for replies to the most urgent appeals for instructions, as contrasted with the almost immediate answers reported by Dr. Sze. The use of these tactics continued throughout the October meetings by the close of which the question of a settlement on "fundamental points" became the chief issue between Japan and the Council.

In all of this, Kenkichi Yoshizawa is an important factor. It was then taken for granted both in Geneva and in Washington that he was a loyal adherent of Baron Shidehara and the Foreign Office. Later events cast doubts on this. Recalled from Paris and Geneva after the fall of the Wakatsuki cabinet he became Foreign Minister under the premiership of his father-in-law, Takeshi Inukai, leader of the Seiyukai party which was more inclined to support the military element. Still later, his extremely competent handling of negotiations between Japan and the Netherlands East Indies would indicate that one of the many mistakes made in 1931 was the underestimating of this smiling, inscrutable "Mr. Moto." [3] Halting in speech he may have been,[4] but he knew exactly what he was doing and he played the army's game throughout. On more than one occasion, it is said, he went to the Council meeting carrying in his pocket authority to vote for the action proposed and did the opposite—notably on October 15 and 16 when he refused to approve the invitation to the United States [5] and on October 23 and 24 when he turned down every compromise offered and voted against the resolution [6] which brought the second session of the Council to a close.

[2] *Official Journal*, Minutes, pp. 2267–69; see also Chap. II, above.
[3] J. P. Marquand's famous character.   [4] See Chap. I, above.
[5] Public opinion in Japan was divided on this issue. See pp. 103–4, below.
[6] See p. 121, below.

In Tokyo the Cabinet itself played into the army's hands. Shidehara could no longer be counted on by the friends of Japan to carry the counsels of moderation. By their acceptance of the bombing of Chinchow and of the army's avowed purpose to put an end to the administration of Chang Hsueh-liang in Manchuria they aligned themselves with those who favored these tactics and their ultimate objectives. Ample evidence of this is found in the official statement of October 12.[7] Therein lies perhaps the greatest difference in the situation which faced the Council when it met on October 13.

In part by design, in part as the result of fortuitous circumstance this Council was stronger both officially and personally than the body which had assembled in Geneva prior to September 19. The small powers did not change their delegations, having sent of their best in September. The same was true of Italy, which was again represented by her Foreign Minister Dino Grandi,[8] while Dr. Bruening, then acting as both Chancellor and Foreign Minister of Germany, sent an able substitute in the person of Herr von Mutius. Alejandro Lerroux was compelled to remain in Madrid, with two fortunate consequences: Salvador de Madariaga, one of the League's great lights, replaced him as the representative of Spain, and Aristide Briand, at Spain's request, took the chair as President of the Council. Because of the many pressing problems facing the Quai d'Orsay it had not been expected that Briand would attend the meeting, but immediately after the events of October 8 it was announced that he would drop everything at home and go to Geneva: [9] the prestige of the League was at stake and no lesser person could speak for France. He was accompanied by Alexis Leger, his chef de cabinet, and René Massigli.[10] Heading the British delegation was the Foreign Secretary, the Marquis of Reading, but with him, at the special request of the Cabinet, went Lord Cecil who was expected "to throw the weight of his unrivalled League experience into the task of making a settlement." [11]

Conservative sentiment in both Great Britain and France seemed more adverse to Japan than at any other period in the negotiations.

[7] *Official Journal*, Annex 1334, p. 2484.
[8] Scialoja substituted for Grandi, Oct. 22 to 24.   [9] New York *Times*, Oct. 11.
[10] *Ibid.*, Oct. 13.   [11] *Ibid.*, Oct. 14.

In striking contrast to its editorial of September 26 [12] commending Mr. Stimson for his refusal to approve a commission of inquiry *The Times* of London launched a vigorous attack on Japan in its issue of October 12:

> . . . it is a particularly disquieting feature of the present crisis that the Japanese Government appears both to deprecate the League's intervention on the ground that it will encourage China to postpone or refuse direct negotiations and to be unable to prevent its soldiers from making direct negotiations increasingly difficult. Granted that the Japanese troops in Mukden exceeded instructions, are they to continue to exceed them without any effective check from Tokyo until the Chinese surrender or explode? The army of a first class power is not expected to remain out of hand.
>
> The Japanese have put themselves in wrong by permitting or failing to prevent repeated military action without submitting the dispute to the arbitration of the League. To this breach of the Covenant is added a clear departure from the spirit of the Kellogg Pact.[13]

A Paris dispatch of October 10 to the New York *Times* characterizes French comment as restrained but "inclined to blame the Japanese for enlarging the scope of the dispute. The *Journal des Debats*, for example, points out that while it is difficult to render a definite judgment all events would lead to the conclusion that the Japanese are operating on a well conceived plan of action." [14]

Chronologically the October meetings fall into three distinct groups:

1. October 13 to 16. Interest centers on the question of the invitation to the United States; five plenary sessions of the Council are held, three public meetings and two private.

2. October 17 to 21. No open meeting is held, the work being carried on through secret sessions, individual conferences, meetings of the Committee of Five, and so on.[15] On the seventeenth, attention is focused on the invocation of the Kellogg Pact, while the remaining time is spent on unsuccessful attempts to get the Japanese to accept a definite date for the withdrawal of their troops within the railway zone.

---

[12] See Chap. II, above.   [13] New York *Times*, Oct. 12; London *Times*, Oct. 12.
[14] New York *Times*, Oct. 11.
[15] The various types of meetings are discussed on pp. 104–6, below.

3. October 22 to 24. The Council is again in open session, with two main points of interest, the question of "fundamental points" and the abortive resolution of October 24.

Opening the eighth meeting [16] at twelve noon on October 13, M. Briand summed up the situation as it had developed since the Council last met. Both sides were reported with the utmost care and impartiality. Nevertheless, the President made clear the keen disappointment resulting from the unrealized hopes of September 30. Nor is it reading too much between the lines to say there was a strong implication that Japan was responsible for that disappointment. He then called on Dr. Sze who reviewed with brevity the history of the case from September 21 through October 9. The immediate issue, he said, was the devising of means for a complete withdrawal of Japanese troops to their treaty zone and the restoration of the *status quo ante*. He cited again the precedent of the Greco-Bulgarian case of 1925 in support of his contention that a state could not justify the invasion of another state on the grounds of legitimate defense and protection,[17] and closed with a solemn appeal for the preservation of the structure of collective security, an appeal strangely prophetic when read today:

The Covenant and the Pact of Paris are our two sheet anchors to which we have moored our Ship of State and with the help of which we believe we shall ride out the storm.

Nevertheless the Covenant and the Pact of Paris are also the cornerstones of the world wide edifice of peace that had been so laboriously erected in the twelve years since the World War, and if they crumble the edifice collapses.

For is it likely that the nations who had witnessed this tragic collapse of the Covenant and the Pact of Paris at the first great test, with all its dire consequences throughout the East—is it likely that these nations would assemble quietly at Geneva in February to disarm? [18] Would they not rather draw the conclusion that, after all, each state must rely on its own armed forces, and on these alone? To say more on this point would be to labor the obvious—it is clear that if the members of the League and

[16] *Official Journal*, Minutes, p. 2309.
[17] *Ibid.*, pp. 2270, 2311. For the reference to the Greco-Bulgarian case see the *Official Journal*, November, 1925, p. 1709.
[18] The opening of the General Disarmament Conference had been set for Feb. 2, 1932.

the United States of America cannot cooperate successfully to avert this threat to peace, one of the first results will be a collapse of the disarmament movement.

. . . With the idea of disarmament goes the idea of international security, for the two are indissolubly linked. If we fail now, when America offers her cooperation, and fail in February with disarmament, what chance have we of working out some form of permanent association, some provision for conference under the Pact of Paris to avert threats to peace?

Finally, if we fail in these things and the world is thrown back on suspicious nationalism, hostile alliances and a race in armaments, if the East is plunged into a state of turmoil, what chance have we of securing effective cooperation in connection with the financial and economic crisis that bears so heavily on the world? That crisis widens and deepens daily, almost hourly, and we are aware, all of us, that only far-reaching and close cooperation between the civilized nations can avert disaster.

However remote and irrelevant this disturbance in the Far East may seem to the West, engrossed in its pressing cares—and it is natural that it should so seem—the web of fate binds us all together, and unless we can cooperate effectively in this grave emergency, we shall fail in disarmament, we shall fail to inspire any confidence in international security and order, and by the same notion we shall fail to grapple with the world economic crisis.

China has put herself in the hands of the League and abides the issue with confidence in her destiny and in the moral forces of civilization. The League cannot fail, for its success is bound up with the interests of all civilized nations, with those of Japan and America as well as those of China and the other members of the League.[19]

In his reply to Dr. Sze, Mr. Yoshizawa attempted again to turn the attention of the Council from the immediate issue of Japanese withdrawal to the treaty zone by questioning the accuracy of the Chinese statements and by a lengthy "historical" account of Sino-Japanese relations since 1894, the purpose of the latter being that those who knew nothing of the Far East might learn the "true" facts in the case.[20] Strange to say, he completely overlooked the famous Twenty-one Demands of 1915, a lapse of memory to which Dr. Sze quickly pointed.[21] It was at this time, also, that Mr. Yoshizawa

---

[19] *Official Journal*, December, 1931, pp. 2312-13.   [20] *Ibid.*, pp. 2315-17.
[21] *Ibid.*, p. 2319.

caused to be read into the minutes the statement of the Japanese government with its reference to fundamental points.[22]

Mr. Briand's presence in the chair made itself felt throughout the day's proceedings, in his opening remarks, and in the masterly exposition with which he closed the day's discussion. An expert in the art of diplomatic strategy, he let Mr. Yoshizawa know that he saw through his tactics of delay and confusion, warned him not to create an "irremediable" situation, and hinted at his sympathy with China, all in terms to which no exception could be taken:

> The representative of China has just told us—and I am not surprised—that the situation with which his country is faced naturally causes irritation and may lead to serious events. The Japanese representative has said that certain military acts have been carried through under the influence of anxiety. Soldiers readily feel such anxiety, and when they do so they act. That I understand. But I want to distinguish between facts capable of explanation which do not create an irremediable situation and those which may confront us with such a situation. . . .
>
> Let us not go into details to discover which points are strictly accurate and which not quite so accurate but let us look at the situation as a whole. . . .[23]

The invitation to the United States was not brought up in either of these meetings but the idea of American cooperation was kept in the forefront by remarks of the President of the Council and of the Chinese representative. The latter referred twice to the fatal results to disarmament and international security if the League and the United States together could not avert disaster,[24] while M. Briand pointed out that

> the Government of the United States of America which in circumstances of which you are aware has been kept informed of our discussions, has informed us that it is in full agreement with the Council's action. It also announces that it has sent two officials to Manchuria as observers.[25]

It will be remembered that the Council had considered an invitation to the United States early in September, but gave it up on learning that Mr. Stimson would not accept.[26] Then came the drastic change precipitated by Japanese action at Chinchow. Sec-

[22] *Ibid.*, p. 2314. [23] *Ibid.*, p. 2321. [24] See above.
[25] *Official Journal*, p. 2310. [26] Chap. II, pp. 48–49, above.

retary Stimson conferred with the President and the latter agreed to the sending of a representative provided he took part only in discussions based on the Pact of Paris. The invitation itself thus became a matter of delicate negotiations. The League could not afford to extend the invitation and have it refused, and we could not invite ourselves.[27] It was necessary, therefore, for Mr. Stimson to discover whether our presence was still desired and to let the Council know its invitation would be welcomed. That Japan would oppose the invitation had become known even in September, but this opposition, if it could not be overcome, would be circumvented.[28] There was, moreover, another element in the situation with which Mr. Stimson was seriously concerned, namely to make sure that League initiative as opposed to initiative by the United States should be preserved.

. . . The original suggestion of joint action had come from the nations at Geneva. It arose from their united impulse not from our suggestions. *For the sake of preventing misunderstanding in Japan* it was important not to blur the truth of that situation. Not only should the invitation for the joint session come from the nations who were members of the League, but *it was also important, if as a result of such conference it were decided to invoke the Kellogg-Briand Pact, that it should be the members of the Council who took the lead in carrying out the various steps necessary to set in motion the signatories of the treaty.* Otherwise, I foresaw that America would be represented to the Japanese people as the instigator of the entire matter—of having wormed herself into League councils in order to stir up hostility against Japan.[29]

Here is the stuff of which the mistakes of nearly a decade of Far Eastern policy were made: the desire not to offend Japan—appeasement if you wish, a lack of solidarity of opinion or effort against aggression, a complete unwillingness on the part of every power concerned to take responsibility for action, divided counsels which prevented the effective use of the newly rooted machinery of peace, until it was too late for anything but war. Not only did Mr. Stimson refuse to take the initiative in the matter of invoking the Kellogg Pact but even now when he recognized the growing seriousness of

[27] See article by Clarence Streit, New York *Times*, Oct. 11.
[28] See p. 104, below.   [29] Stimson, *Far Eastern Crisis*, p. 62. Italics mine.

the situation there is no record that he urged the League to take specific action or that he retracted his previous counsel of prudence and caution regarding the sending of a neutral commission to the scene of the conflict.

Obviously an understanding was reached with Geneva, for on October 12 Mr. Stimson let it be known to the press that an invitation to attend the Council for consultative purposes was expected and that Prentiss Gilbert, our Consul in Geneva, had been authorized to accept it. He made it clear that the United States was not advancing a method of settling the dispute and was withholding independent action to avoid "crossing wires" with the League with whose purposes and methods we were in full accord.[30] Just why the choice fell on Mr. Gilbert has never been explained. A Geneva dispatch of October 10 states positively that "on instructions from Washington" either Hugh Wilson or Hugh Gibson would be present for conversations between the League and the United States when the Council met.

Mr. Gibson is now in Brussels and Mr. Wilson was about to sail today for the United States when the directions came from Washington. In view of the importance of the exchanges to take place next week it was deemed essential to have one of the two in Geneva during that period.[31]

It is in no way a reflection upon Mr. Gilbert to say that either of the other men could have filled the seat at the Council table to better advantage. As a former chief of division of the State Department he was sufficiently informed as well as intellectually equal to the task. On the other hand Mr. Gibson and Mr. Wilson were diplomats of the first order with a recognized position in Europe,[32] Ambassador to Belgium and Minister to Switzerland respectively; moreover, they had sat as equals with Council members at many international conferences in Geneva and elsewhere. That Mr. Stimson, to whom protocol and precedence mattered so greatly,[33] should have chosen a consul to sit as the representative of the United States in the midst of Foreign Ministers and Ambassadors is passing strange. Despite Mr. Gilbert's ability, his positive ideas regarding the need

[30] New York *Times*, Oct. 13.   [31] *Ibid.*, Oct. 11.
[32] Bertram Hulen, *Inside the State Department* (New York, 1939).
[33] See Chap. III, above.

for collaboration, his energy and his drive, his position was second rate and although Mr. Stimson did not so intend it, his appointment was looked upon by many as a slap at the League. Perhaps the explanation lies in the restrictions imposed upon our representative. Would either Mr. Gibson or Mr. Wilson have been willing to sit day in and day out at the Council table without a word to say? [34] Yet this was the role assigned to Mr. Gilbert. Mr. Wilson in his memoirs throws no light on the question. He merely says that he was worn out by the strenuous days of September and early October and was delighted when he received instructions to return to Washington for consultations regarding the coming disarmament conference.

Yet another point remains obscure. Why was the shift made from the Nine Power Treaty to the Kellogg Pact? China had appealed to the United States under the latter but from the beginning Secretary Stimson had referred to the Nine Power Treaty as the instrument under which we would probably act if circumstances made it advisable for us to act at all. On more than one occasion he explained fully to the press his reasons for preferring this treaty. Now, however, it is the Pact of Paris which he chooses as the agency for our collaboration with the League. Was it Mr. Hoover who made the decision in the conference of October 10? Was it because the Kellogg Pact was not implemented and recourse to it would result only in the sending of notes to the disputants, whereas the Nine Power Treaty provided for consultation among the signatories, in which the United States could scarcely avoid a leading role? Or was it that having decided to mobilize world opinion—and opinion only— the Kellogg Pact was best suited because of the greater number of signatory powers? [35]

The situation on the morning of the fourteenth, when discussions on the invitation to the United States were begun was substantially as follows.

[34] This has been suggested as one of the reasons why Mr. Dawes did not sit with the Council in November and December. Gilbert's appointment, like that of Dawes, may have been a sop to the isolationists who would have been very pleased over a slap at the League.
[35] New York *Times.*

As between China and Japan the deadlock continued to exist. China rested her case entirely in the hands of the League and the United States and would not agree to direct negotiations so long as Japanese troops remained outside the treaty limits. Japan, on the other hand, insisted that before her troops could be withdrawn the two governments must by direct negotiations reach agreement upon certain underlying points vis-à-vis each other. The Japanese representative, by emphasizing his government's willingness to withdraw as soon as the safety of Japanese lives and property were assured, distracted attention from the question of underlying principles, nor did he draw attention to the fact that Japan alone was to be the judge of how and when that safety was to be assured. M. Briand, feeling that the situation in the Far East must be taken care of speedily, obtained the approval of the "Twelve" to negotiate with the representative of China and Japan in an attempt to break this deadlock and reach an understanding on the preliminary principles of a settlement—the evacuation of Chinese territory by the Japanese and guarantees for Japanese nationals in China. In this he failed because of Japanese insistence on direct negotiations without neutral observers or assistance and Chinese insistence on evacuation as a prerequisite to direct negotiations.

In the matter of the invitation to the United States, opinion in Tokyo did not altogether support the position taken by Japan's delegation in Geneva. The influential *Jiji* says, "It will be approved by everybody wishing to see normal conditions restored in Manchuria," that the attitude of the United States throughout has been correct and friendly toward Japan, and there can be little doubt that her presence at the Council table will be helpful in finding "a solution to the Sino-Japanese conflict in Manchuria." [36] The *Asahi,* another prominent paper of liberal trend, could find no objection from the Japanese point of view to American participation as a nonvoting member, rather there was every reason to welcome it with the wish that it might mean adherence to the League and the right to vote.[37] However, editorials written after the invitation had been extended over the protests of Japan's representatives have a very

[36] *Trans-Pacific*, Oct. 22. [37] *Ibid.* See also Hugh Byas, New York *Times*, Oct. 16.

different tone.[38] And the New York *Times* of October 14 carried a dispatch from Tokyo which declared that all Japan was united to resist the League.[39]

Mr. Yoshizawa's known opposition to the invitation and Mr. Stimson's somewhat premature announcement had created a delicate situation. Great anxiety was felt as the Council members, in secret sessions throughout the fourteenth, endeavored to find a way out. On a matter of principle, of substance, the Council must reach a unanimous decision, whereas in a matter of procedure a majority vote is sufficient. Here was the loophole, but it took men of the caliber of Briand, Cecil, and Madariaga to find it and use it, men who not only knew League technique and procedure but who had sufficient prestige with their fellow members to dare to interpret the letter of the law in such a way that its spirit might not be nullified. The decision of September 22 to keep in constant communication with the United States was the principle, the substance. On this there had been unanimity. Now it was to be merely a matter of procedure, how to make that collaboration most effective, by written communication, cables, and telephone conversations, or through the presence of a representative of the United States at the Council Table. The last thing anyone wanted was to antagonize Japan and every effort was made to win Yoshizawa to this point of view. This would have made possible the holding of a plenary session on the fifteenth at which a unanimous invitation to the United States would have been extended. To Yoshizawa, however, this was too good a chance to miss, a heaven-sent opportunity to hold up proceedings, to delay resumption of hearings on the main dispute, and he made the most of it. He first asked for time to consult his government, as he was without instructions. This, of course, was granted. By midafternoon of the fifteenth the situation remained unchanged and all thought of a public meeting had to be abandoned. As a last resort a private meeting of the full Council was then called for 5:30 P.M. at which it was decided by a majority vote to extend the proposed invitation to the United States.

The student who reads the minutes of the Council meetings ex-

[38] *Trans-Pacific*, Oct. 22.   [39] New York *Times*, Oct. 14.

pecting to get the full story of that body's actions is sure to be disappointed and sometimes greatly perplexed, for a large part of the work is done elsewhere. The October meetings are an excellent illustration of this. The full plenary sessions were held only after attempts had been made in secret and private meetings to iron out difficulties and reach a unanimous decision. When that was found impossible a public meeting was held at which the views of both sides were presented and placed on record. At such meetings the full delegations of all States Members of the Council may be present, also observers from any other countries who care to attend, press correspondents, and the general public so far as there is room for them. At private meetings, such as that held on the evening of October 15, members of the press and the general public were excluded, and only so much information was given out as the Council thought advisable.[40] Minutes were kept, however, and printed together with those of the public meetings in the *Official Journal.* When very ticklish problems were to be handled, when it was necessary to speak plainly but confidentially, secret meetings were held composed of the chief of delegation, one alternate and a secretary from each State Member. The Secretary General attended exofficio, but no outsiders were permitted and no minutes were printed. In this situation we find what is perhaps the real advantage of American presence at the Council table in October. Hugh Wilson, for all his intimacy with the Secretary-General and his almost universal acceptance by Council members, could not attend the secret meetings. For him to have done so would have been an unthinkable breach of Council etiquette. Prentiss Gilbert had this privilege after October 16, and as there were only secret meetings and conferences from October 17 to October 22 his presence there was necessary if we were to have any part at all in what was going on.

Probably the most important work of all was that of the special committees appointed by the President of the Council, such as the Committee of Five in this case. As was said earlier [41] these committees were coming to be one of the chief agencies through which

---

[40] The communiqué issued on Oct. 15, following the private meeting, is an excellent example of this. New York *Times*, Oct. 16. See p. 109, below.
[41] See Chap. II.

the Council reached its decisions and more often than not were made up of the representatives of the Great Powers having permanent seats on the Council. In the Manchurian case, Japan, as an interested party, was not on the Committee, and Spain, not a permanent member, was, through the accident of holding the presidency at that moment. As the Committee held over for the entire 65th Council, Salvador de Madariaga took Lerroux's place there even though the presidency of the Council passed to France. Prentiss Gilbert was included in these meetings after October 16.

Having reached a decision among themselves, the Committee of Five then called a meeting of the "Twelve," that is, of the Council with the exception of the interested parties. There, a plan of action, usually the same as that proposed by the Committee, was agreed upon. The exclusion of the disputants from these meetings does not mean they were in ignorance of what was being done. Quite the contrary. Either through the Secretary-General, the President of the Council or some influential member of the Committee, they were kept informed and consulted as to their wishes, which were given every consideration. In September it was usually Sir Eric Drummond or Lord Cecil who maintained this liaison, in October it was M. Briand himself. Also it must be remembered that many questions were threshed out over informal luncheon tables and at late evening sessions in hotel suites, in much the same manner as at American political conventions.

Thus on the afternoon of October 15, after vain attempts had been made to obtain Yoshizawa's consent to the presence of the United States at the Council table, the private meeting of the full Council was held.[42] There was still hope that, confronted with a united body he would see that opposition was futile and would retire gracefully from what the other Members considered an untenable position. This was probably the last opportunity for such a withdrawal. By acceding to the repeated appeals to her generosity, to her cordial relations with the United States, and to her good standing in international affairs Japan would have gained rather than lost prestige. No question of forcing her by undue pressure,

[42] See *Official Journal*, pp. 2322–29, for a full account.

or of overriding her wishes, would have arisen had Yoshizawa yielded at this time, while the praise and acclaim of the entire world would have followed such action. National feeling in Japan, highly sensitive to either praise or fancied slight from the West, would have responded favorably and the chances of the Shidehara government to reestablish itself would have been increased.

In the light of the decision of the Committee of Five and of the "Twelve," that the invitation to the United States could be treated as a matter of procedure,[43] M. Briand opened the meeting by recalling the action of September 22 and the subsequent steps taken by the Council and the United States toward closer collaboration. With this in mind he had drafted an invitation to that country based on the obligations arising from the Pact of Paris. This invitation, the text of which was open to amendment, he then read. In the conferences preceding this meeting the Japanese representative had raised a constitutional question as to American participation, basing his argument on Article 4, paragraph 5, of the Covenant. M. Briand had countered by stating that this paragraph did not enter into the matter at all as there was no question of asking the United States to act as a full voting member. A formal interchange of notes had taken place and Mr. Yoshizawa now asked that these be read.[44] He then said that, in his opinion, this was not a matter of procedure, that all decisions under Article 11 must be unanimous, in support of which he quoted an opinion of the Permanent Court of International Justice of 1925.[45] Following this he had read a memorandum embodying his government's views on the question.[46] A great part of this consisted of a long and complicated legalistic argument concerning the rights and duties of members and nonmembers of the League when invited to send a representative to the Council, and as to whether the Council had the constitutional right to invite a nonmember when the case before it arose under Article 11. So involved was it that Lord Reading remarked at its close that he still was not sure whether the Japanese representative did or did not object to the invitation which

[43] See pp. 43, 103–4, above.　　　[44] *Official Journal*, p. 2323.
[45] *Ibid.*, pp. 2323, 2325; also *Opinion of the Permanent Court of International Justice*, Series B, No. 12, pp. 28 ff.
[46] *Official Journal*, pp. 2324–25.

the President proposed; if he did not object the question was settled. Mr. Yoshizawa replied that he was not prepared to say whether or not he had any objections until his doubts on the constitutional and legal questions were resolved. He, therefore, asked the Council to refer the matter to a committee of legal experts.[47]

With this request it became evident that Mr. Yoshizawa was continuing his usual tactics of delay and confusion. In the long and involved memorandum he had tried to draw the red herring of the constitutional question across the trail of the immediate issue—this time the invitation to the United States. Nothing would have suited his purpose better than for the Council to have become hopelessly entangled in an argument over the points he had raised. But Lord Reading prevented this by his simple question. Now Yoshizawa tried to delay matters by proposing a committee of legal experts.

M. Briand then stated the case as it had developed to that point. The Council, he said, now had two questions before it:

one, a question of principle, on a constitutional question, and the other a question of fact; the latter could be settled by a vote. If it appeared that there was opposition to the proposed invitation, the question arose whether a simple majority vote was sufficient for the acceptance of the proposal. The best solution in so delicate a matter would be unanimous agreement.[48]

He followed with a persuasive appeal for the reservation of the constitutional question and approval of the invitation to the United States. This Mr. Yoshizawa felt unable to accept. In the course of his remarks M. Briand had made much of the cordial relations existing between Japan and the United States and of the fact that Yoshizawa had welcomed American collaboration in its earlier stages. He pointed out again that the United States was not being asked to sit as a Member of the Council; if such were the case he could understand the hesitation, but the fact was they were merely trying to improve the communication decided upon by the previous unanimous vote. When M. Briand failed to make any impression, Lord Reading and M. de Madariaga took up the argument. They pointed out how unfortunate it would be if the solution of the real question,

[47] *Ibid.*, p. 2325.   [48] *Official Journal*, p. 2325. See also pp. 43, 103-4.

that of Manchuria, should be put aside or postponed because of the raising of an accessory constitutional point. Madariaga went straight to the heart of the matter when he said that the chief issue confronting the Council was the question of time. It was now October 15; for nearly a month a state of affairs had prevailed in Manchuria which was very difficult to define and as to which he would only say it was not exactly in conformity with the spirit of the Covenant,[49] yet Mr. Yoshizawa insisted on that spirit being acted upon in a purely legal matter. The delicacy of the position as to the United States was emphasized; it was already an open secret that the Council had proposed the invitation; it had to be settled at the earliest possible moment, and it was highly desirable that the decision be unanimous.

The President again stated the case. There were two possibilities. The Council could vote on the proposal for the invitation and in the event of its being accepted take the necessary action, or it could accept the Japanese proposal to appoint immediately a committee of jurists to settle the constitutional question as quickly as possible. Would the Japanese Government, he asked, accept and defer to the Committee's opinion whatever this might be? He closed with another urgent appeal for generous action by that country. Mr. Yoshizawa ignored both question and appeal, merely repeating his demand for the appointment of a committee of legal experts. Lord Reading pressed for an answer to the President's question. This was refused and further discussion showed conclusively that the Japanese representative had no intention of committing himself and that valuable time would be wasted if the committee were appointed. The President, therefore, asked for a vote on the two questions. The Japanese proposal was rejected twelve to two, Germany voting with Japan. On the principle of the invitation to the United States the vote was thirteen to one, Japan standing alone. Following the meeting there was issued a brief communique [50] summarizing the positions taken and giving the results of the voting. Everything of a controversial character was excluded from this but something of the nature of the discussions got out and excitement ran high in Geneva. The growing seriousness of the situation in Manchuria and the prospect

[49] *Official Journal*, p. 2327.   [50] New York *Times*, Oct. 16.

that an American representative might take a seat at the Council table the next day combined to create an extraordinary state of tension. Consequently the hall was crowded when the delegates assembled at ten o'clock the next morning. If there were any who still hoped for a change of heart by the Japanese they were disappointed. Nothing new was added to the arguments of the previous day; there were no further appeals to Japanese generosity. Only the most formal statements of the positions taken were made after which the President informed the Council that the invitation "which had been adopted unanimously apart from one vote" would be sent to the United States.[51]

At this point critical readers may well ask why Yoshizawa fought the invitation to the United States with every weapon at his command if, as has been stated, Mr. Stimson's course of action throughout September and early October was so greatly to Japan's advantage. The answer is, in part, to gain time. Japan's motives were undoubtedly obstructionist, but, coupled with an attempt to delay matters there was probably a very real objection to our presence at the Council table, for it threatened to close the gap between the United States and the League and to put the United States in a position not only to receive direct information but to transmit to the Council confidential reports from our representatives in the Far East, particularly those resulting from the Salisbury-Hanson mission. As a matter of fact Japanese fears on this score were groundless, as will be seen as the story of our "close cooperation" unfolds. Nevertheless, as an American member of the Secretariat has said, a bizarre situation developed, in which one nation acting on the principles of the Kellogg Pact sat with others acting on an entirely different Pact—the Covenant of the League—an excellent example of the whole abnormality of our position vis-à-vis the League.

A second public meeting was called for 6 P.M. of the same day for the purpose of receiving the representative of the United States. Again the Council room was filled to capacity, for this was indeed an epoch-making event and one from which much was expected. The message from the Government of the United States was read,[52]

[51] *Official Journal*, pp. 2329–32.
[52] *Ibid.*, pp. 2335–36; also *Conditions in Manchuria*, p. 18.

after which Mr. Gilbert was invited by the President to take his place at the table.[53] A hush of expectancy fell over the room as Prentiss Gilbert stood to answer M. Briand's warm words of welcome. But as he spoke the tension slackened and sagged, the excitement died down, to be followed by an almost equal disappointment as the import of Mr. Gilbert's instructions were grasped.

I wish to thank you, Mr. President, for the kind words you have spoken in your own name and in the name of the Council.

May I be permitted first to convey to you, Mr. President, the sentiments of deep admiration and respect which the Government and the people of the United States entertain towards you as the untiring artisan of peace and the co-author of the Pact of Paris. It is indeed a happy augury that you should be presiding over the deliberations of this body at this time; and I wish to assure you of our deep gratification at being once more associated with you in the cause of peace.

At this moment of deep international concern, I thank you for your invitation to sit in your deliberations and *participate in your discussions in so far as the Pact of Paris,* to which my country is a party, *is concerned.*

The Government of the United States of America has been following with the closest attention the proceedings before the Council for the settlement of the dispute at present unhappily existing between China and Japan. *My government does not seek to intrude with respect to such measures as you may propose under the Covenant of the League of Nations; and is not in a position to participate with the members of the Council in the formulation of any action envisaged under that instrument* for the composing of differences existing between two of its members. It has already conveyed to you its sympathetic appreciation of your efforts and its wholehearted accord with the objective you have in view; and it has expressed its hope that the tried machinery of the League may in this case, as on previous occasions, be successful in bringing this dispute to a conclusion satisfactory to both parties. Moreover, acting independently and through diplomatic channels my Government has already signified its moral support of your efforts in this capacity to bring about a peaceful solution of the unfortunate controversy in Manchuria.

In your deliberations as to the application of the machinery of the Covenant of the League of Nations, I repeat, we can take no part. But the Pact of Paris, bearing as it does, the signature of the President of this meeting, together with that of our former Secretary of State, as joint proponents, represents to us in America an effective means of marshall-

[53] *Official Journal,* p. 2336.

ing the public opinion of the world [54] behind the use of pacific means only in the solution of controversies between nations. We feel, not only that this public opinion is a most potent force in the domestic affairs of every nation, but that it is of constantly growing import and influence in the mutual relations of the members of the family of nations.

The timely exercise of the power of such opinion may be effective to prevent a breach of international peace of worldwide consequences. We assume that this may be the reason why the consideration of the relationship between the provisions of the Pact of Paris and the present situation has been brought forward in this body; and the purpose which has moved my Government to accept your invitation is that we may most easily and effectively take common counsel with you on this subject. [55]

Having made this very plain statement as to the part the United States would take in the deliberations of the Council, Mr. Gilbert took his seat, breaking his silence only twice thereafter in public meetings. [56] With the exception of Mr. Yoshizawa every member of the Council followed the President with remarks appropriate to the occasion and the meeting ended.

What were the net results of these days of negotiations? What had happened to the original idea of American participation? To what extent was there greater collaboration after October 16? What was actually accomplished by our presence at the Council table in the person of Prentiss Gilbert?

Let us look first at the idea of American participation. Apparently what the Council wanted and what, in the light of Mr. Stimson's letter circulated to them under date of October 12, they had reason to believe they would receive was the greatest possible degree of American support in the new crisis. The Secretary-General urged that we be invited to take part as a full member, citing as a precedent the case of Turkey in 1924. This, however, was rejected as that country had been a directly interested party while the United States was not. Lord Cecil, Lord Reading, and M. Briand took the position that as a signatory and one of the originators of the Pact of Paris, we were entitled to the invitation. They seem to have pictured our representative as having equality with the member dele-

---

[54] See p. 102, above.
[55] *Official Journal*, pp. 2336–37; *Conditions in Manchuria*, pp. 18–19. Italics mine.
[56] See below, pp. 115, 121–22.

gates *in voicing and recording our position in any phase of the discussions* but without the right to vote and without incurring the obligations of membership in the League.[57] They saw clearly that if Japan were to be stopped without the use of force it could only be through the combined and unified efforts of the League and the United States. As to the use of force it must be kept in mind that not only was this never suggested, the very idea of it was abhorrent to the majority of the governments represented on the Council, and, moreover, it was precluded by consideration of the case under Article 11. But the thought of it was always there, hovering in the background, a specter which no one wanted to face, least of all the powers having interests in the Pacific. There was always the possibility that China might shift her appeal to Article 15—it was the hint of this which had brought such a sharp rejoinder from Lord Cecil in September [58]—and Article 15 envisaged the use of economic and military sanctions under Article 16. The Council, the Secretary of State, and the President of the United States were in agreement on this point. Mr. Hoover, however, differed from the others in one very important respect. He foresaw the eventual use of force if Japan were to be stopped in her tracks, and, like Sir John Simon in 1935, he was determined to avoid that for his country no matter what the cost to China, to collective security, or the coming disarmament conference. The decision as to the capacity in which our representative should act was undoubtedly his; his reasons were set forth in a memorandum to the Cabinet [59] and in his message of December 10 to Congress on the subject of Foreign Affairs.[60] In the end, therefore, the Council, restricted by the Covenant itself, by the objections of Japan,[61] and by the American decision, was forced to accept a pale shadow for the substance of American support, a far less effective participation than had been hoped for originally.

[57] New York *Times*, Oct. 16, 1931.   [58] See Chap. II, above.
[59] R. L. Wilbur and A. M. Hyde, *The Hoover Policies* (New York, 1937), pp. 600–602; W. S. Myers, *The Foreign Policies of the Hoover Administration* (New York, 1940), pp. 159–60. For discussion of this memorandum see Chap. V, below.
[60] W. S. Myers, ed., *The State Papers of Herbert Hoover* (New York, 1934), II, 76–77.
[61] See the interesting discussion on this subject by Clarence Streit, New York *Times*, Oct. 11, 1931.

What were the results of our presence at the Council table? On October 17 the Council without the disputants but with Mr. Gilbert met in secret session to discuss the question of invoking the Pact of Paris. It was decided that members who were also signatories would send notes to China and Japan calling attention to their obligations under the Pact. As President of the Council, and one of the authors of the Pact M. Briand, through his government's diplomatic representatives, was to notify those signatories not present *and the United States* of the decision requesting that they take similar action.[62] France, Spain, Great Britain, and others dispatched notes on the same day. Mr. Stimson followed on October 20, after three days' delay. Mr. Gilbert attended the Council meetings for the express purpose of participating in the discussion of obligations under the Pact of Paris. Council action was immediate, but Mr. Stimson in Washington did not act on receipt of news to that effect from his official representative. He had to wait for formal notification from M. Briand through Paris that the decision had been taken and acted upon by the others. Granted that Mr. Gilbert, a Consul, could not have formulated and dispatched the note directly from Geneva as was done by members having authority to act for their governments, nevertheless, the transatlantic telephone, which Mr. Stimson had used before and was to use again, was still in operation, and surely Mr. Gilbert used it and just as surely Mr. Stimson, had he so desired, could have acted on the seventeenth in conjunction with the governments of France and Great Britain. As a matter of fact the note should have been ready for dispatch as soon as the State Department received word of the decision to invoke the Pact. Why was Mr. Gilbert there if not for the purpose of overcoming the time lag between action by the Council members and by the United States? It simply doesn't make sense. Time, as Madariaga said, was the issue, but we stood on form and precedent and, perhaps in fear of isolationist sentiment in this country we let three precious days go by before we acted. Is it any wonder the Japanese militarists felt perfectly safe in going ahead with their plans, confident that no one would stop them? To state the case bluntly, there was no more effective col-

[62] *Official Journal*, p. 2339.

laboration after October 16 than before. We did know just what was going on in secret meetings and conferences; Mr. Stimson was better informed as to the precise attitude of Japan and other Council members, but this knowledge was not converted into action.

Five days and nights followed in which the leading members of the Council worked indefatigably to reach a compromise satisfactory to both parties. Try as they would they could gain no concession from Japan. Yoshizawa would neither consent to a definite date for the withdrawal of Japanese troops to the treaty zone nor would he yield one iota in the matter of direct negotiations without neutral assistance between his country and China. Finally realizing the futility of further argument and thoroughly exasperated, they determined to call a public meeting on the evening of October 22, not for the purpose of recording a difference of views, as on October 16, but to make Japan play her hand in the full light of publicity and, if she still would not yield, to place squarely on her shoulders the opprobrium consequent upon the Council's failure to reach a unanimous decision.

The meeting opened with an interchange of compliments between the Japanese and American representatives in which the former, while maintaining the legal position assumed on the fifteenth and sixteenth, assured Mr. Gilbert of the friendship of Japan for the United States. Mr. Gilbert responded appropriately, closing with these words:

We look upon the long record of peace and friendship between our people and the people of Japan as among the happiest pages of our history, and the thought is furthest from our mind that that record should ever be broken.[63]

M. Briand reported on the action taken under the Pact of Paris including the reading of a note which he had that morning received from the Chinese Government in answer to the communication of the French Government. He then recounted the efforts of the preceding week to put an end to the "regrettable situation with which we are now confronted" and the attempts to work out a draft

[63] *Ibid.*, p. 2339.

resolution satisfactory to all. In the course of this he summarized the positions taken by the parties to the conflict in the following terms:

> On the one hand, we have the Japanese Government protesting that it has no desire to encroach on the territorial integrity of China. It is prepared to evacuate the territories into which it has introduced its troops. It is only anxious as to the security of its nationals and their property. As soon as guarantees are received in this respect, it asserts its readiness to withdraw the troops. That is the Japanese contention. I believe I do not misrepresent it.
>
> On the other hand, the Chinese representative says: "We quite understand that guarantees should be required for persons and property and we are prepared to give these guarantees. We have studied and will continue to study the best means of doing so, and we place ourselves entirely at the Council's disposal for that purpose. We are even anxious to take advantage of its benevolent authority to facilitate matters." [64]

The draft resolution finally agreed upon by the "Twelve" and submitted to the parties concerned shortly before the meeting was then read.

The Council,

In pursuance of the resolution passed on September 30th; noting that in addition to the invocation by the Government of China, of Article 11 of the Covenant, Article 2 of the Pact of Paris has also been invoked by a number of Governments;

(1) Recalls the undertakings given to the Council by the Governments of China and Japan in that resolution, and in particular the statement of the Japanese representative that the Japanese Government would continue as rapidly as possible the withdrawal of its troops into the railway zone in proportion as the safety of the lives and property of Japanese nationals is effectively assured, and the statement of the Chinese representative that his Government will assume the responsibility for the safety of the lives and property of Japanese nationals outside that zone —a pledge which implies the effective protection of Japanese subjects residing in Manchuria;

(2) Recalls further that both Governments have given the assurance that they would refrain from any measures which might aggravate the existing situation, and are, therefore, bound not to resort to any aggressive policy or action and to take measures to suppress hostile agitation;

[64] *Ibid.*, p. 2340.

(3) Recalls the Japanese statement that Japan has no territorial designs in Manchuria, and notes that this statement is in accordance with the terms of the Covenant of the League of Nations, and of the Nine-Power Treaty, the signatories of which are pledged "to respect the sovereignty, the independence, and the territorial and administrative integrity of China";

(4) Being convinced that the fulfilment of these assurances and undertakings is essential for the restoration of normal relations between the two parties;

(a) Calls upon the Japanese Government to begin immediately and to proceed progressively with the withdrawal of its troops into the railway zone, so that the total withdrawal may be effected before the date fixed for the next meeting of the Council;

(b) Calls upon the Chinese Government, in execution of its general pledge to assume the responsibility for the safety of the lives and property of all Japanese subjects resident in Manchuria, to make such arrangements for taking over the territory thus evacuated as will ensure the safety of the lives and property of Japanese subjects there, and requests the Chinese Government to associate with the Chinese authorities designated for the above purpose, representatives of other Powers in order that such representatives may follow the execution of the arrangements;

(5) Recommends that the Chinese and Japanese Governments should immediately appoint representatives to arrange the details of the execution of all points relating to the evacuation and the taking over of the evacuated territory so that they may proceed smoothly and without delay;

(6) Recommends the Chinese and Japanese Governments, as soon as the evacuation is completed, to begin direct negotiations on questions outstanding between them, and in particular those arising out of recent incidents as well as those relating to existing difficulties due to the railway situation in Manchuria. For this purpose, the Council suggests that the two parties should set up a conciliation committee, or some such permanent machinery;

(7) Decides to adjourn till November 16th, at which date it will again examine the situation, but authorizes its President to convoke a meeting at an earlier date should it in his opinion be desirable.[65]

The representatives of both parties asked for time to consult their governments and this was granted. Mr. Yoshizawa, however, could not resist the temptation to go into the history of the case, reverting

[65] *Ibid.*, pp. 2340-41.

again to the underlying situation, to the tension which had existed before September 18 and giving reasons why his government could not fix a definite date for complete withdrawal of its troops to the treaty zone.

When the Council met the next evening the Japanese reply to the Kellogg Pact note had been received and was read. M. Briand then asked if the representatives of China and Japan had received instructions from their governments and were in a position to discuss the text of the draft resolution. Dr. Sze spoke first. He pointed out the objections to extending Japan's time for three more weeks but bowed to "the Council's view of its necessity" and in the name of his government accepted the resolution "as a bare minimum, as marking merely the present stage in the League of Nations' handling of this problem and as a proposal, which, because it is put before us publicly by all the members of the Council, except the parties, as the outcome of their prolonged discussions, must be regarded as fixed in its main lines and subject to amendment only on minor details." He followed this with a detailed discussion of the bases of his government's acceptance of the resolution.

The President then put before the Council a document containing certain modifications in the text of the resolution suggested by the representative of Japan. As M. Briand remarked, these were so drastic as to constitute a counterproposal [66] rather than a series of amendments, and therefore it would be necessary to discuss them and arrive at a decision regarding them before the Council's draft could be voted on. The first three points were similar to those framed by the Council and in the course of the discussion Mr. Yoshizawa agreed to accept the original version. Points 7 and 8 having to do with information to the Council and the date of the next meeting offered no serious obstacle. The real stumbling blocks were points (4), (5), and (6), which would have so altered the character of the resolution as to give Japan a complete diplomatic victory and force China to accept direct negotiation on the "fundamental principles" previous to the evacuation of her territory. These points were:

[66] *Ibid.,* p. 2346.

The Council of the League

(4) Again notes the statement by the representative of Japan made on October 13th to the effect that the Japanese Government would withdraw those of its troops still remaining in a few localities outside the said zone as the present atmosphere of tension clears and the situation improves, by the achievement of a previous understanding between the Chinese and Japanese Governments as regards the fundamental principles governing normal relations. That is to say, affording an assurance for the safety of the lives of Japanese nationals and for the protection of their property.

(5) Recommends the Chinese and Japanese Governments to confer together at once with a view to arriving at the understanding mentioned in paragraph 4;

(6) Recommends the Chinese and Japanese Governments to appoint representatives to arrange the details of execution of the evacuation and of taking over the districts evacuated.[67]

In arguing for the acceptance of these points Mr. Yoshizawa said his government considered a calmer frame of mind essential to a solution and "has carefully thought out what points were necessary to bring about such a *détente* and has determined a number of fundamental points upon which normal relations between China and Japan should be based." Later he said it was "materially impossible for the Japanese Government to fix an exact date" for the withdrawal of troops.[68] Lord Cecil then attempted to obtain an explanation of the fundamental principles mentioned. "It is very difficult," he said, "for us even to consider a resolution pledging us to the proposal that there should be preliminary understanding on fundamental principles unless we know what is meant by those fundamental principles." [69] Mr. Yoshizawa evaded a direct answer to this but M. Briand pressed the point, going a step beyond Lord Cecil with these words:

When reference is made to "fundamental principles" in Point 4 of the Japanese text, is there any idea of bringing under this term any of the questions which are to form the subject of the fundamental negotiations, as an element of security? If so, the whole problem with all its difficulties, is again before us.

If on the contrary, the question relates only to the question of security

[67] *Ibid.*, p. 2346.   [68] *Ibid.*, p. 2349.   [69] See Chap. III.

I note that we would be much nearer agreement and I should be very glad of it. That is a point which must be elucidated.[70]

Because of the lateness of the hour it was necessary to adjourn the meeting until the next morning. When the debate was resumed, Lord Cecil, M. Briand and M. de Madariaga endeavored time and again to persuade Mr. Yoshizawa either to accept the text of the Council resolution, to withdraw his term "fundamental principles," or to clarify its meaning. The Japanese representative stubbornly resisted all of these appeals, the last of which was made by Salvador de Madariaga, who said:

> I should like to ask the Japanese representative, before I am faced with the painful necessity of voting against his proposal, whether he would be prepared to withdraw his proposal if we were prepared to amend our proposal in such a way as to bind the two parties to the case by a solemn and formal undertaking to begin negotiations on all the questions at issue on the very day the evacuation is concluded.
>
> A declaration to that effect, if made immediately, would be so effective in relieving tension and pacifying public opinion as to safeguard the security of Japanese nationals in Manchuria and allow of the evacuation.[71]

Mr. Yoshizawa replied:

> My government thinks it preferable not to enumerate the fundamental principles in the resolution, *nor to discuss the details of these principles* at the Council table. . . .
>
> I therefore regret that I am unable to withdraw the words "fundamental principles" in our counter proposal.[72]

M. Briand then closed the morning session with these words:

> I think we should now adjourn until this afternoon. At this afternoon's meeting we shall vote on the resolutions.
>
> Before concluding, may I draw the Japanese representative's attention to the fact that it would be a difficult matter—indeed, an impossibility—for the members of the Council to accept the inclusion in a draft resolution, in a spirit of conciliation, of a reference to fundamental principles, without knowing what they are and without having the right to formulate and discuss them. That would be asking the members to make too great a sacrifice. No member of the Council would agree to insert in a

---

[70] *Official Journal*, p. 2350.   [71] *Ibid.*, p. 2357.   [72] *Ibid.* Italics mine.

text a fundamental principle if he is ignorant of its precise meaning. I quite understand our colleague's reservation but he for his part must understand how difficult it is for us to entertain the solution he is putting before us.[73]

In the interval between the morning and afternoon sessions of the twenty-fourth, M. Briand again attempted a compromise and, for a time, thought he was on the verge of success. According to his report [74] to the Council he found a new desire on the part of the Japanese delegation—he did not specify Mr. Yoshizawa—to join the other members in the view adopted by them. In the end this effort failed as had all others, and when the Council reconvened at five o'clock the two resolutions were submitted to a vote. The Japanese counterproposal was rejected by thirteen votes to one, following which a roll call vote, an unusual procedure in this body, was taken on the Council resolution with all members except Japan voting in the affirmative.[75]

Announcing the results, M. Briand stressed the point that although the Council had not achieved unanimity their efforts were not without results. They had come near to their goal; the conflict remained, which was serious enough, but it no longer amounted to a threat of war. As to the immediate future he said:

We shall adjourn until November 16th. The draft resolution which has been adopted after a very long discussion is now on the Council table. It is in the hands of our colleague, the Japanese representative, and of his Government. . . . I still venture to hope that between now and November 16th the evacuation already begun will be continued, the Japanese Government thereby proving by its acts that it is straining every effort to end the conflict. . . .

There is no need for me to add that the resolution of September 30th . . . is maintained.[76]

Prentiss Gilbert had preserved complete silence during the three days of almost continuous public debate on the resolution. Under his instructions he could not do otherwise. But at the close of this last meeting, after M. Briand had asked him to convey to his government the warm and sincere thanks of the Council for the "valuable assistance" rendered, he rose to his feet. Every eye was upon him,

[74] *Ibid.*, p. 2358.   [75] *Ibid.*   [76] *Ibid.*, p. 2359.

and observers and Council members alike leaned eagerly forward in the hope that he had been authorized to make some declaration as to the policy of the United States regarding the resolution just adopted. Something like a sigh of disappointment passed over the room as in two short sentences Mr. Gilbert thanked the President of the Council for their kind words which he would have the honor of transmitting immediately to his government.[77]

Despite the general disappointment over Mr. Gilbert's enforced silence at the public meetings of the Council, M. Briand's reference to his "valuable assistance" was not unwarranted. He was present, it will be recalled, at the secret sessions, at the meetings of the "Twelve" and of the Committee of Five, and at these he seems to have played an important role. William Martin, editor of the *Journal de Genève*, goes so far as to attribute to his influence [78] the decisions embodied in the drastic resolution presented on October 22. Even the colorless nature of his remarks at the close of the last meeting was considered entirely appropriate under the circumstances and there was a general feeling that this would serve only to emphasize any statement from the Secretary of State. That such a statement would be immediately forthcoming was confidently expected. The Council had taken literally Mr. Stimson's words, "it is most desirable that the League in no way relax its vigilance and in no way fail to assert all the pressure and authority within its competence toward regulating the action of China and Japan." [79] They had adopted a resolution which, although robbed of its juridic value by Japan's negative vote, demanded complete evacuation of Chinese territory by November 16. "The most satisfactory of all documents worked out by the League of Nations" one writer [80] calls it, while another terms it "the most categorical warning ever sent to a major power in the entire history of the League of Nations." [81] They now looked

[77] *Ibid.*, p. 2362. In *The Far Eastern Crisis* (p. 66) Mr. Stimson writes: "As soon as this invocation of the Kellogg-Briand Pact was concluded and nothing remained before the Council except the transaction of its League business, I directed Mr. Gilbert to retire on October 24th from his temporary seat at the Council table and to resume the normal position which he had always occupied in the Council room as one of the observers."
[78] "The League and the Far Eastern Crisis," *Asia*, July–August, 1932, p. 407.
[79] *Conditions in Manchuria*, p. 14.   [80] William Martin, *op. cit.*, p. 407.
[81] Drew Pearson and Constantine Brown, *The American Diplomatic Game* (New York, 1935), p. 315.

to Mr. Stimson to fulfill the promise contained in these words:

> On its part the American government acting independently through its diplomatic representatives will endeavor to reinforce what the League does and will make clear that it has a keen interest in the matter and is not oblivious to the obligations which the disputants have assumed to their fellow signatories in the Pact of Paris as well as in the Nine Power Pact should a time arise when it would seem advisable to bring forward these obligations.[82]

The Council—and Mr. Gilbert, it would seem—did not interpret the reference to the two Pacts as meaning that American support would be confined to action under those treaties. Nor is there any evidence that Mr. Stimson was thinking in such restricted terms on October 5 (or was it the ninth?).[83] As early as the twenty-fifth, however, a change of attitude was apparent in Washington.[84] The State Department, the press was told, regarded the action of the Council "with intense but *detached* interest."[85] On October 28 and again on the thirtieth the public was informed that no new move by the United States was in prospect, that the moral pressure of the world was the most practical approach to the problem and this had already been registered through invocation of the Pact of Paris. By now League circles were not a little disturbed, so much so that Sir Eric Drummond was reported to have postponed a scheduled trip to London for consultation regarding the Disarmament Conference. Mr. Stimson's silence at this time seems even more serious than his failure to follow up the September resolution. That had been unanimously adopted and, in theory at least, its provisions were binding commitments; the abortive resolution of the twenty-fourth, on the other hand, had only moral force, and, lacking American support, not much of that. On the thirty-first a spokesman for the State Department scoffed at these unofficial rumors from Geneva saying the League had not solicited any action by this country in the matter. Moreover, he continued, any idea that the United States by its silence

---

[82] *Conditions in Manchuria*, p. 14.   [83] See Chap. III, note 14.
[84] Herbert Elliston says Washington considered the resolution a mistake. See Elliston, "Realities in Manchuria," *Asia*, January, 1932, p. 8.
[85] New York *Times*, Oct. 25. (Italics mine.) The succeeding references are to the New York *Times* of the dates specified unless otherwise indicated by footnotes.

was indirectly aiding Japan in its opposition to withdrawal was unfortunate because this government was pursuing "a policy of strict and·undeviating neutrality in regard to Manchuria" [86] and was interested only in the preservation of peace in the Far East. On November 2 the correspondent of the New York *Times* wired his paper that although the State Department was definitely concerned over reports from Manchuria regarding the Nonni River crisis, the only move being considered was the publication of the notes recently [87] sent to Tokyo and Nanking invoking the Kellogg-Briand treaty. On November 4 Mr. Stimson was reported to be undertaking a new study of the situation, and on November 5 Ambassador Forbes, within a few hours after his return to Tokyo, visited Baron Shidehara and communicated a note just cabled from Washington containing "the momentous announcement that the United States Administration had associated itself with the League of Nations resolutions." [88]

The State Department admitted the call of Ambassador Forbes, as well as its serious concern over the turn of affairs in Northern Manchuria, but denied that a note had been sent and gave the press to understand that while indicating its sympathy with the Council's efforts to hasten the withdrawal of Japanese troops from Manchuria it had not adhered to the resolution calling for complete evacuation by November 16. The "note" characterized by Mr. Byas as momentous, was in fact a memorandum or "aide-memoire" acknowledging and commenting on the reply, dated October 24, of the Japanese Government to Mr. Stimson's invocation of the Pact of Paris on October 20. It does not adhere to the Council Resolution of October 24 in any technical sense, nor does it at any point mention a specific date for the withdrawal of Japanese troops, which was the very heart of that resolution. Nevertheless, like the memorandum of September 22, also unpublished, it is far stronger than either the American or Japanese public was led to believe and, had it been sent within a day or two of the Council's action, would have

[86] An Associated Press dispatch in the New York *Times* attributes this remark to W. R. Castle, Jr., Under Secretary of State.
[87] These notes were sent on Oct. 20.
[88] Hugh Byas, New York *Times*, Nov. 5, 1931.

been considered strong evidence of the united opinion and effort of the League and the United States. In it Mr. Stimson says his government cannot escape the conclusion that Japanese occupation of South Manchuria has destroyed Chinese administrative integrity in that area, and that the broader matter of direct negotiations between the two countries in respect to treaty rights cannot be settled until there has been effective withdrawal of troops within the railway zone. The Council action is directly referred to in this concluding paragraph:

My Government finds confirmation of its views as expressed above in its scrutiny of the position taken by the Council of the League of Nations as expressed in the resolution adopted by the Council on September 30th and in the draft resolution upon which thirteen members of the Council gave affirmative vote on October 24th. My Government hopes that the Japanese Government will find it possible to share the view of those nations that negotiations looking to the settlement of long standing issues between Japan and China ought not to be made a condition precedent to the evacuation of the occupied positions and by so doing avail itself of the opportunity presented to refute conclusively any implication that exertion of military pressure was in any way intended to affect the process of arriving at a settlement of the points at issue. My Government confidently hopes that both China and Japan will be guided by the spirit of the resolutions above referred to and will make every possible effort to follow a course consistent therewith.[89]

Unfortunately Mr. Stimson's "keen interest" in the matter had permitted twelve of the twenty-two days allowed for Japanese withdrawal to elapse before he took this step. If not too little it was certainly too late; for in the meantime the fighting over the Nonni River bridge of the Taonan-Anganchi Railway had taken place and Tsitsihar was endangered (it was occupied by the Japanese on November 18). Just as in the first week of October the adjournment of the Council had been followed by an extension of hostilities, this time to the north. The note of warning sounded by those concerned with keeping the peace (and Mr. Stimson's communication of November 5 undoubtedly belongs in this category

---

[89] *Conditions in Manchuria*, p. 32. In the *Far Eastern Crisis* Mr. Stimson refers to this as a "note," and the fact that it was an "aide-memoire" probably does not make any difference—Japan knew exactly where we stood.

along with M. Briand's telegram of the sixth) brought a slight with-drawal by the militarists. For a short space they walked more softly, but it cannot be too greatly stressed that whenever they thought the time was ripe they broadened the field of operations; when protests were raised they drew back but never to the immediate starting point, so that always there was a net gain. In September they oc-cupied Mukden and spread beyond the railway zone. Under pressure from the Council they shifted their forces about but there was little if any actual withdrawal. In October they bombed Chinchow and destroyed the civil administration of Chang Hsueh-Liang. In No-vember they moved north toward Anganchi and the Chinese Eastern Railway. Chinchow and Tsitsihar did not fall until later, but fall they did to the accompaniment of Japanese assurances that they had no intention of violating Chinese administrative or territorial in-tegrity. The same policy of extending the scope of operations was carried into the field of political and diplomatic relationships. In September the Japanese argued that they were acting only in self-defense, then they asserted that no withdrawal within the railway zone could take place until China had given effective guarantees of the safety of the lives and property of Japanese nationals in Man-churia. Little by little the security of Japanese subjects in all of China crept into the discussion, and by October 24 the "fundamental points" had become the basis of a settlement prerequisite to evacua-tion.

Mr. Yoshizawa had refused to discuss these principles with the Council to the great irritation of its members and the utter mystifi-cation of Tokyo where the Foreign Office announced [90] that he had been instructed as early as October 20 that there was no ob-jection to his revealing their nature. However, the Japanese repre-sentative in Geneva was still playing the army's game, and even now it did not suit their purpose to come to any agreement with China or the League. Had they really desired to achieve their objectives as originally stated, and those objectives only, Japan could have ap-pealed to the League or issued an ultimatum to China before Muk-den, and would then have had the support of a considerable section

[90] Hugh Byas, New York *Times*, Oct. 26.

of world opinion on its side. But this was not what the army wanted. For months they had been preparing the public mind in Japan for war because of the twofold political struggle in which they were engaged with the civilian element in the cabinet. The immediate issue of that fight was the army appropriation which the Minseito party wanted to cut and which the army was determined should be increased; but the ultimate objective was the control of foreign policy by the War Office along the lines laid down in the Tanaka Memorial. Through the summer of 1931 the Chinese gave them ample fuel for their fires, especially in the death of Captain Nakamura,[91] but in spite of it all it looked in September as if Premier Wakatsuki and Baron Shidehara would carry the day. On September 17 it was announced that a settlement was about to be reached over the Nakamura case. The Japanese militarists must have echoed the sentiments of Generals Moltke and von Roon when Bismarck read them the original telegram from Ems, "There goes our fine war"; and as in that historic incident they set about to remedy the situation. And so, Mukden. Having set their course they let nothing stop them until they saw their first victory within their grasp. That is why the fundamental points were not made public before the Council adjourned, that is why Mr. Yoshizawa would make no real concessions as to the October 24 resolution, and that is why it was Mr. Yoshizawa who, at the Paris meeting in November, proposed [92] the sending of a Commission of Enquiry to Manchuria to study and investigate the situation there and report its findings to the Council. By that time the Wakatsuki-Shidehara group was doomed, the political struggle at home won, and the Japanese populace aroused to the necessary pitch of national fervor by military victories, by stories of Chinese atrocities and of how the world was leagued against Japan. The army no longer had anything to fear from a Commission of Enquiry and Yoshizawa could make his fine gesture.

[91] For a detailed account of the Nakamura case see *Lytton Report*, pp. 63–66. See also Chaps. I and II, above.
[92] Chap. VI, p. 184, below.

V

SECOND INTERLUDE

October 24 to November 16

MILITARY AND DIPLOMATIC DEVELOPMENTS.—As has been previously indicated the three weeks between the October and November meetings of the Council were marked by momentous developments regarding Manchuria: military operations were extended northward with a view to destroying the last vestige of Chang Hseuh-liang's authority in the three eastern provinces; the scope of the proposed settlement with China was expanded to include the whole field of Sino-Japanese relations; and a new phase of the violation of Chinese administrative integrity was initiated with the seizure of the salt and other public revenues.[1]

Quite apart from the Manchurian Question certain national situations were evolving in ways which drastically affected the next meeting of the Council and the attitudes of the countries concerned. In Japan the inability of Finance Minister Inouye to stabilize the serious financial and economic situation was loosening the tenuous hold of the Wakatsuki cabinet. Indeed it was this failure rather than the international crisis in which Baron Shidehara found himself involved which was to give the *coup de grâce* to the Minseito party and bring the Seiyukai with their powerful military backing into control immediately after December 10.[2]

In Great Britain the general election on October 27 resulted in the utter debacle of the Labour Party, a "violent redistribution of political power" which was followed by a "proportionately violent

---

[1] There is no question that this seizure of the salt revenues involved a serious violation of Chinese administrative integrity, but it did not materially affect the case before the Council or American cooperation. It has therefore been omitted from this study. Excellent short discussions of this question are found in Willoughby, *The Sino-Japanese Controversy and the League of Nations* (Baltimore, 1935), pp. 102–3, *The League and Manchuria, the Third Phase of the Chinese-Japanese Conflict* (Geneva Special Studies, Vol. II, No. 12, December, 1931), pp. 19 ff., the *Lytton Report*, pp. 102–3. The considerable correspondence carried on between M. Briand and the two governments is given in the *Official Journal*, Annex 1334, pp. 2524–28.

[2] See Chap. VII, below.

reversal" of more than one established national policy, including that which governed the relations between Great Britain and the League of Nations.[3] The National government with Ramsay MacDonald as Prime Minister remained but was no longer truly National, in everything but name it was Conservative, arch-conservative in fact, and Sir John Simon was its Secretary of State for Foreign Affairs.

In the United States, too, there was a change. During September and October Secretary Stimson seems to have been fairly free from political pressure, but as the first of December drew near the shadow of that lame-duck Congress [4] which was to embitter Mr. Hoover's last year in the White House cast its gloomy length over the foreign as well as the domestic situation. Isolationists, particularly those of Mr. Hoover's own party, were speaking more freely and could no longer be ignored. To this may be due in some measure the apparent weakening of American cooperation with the League, the "detached" [5] interest with which the State Department watched events and its failure to associate this government with the Council's demand for the evacuation of Manchuria by November 16.

Add to these the military events in Northern Manchuria and the result is a situation far more exigent and fraught with disaster than that precipitated by the bombing of Chinchow on October 8.

Early in October trouble had broken out in the province of Heilunkiang between the governor, General Ma Chan-shan, and General Chang Hai-peng, commander of the garrison at Taonan.[6] To delay the advance of his rival while he prepared his own defenses, Ma had blown up the bridge over the Nonni River some thirty miles south of Anganchi, junction of the Chinese Eastern Railway with the Taonan-Anganchi line.[7] As this interfered with the flow of traffic, especially of much needed food supplies, to the South Manchuria Railway the authorities of that road demanded the immediate repair of the bridge, but General Ma delayed. On October 28 General Honjo demanded completion of the repairs by noon of November

[3] Arnold J. Toynbee, ed., *Survey of International Affairs,* 1931 (London, 1932), p. 399.
[4] See Chap. VI.   [5] See Chap. IV.
[6] In the Japanese-controlled province of Liaoning.
[7] Built by China with a Japanese loan.

3, otherwise these would be undertaken by laborers of the South Manchuria Railway under protection of Japanese troops. Ma was in a tight place. To repair the bridge immediately was to give his Japanese-supported rival the advantage; [8] to permit the Japanese to repair it under protection of armed forces was regarded as equivalent to giving them command not only of the Taonan-Anganchi line but of a key section of the Chinese Eastern as well; to refuse the Japanese demand entirely meant that he would face a pitched battle with a force far superior to his own in everything but numbers. Ma still tried to delay by asking for an extension of time, but to this he received no reply. By November 2 no decision had been reached, although it was reported Ma had promised to repair the bridge within a week. Both Ma and Chang were then notified by Honjo that they were to withdraw their troops six miles from each side of the river and that neither was to use the railway for tactical purposes. According to the account given in the report of the Lytton Commission, [9] Ma seems finally to have accepted the ultimatum but so late that there was much confusion, conflict in orders, and misunderstanding on the part of both Chinese and Japanese officers in the field. The truce was not observed and a serious clash took place on November 4. Hot fighting continued for several days. Honjo's forces, having received reinforcements from Korea and Japan, were victorious and on November 6 crossed the Nonni River and occupied Tahsing Station. Ma's retreating army was not pursued but the Japanese remained in the vicinity of the station, although the Japanese government was reported to have authorized the dispatch of troops only on condition they would not go beyond the river and would be withdrawn as soon as the repairs were completed. [10]

There was little fighting during the following week but the atmosphere remained tense and the situation was complicated by the outbreak of trouble in Tientsin [11] and by rumors that the Japanese Consul and his staff at Tsitsihar were in danger of attack from the Chinese. Japanese military authorities demanded General Ma's resig-

[8] *Lytton Report,* pp. 72–74.   [9] *Ibid.,* p. 73.
[10] Hugh Byas, New York *Times,* Nov. 5.
[11] *The League and Manchuria, the Third Phase,* pp. 17, 24.

nation four times during the week,[12] each time stiffening their terms. None of these was accepted and on November 14 and 15 the Japanese attack was renewed. On the fifteenth Ambassador Debuchi in Washington had assured Secretary Stimson [13] that Japan would launch no offensive from the Nonni River and that there was no plan for an advance upon Tsitsihar, but on the sixteenth, the day the Council reconvened, the day when according to the resolution of October 24 the withdrawal to the railway zone was to have been completed, the United Press reported the heaviest fighting yet in the Nonni region. The next day there was a lull in the fighting: General Ma was playing for time before replying to Honjo's demand that he evacuate his capital while the Japanese were preparing a large-scale movement to drive him out. Once again the Japanese commander in Manchuria seems to have ignored orders from Tokyo, for on the fourteenth Hugh Byas reported that the Cabinet knew nothing of Honjo's ultimatum and if, as was said, he had asked that a Japanese force be stationed east of Tsitsihar he knew his positive orders prohibited him from passing a clearly defined line nearly fifty miles from that city.[14] It was reported also that Honjo had asked to be released from these orders but the government had refused and had instructed him to negotiate for mutual withdrawal. However there was no hint of withdrawal in Honjo's ultimatum [15] of the sixteenth, which demanded that Ma retire from Tsitsihar, his capital, withdraw all Chinese troops north of the Chinese Eastern Railway, and undertake not to interfere in any way with the traffic and operation of the Taonan-Anganchi line. Remarking that he remembered only too well what had happened to Chinese administrative authority when Chinese military forces were compelled to retire from Mukden and Kirin, Ma rejected the ultimatum. A new general attack was begun. Ma was decisively defeated and on November 19 Tsitsihar was occupied by the Japanese.

One of the first consequences of the fighting on the Nonni River was the announcement by M. Briand on November 5 that he would probably ask the Council to meet in Paris instead of Geneva, as his

---

[12] *Lytton Report*, p. 74.
[14] *Ibid.*, Nov. 15.

[13] New York *Times*, Nov. 16.
[15] *Lytton Report*, p. 74.

presence there was made necessary by his Parliamentary duties. This did not meet with unanimous approval. Dr. Sze and the League Secretariat were opposed to it for several reasons. The French capital was not neutral ground and it would be much more difficult to keep extraneous matters, such as the world economic situation and the increasing strain in Franco-German relations, from intruding on the delicate negotiations. Paris, moreover, was considered pro-Japanese. From the beginning, the French press, at least that section which had official backing, had supported the Japanese, picturing that government as a good gendarme who sought only to maintain order in a chaotic and lawless region.[16] Italy and Germany also preferred Geneva. Tokyo, quite naturally, was well pleased with the prospective change, and the opinion was freely expressed there that Paris might prove more patient and understanding than Geneva had been.[17] In the end it was generally felt that Paris with Briand was better than Geneva without him and the decision was left entirely in his hands.[18]

The gravity of the situation in northern Manchuria impelled M. Briand to dispatch on November 6 an urgent appeal to the governments of China and Japan reminding them of their solemn obligations under the resolution of September 30 and suggesting a course of action which he felt might prevent further trouble there:

[16] Karl Radek, "War in the Far East," *Foreign Affairs*, July, 1932: "The attitude of France toward Japan is plain. It is determined by French hostility toward the nationalistic movement in the Orient, a movement which threatens the French position in Indo-China. It is also determined by France's hostility to the Soviet Union. French imperialism would like to see Japan strengthened in the hope that this will lead to a struggle with the Soviet Union."

Sir Wilmot Lewis (Washington correspondent) in the London *Times*, Jan. 29, 1932: "No doubt is entertained regarding the sincerity with which M. Briand spoke for the League as the representative of France . . . but it is believed here that the France which speaks at Geneva and the France which speaks through the Quai d'Orsay and, by way of the Metropolitan press, to the French opinion are not entirely the same."

See also Constantine Brown, "French Foreign Policy in the Far East," *Asia*, May, 1932; William Martin, "The League and the Far Eastern Crisis," *Asia*, July–August, 1932; Clarence Streit, "The Far Eastern War in Geneva," *Asia*, February, 1933.

[17] Byas, New York *Times*, Nov. 6.

[18] This decision may have been influenced by the knowledge that neither Cecil nor Madariaga would head the delegation of their respective governments, thus leaving the Council without a leader versed in League technique and procedure. More serious still, the absence of Briand might have thrown the presidency in doubt, after the precedent set by Spain when, Lerroux being detained in his own capital in October, France had been asked to take the chair.

To fulfill those undertakings it now seems to me necessary for the two Governments to issue instructions without delay to the officers commanding their forces in order to remove all possibility of sanguinary engagements between Chinese and Japanese troops as any further serious incidents may make it even more difficult for the Council to pursue its efforts for the maintenance of peace and the settlement of the dispute with which it is called upon to deal.[19]

Dissatisfied with the responses [20] in deeds if not in words, on November 11 he addressed another appeal, more peremptory in tone, to the two governments, insisting that every effort should be made to avoid any aggravation of the situation and that commanders in the field should receive the "strictest orders to refrain from initiating any fresh action." [21] To this the Chinese Government replied they would refrain from using force except where "absolutely necessary for defence against deliberate attacks by Japan." Tokyo declared that Japanese troops had received "instructions not to extend military operations as long as Chinese forces undertake no acts of hostility." Each note [22] points to the danger inherent in the presence of the armed forces of the other party. Unfortunately the situation remained acute, and when the Council reconvened in Paris on November 16 it was to be confronted almost immediately with the *fait accompli* of the Japanese occupation of Tsitsihar.

In an editorial of October 25 the New York *Times* had commented: "At last the fact is gradually coming to the surface that the Manchurian quarrel is over the 1915 treaties—the Twenty One Demands." And to a great extent this was true. Certainly these treaties and their predecessors of 1905 play an important part in the events and discussions throughout November and December. Hugh Byas writing from Tokyo on November 2 says: "If China is prepared to respect the 1915 treaty the Manchurian question is finished but Dr. Sze's letter [23] here is regarded as a verbal repudiation of the pact." [24]

Had the 1915 treaty been the only thing at stake there might have been hope for some compromise solution, difficult as that would have

[19] *Official Journal*, Annex 1334, XXVIII, p. 2521. This note coincides with the visit by Forbes to Shidehara with Stimson memorandum.
[20] Chinese reply, *ibid.*, XXIX, pp. 2521–22; Japanese reply, *ibid.*, XXX, p. 2522.
[21] *Ibid.*, p. 2523.   [22] *Ibid.*, pp. 2523–24.
[23] *Ibid.*, p. 2513. See also pp. 174–75, below.   [24] New York *Times*, Nov. 3.

been for both parties; but the military faction in Japan had wagered its very existence as well as the future direction and control of national policy on the outcome of the Manchurian quarrel.[25] Their determination to make no concessions and to put themselves in a position to dictate the final settlement becomes more and more evident from the beginning of the conflict with General Ma's forces. Neither the remonstrances of the United States, appeals from the President of the Council of the League, nor direct orders from their own government deterred them.[26]

As military victories increased, the temper and will of the Japanese people hardened, the long-cultivated reverence for the military [27] began to work, and national feeling was inflamed. As the army advanced in Manchuria, the War Office in Tokyo through the chauvinistic section of the press aroused bitter animosity against anyone who opposed them, pouring out their invectives, now on the United States, now on Great Britain, quite frequently on their own Foreign Office, but always and continuously on the League, which they accused of interfering on the wrong side in a quarrel entirely outside its sphere.[28] At the same time every foreign comment which put Japan in a favorable light or evidenced the slightest sympathy with her position was seized upon and played up, even to the point of issuing special editions with reprints from British conservative papers, the French press, and some American papers.[29]

The course of diplomatic discussions and communications was much the· same, stiffening, hardening, demanding more and more as the military won their battles in Manchuria and in Tokyo. We have already pointed out the shift in the Japanese position from September to late October,[30] that whereas in September Japan professed a readiness to evacuate the illegally occupied portions of Man-

[25] See pp. 126–27, below.
[26] For the single exception to this see Chap. VI, p. 190, below.
[27] See Nathaniel Peffer, *Basis for Peace in the Far East* (New York, 1941), Chap. V, for an excellent analysis of Japanese character and the place held by this cult of the military.
[28] Byas, New York *Times*, Nov. 10.
[29] Dispatches of Hugh Byas in the New York *Times* through November and excerpts from the Japanese press, published in *Trans-Pacific*, attest the influence of these.
[30] See pp. 125–26, above.

churia as soon as China could make proper provision for the protection of Japanese nationals, that government at the close of the October Council meetings was insisting that China must accept the "fundamental principles" as a prelude to evacuation.

On October 26, two days after the Council adjourned, the Japanese Government published in Tokyo a statement regarding these fundamental principles of which Mr. Yoshizawa had made such a mystery. As summarized in section 4 of the statement, they were: [31]

(1) Mutual repudiation of aggressive policy and conduct;
(2) Respect for Chinese territorial integrity; [32]
(3) Complete suppression of all organized movements interfering with freedom of trade and stirring up international hatred;
(4) Effective protection throughout all Manchuria of all peaceful pursuits undertaken by Japanese subjects;
(5) Respect for treaty rights of Japan in Manchuria.

Copies of the statement were circulated to all members of the Council. On October 29 M. Briand wrote [33] Mr. Yoshizawa that in his opinion the governments of China and Japan and the Council of the League of Nations had shown themselves to be in complete agreement as to the first four of these points inasmuch as they were embodied in principle in the resolution of September 30 (which was still valid from a juridical standpoint), as well as in both the Council's draft resolution of October 24 and the Japanese amendments thereto. The fifth point, he argued, was amply covered by Dr. Sze's arbitration proposal, made shortly [34] after the Council adjourned on October 24. In proof of this he quoted from Dr. Sze's letter as follows:

China, like every member of the League of Nations, is bound by the Covenant to a "scrupulous respect for all treaty obligations." The Chinese Government, for its part, is determined loyally to fulfill all its obligations under the Covenant. It is prepared to give proof of this intention by undertaking to settle all disputes with Japan as to treaty interpretation by arbitration or judicial settlement, as provided by Article 13 of the Covenant.

M. Briand therefore urged the Japanese Government to conform to the terms of the September 30 resolution and its own repeated decla-

[31] *Official Journal*, Annex 1334, p. 2514.
[32] No mention is made here of administrative integrity.
[33] *Official Journal*, p. 2515. [34] *Ibid.*, p. 2513.

rations at the Council meetings of October 22, 23, and 24, to "continue as rapidly as possible the withdrawal of its troops into the railway zone." In conclusion he called attention to paragraph 5 of the resolution submitted on October 24 recommending that the two governments "appoint representatives to settle the details relating to the carrying out of the evacuation and to the taking over of the evacuated territories in order that these operations may be carried out in a regular manner and without delay."

Foreign Minister Shidehara did not reply to this until November 7 and then it was to reject almost in their entirety the arguments advanced by the President of the Council. He assured M. Briand that his government respected the validity of the September resolution but had regretfully concluded that "the dangers involved in precipitate recall of Japanese troops could not be averted by measure of supervision such as are recommended in opposed resolution of October 24." Concerning the fundamental principles he asserted that the terms used in that resolution "are not sufficiently explicit or comprehensive to cover all the implications of the four points in question," while the Chinese offer of arbitration was cast aside as amounting to a repudiation of treaty rights:[35]

. . . As regards final point—viz., guarantee of respect for Japanese rights in Manchuria, terms of letter addressed to you on October 24th by Chinese representative seem to give doubt whether it is contemplation of Chinese Government to call in question validity of some of treaties constituting basic embodiment of relations between Japan and China. It may be needless to state that Japanese Government could not for a moment entertain such contention. . . . Unless and until arrangement is reached between Japan and China on bases of these principles no measure of security for·lives and property of Japanese subjects sufficient to enable withdrawal of Japanese troops to railway zone can possibly be assured.

Although it is true that in this note Baron Shidehara indicates that Japan will not ask for a settlement of all pending questions before evacuation, nevertheless, he insists on "frank recognition by direct negotiation between the two parties of the fundamental principles that should govern the normal relations between any two nations." It has been argued that Shidehara was thus holding open the door

[35] *Ibid.*, pp. 2516–17.

for a reasonable settlement. Nor would the Foreign Minister of his own accord have closed that door. Two points, however, must be taken into consideration: first, in section 3 of the note he rejects the proposal for League supervision of evacuation as proposed in the October resolution; second, the fundamental principles as defined in the statement of October 26 demanded recognition of treaties which China had never considered legitimate and her interpretations of which she had offered to submit to arbitration. This offer Shidehara also rejects.

The note, coinciding as it did with the height of the Nonni River fighting, gave the American State Department and League officials cause to view the situation with increasing gravity. A technical state of war was still avoided, but the events of the last few days could not be considered other than as a deliberate flouting of both the League Covenant and the Kellogg-Briand Pact. Considered together the note and the military events constituted a flat refusal to evacuate the occupied territories by November 16.

Although there is no marked extension of the basis of settlement acceptable to Japan between November 7 and 16, there is ample evidence of a hardening of the Japanese attitude. Describing a Foreign Office press conference of November 8, Hugh Byas stresses the emphatic expression of "dissatisfaction with the methods of the League Secretariat, which is accused of uncritical readiness to accept at face value every unverified statement of Dr. Alfred Sze, even to the point of allowing these to be used as a basis for action by the Council president." [36] The Seiyukai and the chauvinistic press had been saying for some time that Japan should withdraw from the League rather than withdraw her troops before her rights were assured. Now, for the first time the possibility of such action is hinted at by the Foreign Office spokesman and the Associated Press on November 9 reported [37] that "authoritative sources" stated it was Japan's intention to secure from China a signed agreement covering the five fundamental points with the League of Nations as witness.[38]

---

[36] New York *Times*, Nov. 9. This outburst seems to have been occasioned by the controversy over the salt revenue.
[37] *Ibid.*, Nov. 9 and 10.
[38] In his dispatch of Nov. 10 (New York *Times*, Nov. 11), Hugh Byas points out that the Japanese press in its leading of public opinion failed completely to grasp

Undoubtedly the no-compromise faction was encouraged in its stand by reports of the conciliatory attitudes of the British and American governments found in the press of those countries and of Japan. Writing from London on November 11, Charles A. Selden [39] stated that the British Government was concerned primarily with preserving the appearance of absolute impartiality in the controversy so as to avoid the awkward situation attributed to the apparent bias of Viscount Cecil at Geneva [40] which created the feeling in Tokyo that Britain was championing the cause of China. "If London had its way," Mr. Selden continues, "it would persuade China to accept the Japanese offer for direct negotiations without insisting that Japan first withdraw her troops from the disturbed area." [41] The Beaverbrook and Rothermere papers in the meantime were attacking the League "not because it has failed to end the Manchurian war but because it is trying to do so, thereby involving Great Britain in futile negotiations." As for Washington, the tendency toward appeasement was, in all probability, more apparent than real. Mr. Stimson's message of the fifth, although it failed to associate this government with the Council resolution of October 24, was firm and unyielding in its disapproval of Japanese actions. Unfortunately it was not made public, and the tone of the State Department's press conferences was decidedly conciliatory, making it possible for the Japanese press to disseminate the idea that the United States disapproved of and was trying to destroy any impression of Japan's moral isolation from the rest of the world, left by the October meetings in Geneva.

Further evidence of the stiffening of the Japanese attitude may be seen in the strong statement made in Washington by mild-mannered little Debuchi to the effect that national opinion would not permit the submission of Japan's position in Manchuria to any outside authority. And on the day before the Council was to open its final sessions in Paris the Associated Press quotes the Foreign Office spokesman as saying:

---

the League's point that negotiation under military occupation is contrary to the new diplomacy.

[39] New York *Times*, Nov. 12.

[40] See also an article on Lord Reading by "Augur," *ibid.*, Oct. 27.

[41] See Chap. VI, below.

The League might recommend direct negotiations between China and Japan. That is about the only thing it can do. We have been insisting on that from the start.

Unless China is ready to accept Baron Shidehara's five points the present state of affairs may continue indefinitely.[42]

There were observers in Paris who thought that had it not been for the successful Japanese advance in Manchuria a compromise settlement might have been arranged before the public opening of the Council on the basis of Chinese consent to some limited form of direct negotiations and Japanese acceptance of a general statement of China's recognition of her treaty obligations rather than a detailed restatement of Tokyo's interpretation of these. Military events, however, made it practically impossible for either government to make an immediate move.[43]

As the time for the meeting approached, suggestions and rumors of proposals for a settlement flew thick and fast, the most important of these and the only one to be seriously considered by the Council being that for parallel and simultaneous negotiations [44] variously attributed to Mr. Yoshizawa, to General Dawes, to Secretary Stimson, to the French Government, and to the League Secretariat. One of the most persistent and most consistently denied was to the effect that Washington had found a formula for a settlement which would satisfy Japan yet leave the luster of League prestige undimmed, a formula, it was hinted, which rested upon concessions to be made by China. Especially numerous were the rumors regarding the application of sanctions and the method and extent of American cooperation with Council during the coming session.[45]

SANCTIONS.—It is generally acknowledged that the most troublesome question the League ever had to face in any dispute

---

[42] New York *Times*, Nov. 16. [43] P. J. Philip, New York *Times*, Nov. 16.
[44] See Chap. VI.
[45] About this time Japanese correspondents in Geneva reported to their papers that an international police force was being suggested to replace Japanese troops in the occupied area. Subsequent comments from the Tokyo press indicate that opinion there was not uniformly behind the military group even at that late date. The liberal *Asahi*, for example, expressed itself as thinking Japan would welcome this as a means of complying with the League demand for evacuation and at the same time safeguarding the lives and property of Japanese nationals in Manchuria; *Nichi Nichi*, on the other hand, took quite the contrary view.

brought before it was that of sanctions. This was particularly true in the present instance due among other things to the instability of the whole structure of world economics, the enormous trade interests of Great Britain and the United States in the Far East, the unwillingness of all countries concerned to take any individual risks, and the ever-present uncertainty as to what the United States might do. The tragic history of Woodrow Wilson and the League Covenant had not been forgotten, and European leaders realized there could be no assurance that Congress would support any form of sanctions even if the President and the Secretary of State were prepared to take action along these lines. The question did not come formally before the Council, but it played an increasingly important part behind the scenes and in the press dispatches, especially during November and December.

Inasmuch as the experiences of this period sowed seeds of suspicion and distrust which affected later consideration of sanctions in and out of the League and will undoubtedly influence the attitude of many public men, especially those of the isolationist variety, whenever problems of peace and world policy are attacked, it would be of the greatest value to present a clear-cut picture of the situation. Unfortunately this is extremely difficult. Indeed, at the present writing it seems impossible to determine just what the situation was. The matter was handled as gingerly as a time bomb which might explode in one's face at any moment. Neither the United States, the Council of the League of Nations, nor the government of any great power represented on the Council, was willing to assume responsibility for initiating such a drastic step, even had they been willing to support it once it had been proposed by others. Since the question did not come formally before the Council in either public or private meetings, the published documents are of little help and one is forced to fall back upon not altogether reliable sources such as contemporary news reports and the published journals and memoirs of men concerned with the events of that day. As to the news reports these, whether from Washington, London, Geneva or Paris, were either strictly anonymous or so carefully worded that authority and responsibility could easily be disclaimed. Some of them were undoubtedly trial balloons, but lacking in the very frank character of President Roosevelt's utterances to the same intent from 1937 on.

The sanctions alluded to were for the most part of an economic nature, but on November 6 it was reported from Geneva that the Secretariat was making a careful study of Article 16 to see whether a diplomatic break could be used to exert pressure on Japan. There must have been an instantaneous reaction to this somewhere, for the very next day it was announced that any talk of withdrawal of ambassadors was premature and unfeasible. And on the eighth Tokyo papers said that the report of diplomatic withdrawal was in itself a form of diplomatic intimidation but Japan would not be moved one inch from the stand she had taken.[46] Nothing came of this but the suggestion continued to appear in print from time to time thereafter.

Scarcely a day went by from November 1 to 16 that dispatches from Washington did not mention sanctions in relation to American policy. During the first week the general trend of these was that the State Department apparently did not feel that any move beyond an appeal to world opinion was practical, but if the League decided on sanctions we might consider the question. Then the tone changes, and the emphasis is on the fact that sanctions are not under consideration here; doubts are expressed as to the ability of the League to exert economic pressure successfully because of the world trade situation; and it is pointed out that it is to Congress and not to the Executive that the Constitution entrusts the control of our foreign trade and therefore anything in the nature of economic sanctions could be undertaken only on the authorization of that body.

On November 11 a London dispatch stated there was not the slightest indication that the British government would agree to withdraw its Ambassador from Tokyo or to resort to any sanctions against Japan. It was about this time that the Beaverbrook and Rothermere papers launched their violent attacks on the Council for its handling of the case, taking much the same position in regard to

[46] New York *Times*, Nov. 7, 8, and 9. See also William Martin, "The League and the Far Eastern Crisis," *Asia*, July–August, 1932.

Japan as did the French press.[47] On the same date Raymond Leslie Buell in an editorial for the Foreign Policy Association [48] urged stronger action by the United States in cooperation with the League, including sanctions if these became necessary, and a petition signed by more than one hundred and fifty prominent persons was presented to President Hoover urging him to support the League and to have the representative of the United States sit at the Council table during the November session.[49] But there is no evidence that either here or in Great Britain any section of public opinion, important in size or political weight, favored the imposition of sanctions. Mr. Stimson makes it clear that he felt public opinion in this country would not support such action.[50]

To complicate the situation further, the latent doubt of Mr. Stimson's sincerity caused by his earlier policy of backing and filling seems to have raised its head again. On November 17, the day after the Council reconvened, the Secretary of State, according to the New York *Times*, personally denied that "he had informally told Ambassador Debuchi that the United States would not participate in an economic boycott of Japan and would not withdraw her Ambassador from Tokyo whatever the developments in the Manchurian situation. The report had no basis he asserted." [51]

Thus far the discussion had been carried on largely through the medium of the press but the renewal of military operations around Tsitsihar brought matters to a climax in this as in other phases of the case. Especially was this true of the Council, which was abruptly faced with the prospect of no longer being able to avoid the issue.

[47] Charles A. Selden, New York *Times*, Nov. 12. See also analysis of F. L. Schuman in *Europe on the Eve* (New York, 1939), a footnote on p. 32 quotes from the *Daily Mail* and *Morning Post* to support this view.

[48] New York *Times*, Nov. 12.

[49] Among the signers were Bernard Baruch, Isaiah Bowman, Carrie Chapman Catt, John W. Davis, Frank E. Gannett, Carlton J. H. Hayes, John Grier Hibbens, Roy W. Howard, Bishops William Manning and R. E. L. Stryder, Owen F. Roberts, Alfred P. Sloan, Charles P. Taft 2d, and William A. White. Later in November another petition urged the President to support more actively the League's efforts to regulate the conflict. This was signed by representatives of 41 national organizations, including the Foreign Policy Association, The League of Nations Association and the National Council for Prevention of War.

[50] Stimson, *The Far Eastern Crisis*, pp. 83–84; also his "Bases of American Foreign Policy during the Past Four Years," *Foreign Affairs*, April, 1933, p. 389.

[51] New York *Times*, Nov. 18.

On the eighteenth of November Dr. Sze wrote the Secretary General: "If the Council declared it could do no more under Article 11 we should not shrink from immediately invoking other articles of the Covenant." [52] Although Dr. Sze was reported as having told members of the Council that China was ready to invoke Article 15 which might lead to the invocation of Article 16 and the use of economic sanctions, the expression "other articles of the Covenant" is as close as anyone came to a formal proposal of such action during the 65th session of the Council. But even this veiled allusion was enough to strike dismay in the minds of some of the statesmen and cause a flurry of efforts to find a formula by which a settlement might be effected. It may have been this which gave the final spur to the slow-moving Yoshizawa who, a few days later, proposed the sending of a Commission of Enquiry to Manchuria.[53] It may have been these same words of Dr. Sze which brought the question of sanctions to a climax in this country, in the carefully guarded discussion of the State Department, of the Cabinet, and between the President and Secretary of State, most of which still remain secret.

The position of the United States is far from clear, and an examination of the few available sources together with secondary accounts merely increases the confusion. The only discussion of any length with any claim to authority is that given by Mr. Stimson in his *Far Eastern Crisis* and this is far from complete. To this may be added a brief excerpt from the journal of Ambassador Dawes, the undated memorandum in which President Hoover gave the Cabinet his analysis of the situation, another memorandum from the President (dated February 23, 1933, and addressed to Mr. Stimson), together with interpretations of these such as are found in *The Hoover Policies* by Wilbur and Hyde, *The Foreign Policies of the Hoover Administration* by William Starr Myers, A. Whitney Griswold's *The Far Eastern Policy of the United States*, Raymond Leslie Buell's *Isolated America*. Because of the complex nature of the question and the dangers of misinterpretation where isolated sentences or phrases

[52] *Official Journal*, Annex 1334, p. 2552.
[53] See pp. 126–27, above, for another explanation of Yoshizawa's proposals.

are used apart from the context it has seemed necessary to quote somewhat at length from both the primary and secondary sources.

Discussing the situation which resulted from the capture of Tsitsihar Mr. Stimson explains the American position in relation to the League and sanctions, both from the constitutional standpoint and from that of the barrier of public opinion which had been built up during the bitter struggle to prevent ratification of the Treaty of Versailles in 1919:

November 19th, when the news came of the Japanese defeat of General Ma, was a day of excitement in Paris. Dr. Sze was reported as being anxious on behalf of China to invoke Article XV of the Covenant with a view to leading ultimately up to the imposition of sanctions. Members of the League were reported to have enquired from Mr. Dawes what our attitude would be in case they should proceed along that line. They were anxious to obtain commitments from us before they even discussed such action themselves. On our part we manifestly could give no such commitment. Our Congress was not in session and there was no statutory authority under which the Executive could impose economic sanctions. Furthermore it was quite unlikely that such authority would be granted. In the public discussions in America a decade before as to joining the League much opposition had been manifested against the provisions for either the military or economic sanctions expressed in the League Covenant. In the treaties to which it had afterwards become a party, viz. the Pact of Paris and the Nine Power Treaty the American government had confined itself to a reliance upon sanctions of public opinion alone. Under such circumstances manifestly we could not commit ourselves to the imposition of sanctions. On the other hand if the League of Nations desired to proceed under Articles XV and XVI of the Covenant and themselves impose such sanctions we were anxious not to discourage them or put any obstacles or dangers in their path. With the authority of the President, after a conference with him on that day, November 19th, I informed Mr. Dawes to that effect and authorized him in his discretion to make known our whole position to M. Briand. The following morning he reported to me that he had done so and that M. Briand was perfectly satisfied with our attitude.[54]

A little further on Mr. Stimson concludes a summary of the failure of efforts at conciliation in the autumn of 1931 with these comments:

[54] Stimson, *Far Eastern Crisis,* pp. 76–77. Far from being satisfied with our attitude, Briand is reported to have been heartbroken: "Collective security is finished," he told a confidant.

For the reasons already pointed out it [the League] could not have had during those early months the same American cooperation in the use of sanctions. Without the United States the League's use of sanctions would have been incomplete and comparatively ineffective—less effective than it could have been in the case of Italy versus Ethiopia. Roughly speaking the United States possessed one third of the world's trade with Japan; all the other nations combined two thirds. Although the League was assured of our moral sympathy and that we would interpose no obstacle to its economic sanctions it took no step to invoke sanctions and even China, the party most concerned, did not insist upon them and did not even discuss them until near the end of November. In short the League leadership was not ready to attempt sanctions in the autumn of 1931 in relation to Manchuria and the government of the United States in its efforts at cooperation with the League under Article XI had gone to the limit of its legal authority and at least to the limit of its popular support.[55]

Certain discrepancies appear between Mr. Stimson's account and that of Ambassador Dawes, who arrived in Paris on November 13 and had his first conference with M. Briand at the Quai d'Orsay the next morning, Saturday, November 14. Describing the interview Mr. Dawes writes in his journal:

> Briand inquired as to the probable attitude of the United States, if instead of proceeding under Article XI as at present the Council hereafter came to consider possible action under Articles XV and XVI of the Covenant, which provides for sanctions.
> My reply was that I had been informed that the United States would not join in the consideration of the question of sanctions or in the enforcing of them if hereafter imposed by the League acting under Articles XV and XVI.[56]

Mr. Stimson definitely dates his conference with President Hoover on the question of sanctions as November 19. Mr. Dawes, on the other hand, just as definitely dates this conference with Briand as November 14, his account of the interview of the twentieth, following a transatlantic telephone conversation with Stimson, being confined to an entirely different subject.[57] If Mr. Dawes, acting upon his chief's instructions, made it clear to M. Briand that the Govern-

[55] *Ibid.*, pp. 83–84.
[56] Charles G. Dawes, *Journal as Ambassador to Great Britain* (New York, 1939), p. 416. Further details of this conference are given on p. 165, below.
[57] See pp. 167–68, below.

ment of the United States was anxious not to place any obstacles in the way of the League Council if that body felt inclined to impose sanctions on Japan he does not mention it in his published journal. He does, however, confirm Mr. Stimson's statement that the question was raised in Paris and not in Washington, the latter being the position taken by A. Whitney Griswold in his study of American policy in the Far East. Mr. Griswold holds that Mr. Stimson in reserving the right to publish the communications [58] between Washington and Tokyo (this was on November 19) was threatening "to invoke that 'most potent sanction' of publicity" and continues:

Nor was that all. After a conference with Hoover, the same day, he sent word (through Dawes) to Briand that in case the League wished to impose the economic sanctions provided for in Article XVI of the Covenant the United States was "anxious not to put any obstacles or dangers in their path." That the United States a non-member of the League had begun to suggest sanctions in advance of the League itself showed the degree to which Stimson's allegiance to the doctrine of collective security was influencing his Far Eastern policy.[59]

On the face of the evidence it seems an unwarranted conclusion to say that the United States "had begun to suggest sanctions in advance of the League." Using the same source material but with the addition of Mr. Dawes's *Journal*, which was published two years later than Mr. Griswold's study, Raymond Leslie Buell reaches a diametrically opposite conclusion:

League members now raised the question whether, if they were prepared to use sanctions against Japan, the United States would do likewise. Ambassador Dawes, who represented the United States at the Paris Council meeting in November, replied that "The United States would not join in the consideration of sanctions or in the enforcing of them if hereafter imposed by the League. . . ." This attitude wilted the League's enthusiasm.[60]

To state positively that Mr. Stimson did or did not wish sanctions imposed upon Japan is not possible on the strength of the evidence now available. In the passages quoted above he discusses sanctions, he

[58] See Chap. VI, below.
[59] A. Whitney Griswold, *The Far Eastern Policy of the United States* (New York, 1938), p. 420.
[60] R. L. Buell, *Isolated America* (New York, 1940), p. 58.

explains why the United States could have no part in them but would place no obstacle in the way of their use by the League, and why he felt that action by the League without the United States would not have been effective. Except by inference, however, he does not say what he himself desired. Perhaps the closest approach to an expression of personal or departmental preference is found in the concluding paragraph of his discussion of the general effect of Japanese acts of aggression upon our diplomatic objectives.[61] Here, as in other instances, we are confronted with the difficulty of determining the period of which Mr. Stimson is writing. Griswold implies that it is October, 1931, and this conclusion is justified if the passage is to be considered only in connection with the Cabinet meeting of October 9 to which Stimson refers and with the account of the October Council meetings which follows. On the other hand the passage immediately preceding [62] deals with Japanese acts of aggression from the bombing of Chinchow on October 9 through the capture of Tsitsihar in November down to the occupation of Chinchow in January, 1932. If, as seems to me necessary, we take this into consideration, his words, quoted below, have a meaning quite different from that imputed to them by Mr. Griswold:

In the face of such a situation certain basic facts had to be faced. The group of interrelated treaties entered into at the Washington Conference in 1922, under which America and Britain reduced the size of their respective navies in relation to that of Japan and agreed to leave their possessions in the Far East without further fortifications, had been intended to make and had made it impossible for any single western nation to intervene by military force in such a matter as the Manchurian dispute even if it should desire to do so. Quite apart from such limitations, no fact was more clear to any observer than that at this period of great depression none of the nations in Europe or America, even if able, had the slightest desire to go to war in such a controversy. These facts had evidently reduced the area of possible action before us to

(1) some form of collective economic sanctions against Japan or in default of that

(2) by the exercise of diplomatic pressure and the power of world public opinion to try to get as fair play as possible for the weaker power, China, in the eventual negotiated settlement, and

[61] Stimson, *Far Eastern Crisis*, pp. 54–58.
[62] *Ibid.*, pp. 52–54.

(3) by a vigorous judgment against Japan backed by the public opinion of the world to save as much respect as possible for the great peace treaties which had been publicly flouted by Japan's action.

These in substance were the objectives which one after another were discussed by us at the State Department during the autumn weeks while the proceedings of the League were taking their course at Geneva and Paris.[63]

Griswold's version of this, directly linked to the Cabinet meeting of October 9 and the bombing of Chinchow, is as follows:

The vigor of Stimson's efforts to bring Japan to account increased in direct ratio with his misgivings. He had at first been apprehensive of forcing Shidehara's hand. . . . The bombing of Chinchow on October 8th dashed some of his hopes. . . . In a cabinet meeting the next day he voiced the fear that "these modern treaties . . . might not be taken very seriously in the Orient." But . . . "these treaties existed . . . and if we surrendered and permitted them to be treated like scraps of paper, the hope of peaceful development in the world would receive a blow from which it would not soon recover."[64]

Accordingly Stimson began to consider means short of armed force by which Japan might be compelled to respect "the great peace treaties which had been publicly flouted by Japan's actions." He began to talk of "some form of collective sanctions against Japan," of "the exercise of diplomatic pressure and the power of public opinion to try to get as fair play as possible for the weaker power, China," of "a vigorous judgment against Japan backed by the public opinion of the world."[65]

The division of Mr. Stimson's last point into two phrases, placing one of them at the beginning of the paragraph and the other at the end as if they were two separate proposals, creates a very different impression in the reader's mind from the original; also to consider means by which Japan might be "compelled to respect" the great peace treaties suggests a far more vigorous policy than Mr. Stimson's words "to save as much respect as possible" for those treaties.

Mr. Griswold is not the only writer who feels competent to speak for Mr. Stimson in this matter of sanctions. In two books dealing with the policies of the Hoover Administration it is flatly stated that the Secretary of State advocated this policy but neither one

[63] *Ibid.*, pp. 56–57.   [64] Quoted by Griswold from Stimson, *op. cit.*, p. 56.
[65] Griswold, *op. cit.*, pp. 416–17.

suggests that Mr. Stimson proposed it to the League. In one case the authors, Ray Lyman Wilbur and Arthur M. Hyde,[66] colleagues of Mr. Stimson in the Hoover Cabinet, were in a position to be well informed as to the policies he advocated, while William Starr Myers seems to have drawn his material very largely from them. The principal subject of their discussion is not, however, the Stimson policy in regard to sanctions but that memorandum, presented to the Cabinet some time in the autumn of 1931, in which President Hoover analyzed the situation and set forth his conclusions:

The whole transaction is immoral. The offense against the comity of nations and the affront to the United States is outrageous. But the Nine-Power Treaty and the Kellogg Pact are solely moral instruments based upon the hope that peace in the world can be held by the rectitude of nations and enforced solely by the moral reprobation of the world. We are not parties to the League of Nations, the covenant of which has been violated.

The problem lies in three parts:

First, this is primarily a controversy between China and Japan. The U.S. has never set out to preserve peace among other nations by force and *so far as this part is concerned we shall confine ourselves to friendly counsel.* In this connection we must remember some essentials of Asiatic life. Time moves more slowly there; political movements are measured in decades or centuries not in days or in months; that while Japan has the military ascendancy today and no doubt could take over parts or all of China, yet the Chinese people possess transcendent cultural resistance; that the mores of the race have carried through a dozen foreign dynasties over three thousand years; that the Chinese are ten to one in population. No matter what Japan does in time they will not Japanify China and if they stay long enough they will be absorbed or expelled by the Chinese. For America to undertake this on behalf of China might expedite it but would not make it more inevitable.

There is something on the side of Japan. Ours has been a long and deep-seated friendship with her and we should in friendship consider her side also. Suppose Japan had come out boldly and said:

"We can no longer endure these treaties and we must give notice that China has failed to establish the internal order these treaties contemplated. Half her area is Bolshevist and cooperating with Russia, the

---

[66] R. L. Wilbur and A. M. Hyde, *The Hoover Policies* (New York, 1937); William Starr Myers, *The Foreign Policies of the Hoover Administration* (New York, 1940).

government of Manchuria is in the hands of a military adventurer who ignores the Chinese Government, and China makes no effort to assert her will. That territory is in a state of anarchy that is intolerable. The whole living of our people depends upon expanding the sales of our manufactures in China and securing of raw materials from her. We are today almost economically prostrate because there is ₙₒ order in China. Beyond this with Bolshevist Russia to the north and a possible Bolshevist China on our flank, our independence is in jeopardy. Either the signatories of the Nine-Power Pact must join with us to restore order in China or we must do it as an act of self-preservation. If you do not join we consider we cannot hold to an obligation around which the whole environment has changed."

America certainly would not join in such a proposal and we could not raise much objection.

Second, our whole policy in connection with controversies is to exhaust the processes of peaceful negotiation. But contemplating these we must make up our minds whether we consider war as the ultimate if these efforts fail. *Neither our obligations to China nor our own interest, nor our dignity require us to go to war over these questions.*

These acts do not imperil the freedom of the American people, the economic or moral future of our people. I do not propose ever to sacrifice American life for anything short of this. If that were not enough reason, to go to war means a long struggle at a time when civilization is already weak enough. To win such a war is not solely a naval operation. We must arm and train Chinese. We would find ourselves involved in China in a fashion that would excite the suspicions of the world.

Third, we have a moral obligation to use every influence short of war to have the treaties upheld or terminated by mutual agreement. We should cooperate with the rest of the world, we should do so as long as that cooperation remains in the field of moral pressures. As the League of Nations has already taken up the subject we should cooperate with them in every field of negotiation and conciliation. *But that is the limit. We will not go along on any of the sanctions, either economic or military, for these are roads to war.*[67]

Commenting on the situation Wilbur and Hyde say:

Our State Department supported the idea that we should participate in certain economic sanctions. The President, however, was adamant that this was simply the road to war itself and he would have none of it. It was at this time that Hoover developed with Stimson the idea that we propose a great moral sanction. That was that all the nations should

[67] Wilbur and Hyde, *op. cit.*, pp. 600–603; Myers, *op. cit.*, pp. 156–69. Italics mine.

agree that they would not recognize the acquisition of territory obtained in violation of the Kellogg Pact.[68]

Mr. Myers writes more positively concerning Mr. Stimson's views:

Meanwhile certain nations that were members of the League of Nations demanded that economic sanctions should be imposed upon Japan. This idea seemed to have the support of the State Department and was especially appealing to the judgment and ideas of Secretary Stimson who continually advocated this policy. Hoover not only strongly opposed this policy but placed his personal veto upon it on the grounds that such a policy would lead directly to war. In place of it he developed with Stimson's assistance the plan that all nations should agree that they would not recognize the acquisition of territory which might be obtained in violation of the Kellogg-Briand Pact.[69]

One point, at least, is clear. Mr. Hoover had at some point in the proceedings assumed a more active direction of our foreign affairs than was indicated on the surface at the time, and it was he who put an end to any talk of the application of sanctions by the United States. It would be interesting, though perhaps not at all important, to know just when this process began, but this is not possible with the material now available. It may be pointed out also that Mr. Myers, for one, takes the view that the demand for sanctions came from members of the League and not from the United States. Another interesting point, not significant to this study, is the connection, indicated in both of these accounts, between this memorandum of the President and the idea of "nonrecognition," of which, according to these authors, Mr. Hoover was the source and originator, and which he "developed with Mr. Stimson's assistance."

One more item is needed to complete this part of the story. As he was about to leave the White House at the close of his term President Hoover felt that he must make clear his position in regard to both nonrecognition and sanctions. For some time he had been busy collecting letters from members of his Cabinet supporting his claim to authorship of the former policy, and on February 23, 1933, he went on record in another memorandum finally and absolutely opposing the latter. In a sense this may be considered a kind of mort-

---

[68] Wilbur and Hyde, *op. cit.*, p. 603.   [69] Myers, *op. cit.*, pp. 162–63.

main document, intended to influence the incoming administration. If it failed to do this and different policies were adopted at least no responsibility could be attached to him. Addressing himself to the Secretary of State, Mr. Hoover wrote:

As you are aware, I have long been inflexibly opposed to the imposition of any kind of sanctions except purely public opinion. The imposition of any kind of sanctions, military or economic, would in the present state of mind of the Japanese people provoke the spread of the conflagration already in progress and might involve the United States. As it is not our intention to ever engage in sanctions other than that of public opinion it would seem to me that some occasion should be taken to make it clear. It would certainly relax the tension to some extent. It would in no way undermine the importance of public opinion in this controversy for under the non-recognition doctrine that would be continuous and will ultimately triumph.[70]

Not only does Mr. Stimson in his *Far Eastern Crisis* fail to mention either of these two significant memoranda from his Chief Executive but Mr. Hoover himself, collaborating with Hugh Gibson in *The Problems of Lasting Peace,* ignores them utterly and by implication repudiates their explicitly stated meaning. Discussing the League's failure to use force when faced with aggression on the part of a great power, Messrs. Hoover and Gibson say:

. . . The Japanese aggression in Manchuria in September 1931, and during the next year at Shanghai, violated every implication of the Covenant in spirit and letter. The authority of the League was here brought to test in dealing with major Powers. The League failed utterly in its dealings with this gross breach of the Covenant, and the real reasons are important to note.

The Council attempted to apply the pacific methods with painstaking persistence. But when these failed, it did not exercise the measures of force. The commercial and political relations of the major Powers in the Council were such, together with the military consequences involved, that they withheld from the League the powers necessary to force effective action.

Following the Council's failure the controversy was then transferred to the Assembly, where the smaller Powers were largely represented. But despite brave talk about applying the economic sanctions through a world-wide boycott of Japan, they also soon discovered that the major

[70] *Ibid.,* pp. 168–69.

European Powers would not follow. . . . Nor could this failure of the League be blamed upon lack of American cooperation, for upon Mr. Hoover's instructions and under the able guidance of Mr. Stimson, the United States *consistently supported the League throughout.* Finally, the United States injected a new moral sanction—that is, an agreement of non-recognition of territory gained by aggression.[71]

To the average reader, cognizant only of the surface facts and familiar with the story so often repeated by press and radio that we did everything in our power to stop Japan but were not supported by others, particularly by Great Britain, this account is completely misleading. Since the sole subject of the Hoover-Gibson discussion is the League's failure to use force or apply sanctions, the plain inference of the words "upon Mr. Hoover's instructions" is that we would have supported the League in such a policy. Mr. Hoover's memoranda to the Cabinet and to his Secretary of State prove without a shadow of doubt that just the opposite was the case.

In an article published in 1933 after his retirement from office Mr. Stimson summarized Mr. Hoover's attitude toward international cooperation as follows:

In 1919 the United States had declined to join the League of Nations. This decision, primarily based upon the policy of the people not to become entangled in the political affairs of the European continent with the activities of which the League of Nations was mainly concerned, also represented the disapproval of many American leaders of the proposal for the use of force by the community of nations against a violator of the League Covenant. Mr. Hoover shared this latter disapproval. He also was fully alive to the wisdom of the traditional policy of this country, shared by other parliamentary nations, not to enter into undertakings binding this government to apply sanctions to the undetermined facts of cases arising in the unknown future, instead of reserving each case for independent judgment of the nation at the time when it arose. On the other hand he was quite prepared to have his government cooperate with moral sanctions in each single instance as it might arise where there was a direct interest of the United States involved and where there was a major danger to the peace of the world.[72]

[71] Hoover and Gibson, *The Problems of Lasting Peace* (New York, 1942), pp. 158–60. Italics mine.
[72] Henry L. Stimson, "Bases of American Foreign Policy during the Past Four Years," *Foreign Affairs*, April, 1933, p. 388.

Thus Mr. Hoover's position has been made quite plain, if Mr. Stimson's has not, and there can be little doubt that he looked upon the nonrecognition doctrine, to which he was so anxious that his name rather than that of his Secretary of State should be attached, as the most powerful form of moral pressure, the sanction of public opinion, and the sole sanction to which the United States under his leadership would be a party.

Whether the Council of the League of Nations as it was constituted at the Paris meetings would have consented to the imposition of sanctions under any circumstances is open to question. Certainly, Sir John Simon would have opposed it as vigorously as Mr. Hoover, though for different reasons. Just as certainly, that section of the French Foreign Office not directly and personally attached to Aristide Briand would not have favored such a step. Late in 1932 Eduard Benes wrote that the League "tried to avoid and did avoid carrying out the sanctions which in this case were justified." [73] And Chester P. Howland says that "the British and French at Geneva in 1931 were unwilling because of their individual risks to have the Council apply sanctions" against Japan and that the Council went to great lengths to escape the necessity of such a decision.[74]

As was said in the beginning the picture is far from clear, many of the details are missing, many of the facts not yet known. Such as they are they have been presented and no attempt is made here to determine whether sanctions were advisable at this time or to fix responsibility for the failure to invoke them. Only the following meager conclusions seem justified:

(1) The League Council, or at least certain of its members, considered the question before or during the early days of the Paris meetings.

(2) The most powerful political elements in Great Britain and France were opposed to sanctions.

(3) Without the active cooperation of the United States sanctions against Japan could not have been made effective.

(4) The question was discussed pro and con by the Hoover administration with the President definitely opposed to any such action on our

[73] Eduard Benes, "Success and Failures of the League," *Foreign Affairs*, October, 1932, pp. 73–74.

[74] C. P. Howland, "Washington's Stand on the Far Eastern Crisis," *Asia*, April, 1932, p. 263.

part. The extent to which our position was made known to the Council is uncertain but considering the convictions and predilections of Ambassador Dawes it seems likely that he would have erred in the direction of discouraging the League rather than the opposite.

If, as some insist, it was in late October and early November that Mr. Stimson began to incline toward strong and coercive measures against Japan, there is no indication of it in the official record of his communications to the American representative or to the Council during the November–December meetings. There are no such assurances of support for the League as are found in his note of September 24, no such urging to action as in that of October 5. The tone of the State Department as reflected in reports emanating from the Secretary's press conferences is definitely cooler and more detached, sometimes almost aloof, and there is a return to the idea that the Japanese Government could be trusted to regulate the situation properly.

Numerous reasons have been advanced for this change. One of these is that the State Department, if not Mr. Stimson personally, felt that the setting of a definite date for evacuation was extremely unwise, that it savored too much of coercion, of rushing the Japanese; [75] another, that in taking a place at the Council table over Japan's objections we had offended that country and created a situation which, if not ameliorated, threatened to bring these two former friends to the brink of war; [76] a third reason, often put forward, has already been mentioned: that, because of the approaching session of Congress the opposition to American cooperation with the League expressed by certain powerful newspapers and by the isolationist sentiments of a small but important group of Senators of both political parties exerted a restraining influence on the President and on the State Department.[77] Judging from the vigor with which Mr. Stimson later condemned Japan and all her works in Manchuria his course in the last months of 1931 probably reflects not so much his own attitude and desires as the position taken by President Hoover.

[75] R. V. Oulahan, New York *Times*, Nov. 15.
[76] Byas, New York *Times*, Nov. 13.   [77] *Ibid.*, Nov. 12 and 24.

THE APPOINTMENT OF GENERAL DAWES.—The Council of the League was to reconvene in Paris on Monday, November 16, and until the middle of the preceding week there had been no indication from Washington as to who, if anyone, would represent this government. On Monday, November 9, Mr. Stimson called Charles G. Dawes, our Ambassador to Great Britain, by transatlantic telephone and informed him that he was to go to Paris for the meetings of the Council.[78] The Secretary explained his views of the situation in some detail and followed this with cabled instructions and the formal announcement of the appointment which was released to the press on the eleventh, as follows:

I have asked General Dawes, the ambassador to London, to go to Paris during the coming meeting of the statesmen who comprise the Council of the League of Nations. Inasmuch as this meeting will consider the present situation in Manchuria and questions may arise which will affect the interests or treaty obligations of the United States, I desire to have at hand in Paris a man of General Dawes' standing, particularly as the American Ambassador to Paris [79] is at home on leave. It is not anticipated that General Dawes will find it necessary to take part in the meetings of the League Council but he will be in a position to confer with representatives of the other nations present in Paris in case such conferences seem desirable.[80]

Neither then nor later did the Secretary reveal to the press the nature of the instructions to the Ambassador although their contents show no reason for their being kept secret. As published in *Conditions in Manchuria* they read:

Confirming telephone conversation, you are requested to be present in Paris during the next few days so that you may be available for conference with M. Briand and perhaps the representatives of other nations who are gathering there for the adjourned meeting of the Council of the League of Nations on November 16 in connection with the situation which has arisen in Manchuria. It is not expected that you will find it necessary to attend the Council meetings, but since the developments in Manchuria and the discussions which will take place in Paris presumably will involve matters affecting the treaty rights and general interests

---

[78] Dawes, *Journal as Ambassador to Great Britain*, p. 411.   [79] Walter E. Edge.
[80] Dawes, *loc. cit.*; New York *Times*, Nov. 12; State Department Press Release of Nov. 11.

of the United States, it is considered desirable that you be available for conference on matters bearing thereon.[81]

Of the appointment and what was expected of Mr. Dawes, Mr. Stimson later wrote:

. . . In the light of the serious problem before us I determined to be represented in our cooperation with the League at this meeting by the most prominent and experienced public man of whose services we could avail ourselves at this moment, our London Ambassador, Charles G. Dawes, the former Vice-President of the United States. His instructions were similar to those which had been given to Mr. Gilbert in October except that it was left entirely to his discretion as to whether and when he should attend in person the actual meetings of the Council.[82] In view of his prominence as a public man, I counted on his having easy opportunities for informal discussions with the representatives of other countries and at the same time I believed that his personality and reputation would do much to assure the people in this country of the importance of his work as well as the discretion with which he would carry it on. In both respects my anticipations were fulfilled.[83]

As in the case of Prentiss Gilbert exactly why the choice fell on Mr. Dawes and why he was not instructed to sit with the Council may never be known. Mr. Stimson says he was chosen because he was "the most prominent and experienced public man of whose services we could avail ourselves at the moment." [84] Most prominent he was without a doubt, but most experienced in diplomacy he just as certainly was not, with all due allowance for the way in which he acquitted himself as head of the commission on reparations in 1924–25 and as Ambassador to Great Britain during the London Naval Con-

[81] *Conditions in Manchuria,* p. 38.   [82] Dawes, *op. cit.,* p. 415.
[83] Stimson, *Far Eastern Crisis,* p. 75.
[84] Hugh Wilson in his *Diplomat between Wars* (p. 263) says of the appointment: "The Council met later in Paris and the Secretary of State sent General Dawes, Ambassador to Great Britain, to attend as American representative. When I arrived in Washington I called on Secretary Stimson. He said: 'It is a pity we ordered you home. I should have preferred to send you rather than General Dawes to the Council meeting in Paris, it would have appeared more normal and would have caused less sensation.' "
    Another qualified observer has commented: "God help us! He was probably the worst representative any nation ever sent abroad to represent it. Who was responsible for the choice?"
    See also Pearson and Brown, *The American Diplomatic Game* (New York, 1935), p. 320; Howland, *op. cit.,* p. 235; Russell Cooper, *American Consultation in World Affairs* (New York, 1934), p. 221 and footnote.

ference of 1930. The former was not altogether a matter of diplomacy and in the latter case the real burden of negotiations fell on the shoulders of the American delegation composed of such able men as Mr. Stimson, Hugh Gibson, Dwight Morrow, and Claude Swanson. For his own part in that conference General Dawes had had the aid of the very competent staff of our London Embassy, whereas in Paris he had with him no American diplomat who had followed the case from the beginning or who was thoroughly cognizant of League technicalities and procedure, his special aides being G. Howland Shaw, Counsellor of our Embassy at Istanbul and former chief of the division of Near Eastern Affairs, and Eugene Dooman of the Tokyo Embassy. It should be noted here that Mr. Dawes did have the advice and assistance of a highly qualified fellow American in the person of Arthur Sweetser, his official liaison with the League Council. Mr. Sweetser, then the senior American member of the staff of the League Secretariat, was particularly charged with liaison regarding the many matters of interest to the United States. Consequently when the Council met in Paris he at once got in touch with the Ambassador and very shortly established a relationship, approved by both sides, whereby he reported everything that happened in both the full sessions of the Council and in the smaller committee meetings of which there were so many. In addition to seeing Mr. Dawes daily, usually twice daily, Mr. Sweetser, at the former's request, put his reports in the form of memoranda which our representative could cable to Washington.[85] The Ambassador was, therefore, fully informed as to developments in and out of Council meetings but this could not compensate for his absence from the meetings, nor could Mr. Sweetser, a member of the Secretariat, fill the place of a confidential advisor in American service.

Mr. Stimson also says he believed the personality and reputation of Mr. Dawes "would do much to assure the people in this country of the importance of his work as well as the discretion with which he would carry it on." Now the people who needed to be "assured" as to the "discretion" of our representative were those who thought Prentiss Gilbert had gone quite too far in cooperation in October;

[85] See pp. 164, 166–67, below for further references to this situation. Mr. Sweetser is the authority for the facts given above.

namely, the isolationists and the anti-League groups. Any fears they may have felt should have been set at rest not only by the appointment of Mr. Dawes and his course of action in Paris but by the very cautious wording of Mr. Stimson's instructions and of the official announcement of the appointment. General Dawes was asked to go to Paris "during the coming meeting of the statesmen who compose the Council of the League of Nations"; he was to be "available for conference with M. Briand and perhaps the representatives of other nations who were gathering there for the adjourned meeting of the Council of the League of Nations"; not to confer with the members of the Council even unofficially as Hugh Wilson tells us he did in September,[86] not to sit as a silent observer at the Council table as Prentiss Gilbert did in October, but merely to "be in a position to confer with the representatives of the other nations present in Paris in case such conference should be desirable."

Although it would seem now that the selection of General Dawes definitely indicated that the peak of American cooperation with, and support of, the League had been passed in October, the immediate reaction was a favorable one in practically all quarters here and abroad. In League circles it was felt that the choice of the Ambassador to Great Britain showed due regard for the prestige of the Council and this, of course, was heightened by the fact that he was also a former Vice President of the United States.[87] In England, Sir John Simon expressed great pleasure that he would be associated with Mr. Dawes in Paris as in London, while the liberal *News-Chronicle* commented:

It is excellent news that General Dawes is going to Paris at Secretary Stimson's request to act as America's mouthpiece in the critical discussions proceeding there. It should be made clear to the world in general and Japan in particular that the United States intends to take an active part by the side of the European powers in preserving the world's peace. The appointment of a special envoy of the standing of General Dawes goes a long way to demonstrate that.[88]

[86] Wilson, *op. cit.*, p. 260.
[87] The authors of *The League and Manchuria, the Third Phase* (p. 29) say the appointment indicated two things: the desire for fullest cooperation; and the desire for fullest independence of judgment.
[88] Reprinted in the New York *Times*, Nov. 12.

In Japan, too, the news was well received; the feeling of satisfaction was strengthened by the realization that Dawes was not to replace Gilbert at the Council table but was merely to be on the spot to confer and look after American interests.[89] In Geneva the reverse was true, for there the early gratification over the selection of a representative of such high rank was soon replaced by uneasiness and even dismay as it was learned that not only would the Ambassador not sit with the Council but none of the diplomatic representatives who were acquainted with the earlier stages of the case would be in Paris to give him the benefit of their experience and information. Hugh Wilson was in Washington, but Hugh Gibson, who had been closely associated with Dawes in London during the naval conference and who had been in Geneva for the meetings of the disarmament commission when the Mukden incident occurred, was at his post in Brussels, and Prentiss Gilbert, who had followed the case from its very inception as well as sitting with the Council in October, was in Geneva anxious to be of whatever assistance he could. But Gilbert, at least, was not permitted to go to Paris. It is said that when he telephoned offering to come up for two or three days to go over the earlier developments with him Dawes refused explosively, saying that he knew all about the case, which was patently untrue as the Ambassador himself seems to have made clear later when he told Dr. Sze he knew nothing about it and very little about diplomacy.[90]

The Ambassador's journal makes it quite clear that he had not followed the case closely prior to his appointment to Paris, for up to that time there are only three references to the situation in Manchuria and not one to the League's handling of the matter. As a matter of fact so great was Dawes's isolationist sentiment that one might say that for him the League simply did not exist. The first entry is on September 27 in reference to a conference with Lord Reading, then Foreign Minister, "about the serious clash between Japan and China in Manchuria which for the time is less disquieting." On October 11 he notes that "the war situation in Manchuria

89 Byas, New York *Times*, Nov. 13; *Trans-Pacific*, Nov. 19, 26
90 Pearson and Brown, *op. cit.*, pp. 320–21.

is most disturbing," and on October 18, "the critical situation in Manchuria is maintained." There is no entry of any sort in the diary from October 18 to 25, although this was the most critical period of the October sessions.[91]

This seeming lack of interest in the Manchurian crisis or in the policy of the American Government in respect to it is thrown into striking relief by the many evidences of Dawes's friendship with the Japanese Ambassador to London, Tsuneo Matsudaira, whom he had known in Washington. The frequent references indicate a close association throughout the four years Dawes spent in London; he seems to have been more intimate with Matsudaira, or on less formal terms with him, than with any other members of the diplomatic corps. During the London Naval Conference they worked together in perfect harmony, each keeping the other informed as to what was going on, and often Dawes seemed most concerned to meet the Japanese point of view, to reconcile Japan's demands with those of the United States and Great Britain, and concerned also with the reaction in Japan if certain differences as to naval limitations were not ironed out and compromises effected before the matters were made public.[92] It is not meant to imply here that there was anything improper in this. Far from it. Any efforts to reconcile the opposing views of the three great naval powers in 1930 were of inestimable value if successful. But there can be no question that Mr. Dawes went to Paris with a definite bias toward the Japanese position and that he was influenced by that bias throughout the whole of the November-December meetings. Any doubt of this is dissipated by his own words written aboard the train and channel boat on his way to Paris on November 13:

I got busy at once [after the telephone conversation with Mr. Stimson] and have been ever since. I first saw my friend Matsudaira, the Japanese Ambassador to Great Britain. Our personal friendship facilitated the frankest kind of a discussion between us. I then saw Sir John Simon, the new Foreign Secretary, with whom also I have had for some time the most friendly relations. After we had gone over the situation I suggested that he meet Matsudaira and me together as we all seemed to

---

[91] Dawes, *op. cit.*, pp. 397, 402, 404.
[92] See for example, *ibid.*, pp. 33, 43, 71, 72, 107.

be united in purpose with about the same views as to the procedure the situation required.

Yesterday the three of us met for a long conference. In the light of possible events, all attitudes and plans are, of course, tentative. Last night at the Embassy Matsudaira and I had another conference. Both he and Simon will be in Paris by Monday.

Through the Chinese Legation, I got in touch with Alfred Sao-ke Sze, the Chinese representative on the League Council at Geneva, and will meet him at my hotel in Paris at noon on Sunday. Through the French Ambassador, I made an appointment to meet Briand at 11:30 tomorrow at the Quai d'Orsay.

In my first talk with Matsudaira we both felt that the League should withdraw its time limit for the evacuation of Japanese troops. To have made it was a serious error in my judgment. We agreed that the immediate objective should be the cessation of hostilities under an armistice pending discussion of the best agencies and methods for final settlement. In my talk with Simon, immediately afterward, he agreed that while the League might have the better juridical argument Japan, notwithstanding, seemed to have the argument in its favor as to the necessary location of troops. His idea was the same as that of Matsudaira and myself, independently formed, *namely that the League had best propose a cessation of hostilities without suggesting any change at present in the location of Japanese troops* pending an agreement upon the agencies and methods of securing final settlement. This, he said, seemed to be the Prime Minister's view on the matter in the short talk he had had with him. Simon instinctively realized, as had Stimson, the unwisdom of the time limit clause for Japanese troop evacuation in the League proposition.[93]

Note particularly the words "that the League had best propose a cessation of hostilities without suggesting any change at present in the location of the Japanese troops," not without change in the location of the troops of either party but of Japanese troops. And this was written on November 13 when General Honjo had announced that his troops would not withdraw from the Nonni River and that he had received instructions from Tokyo to issue an ultimatum to General Ma to evacuate his position at the Nonni bridge by November 25.

---

[93] *Ibid.*, pp. 411–12. (Italics mine.) See also Charles A. Selden in New York *Times*, Nov. 12: "If London had its way it would persuade China to accept the Japanese offer for direct negotiations without insisting that Japan first withdraw her troops from the disturbed area."

On his arrival in Paris Mr. Dawes set up his headquarters at the Ritz Hotel where he seems to have been almost as much cut off from the American Embassy as he was from the Council of the League housed at the Quai d'Orsay across the Seine. There he soon began a wholly separate set of negotiations, seeing first the Japanese, then the Chinese, and occasionally Cecil or Drummond, but being most inaccessible to other Council members who sought to see him.

Mr. Stimson's instructions to Prentiss Gilbert to leave the Council table and resume his seat among the unofficial observers on October 24,[94] coupled with his failure to approve the resolution of that date, had created the fear that Washington might be on the point of dissociating itself from League action. As early as October 25, League officials had said unhesitatingly that the United States, having once occupied a seat at the Council table in the conflict, would do serious injury to the Council's action and to the cause of world peace if the Administration considered withdrawing its representative when the Council reconvened.[95] There had been nothing in the attitude of the State Department during the interim to allay this uneasiness, nor did the respective statements of Mr. Stimson,[96] announcing the appointment of Mr. Dawes, and of the Ambassador on his arrival in Paris set their doubts at rest. Said Mr. Dawes:

The views of my Government correspond with those of the Council of the League of Nations in the Manchurian situation and in the endeavor to prevent war and forward a peaceful settlement.

The Council of the League in this connection is considering matters which presumably affect not only the treaty rights and general interests of the United States under the Nine Power Pact but relate to the Kellogg Pact as well. I will be in Paris to confer with the members of the Council individually with regard to a problem which is of common concern and involves mutual treaty interests. I shall hope to make every contact which is essential to the exercise of any influence we may have in properly supporting this effort to avert war and to make effective the Kellogg Pact.

The United States is not a member of the League and the methods which have been followed on occasions when a matter of mutual concern and self-interest to the League and ourselves is under consideration

---

[94] Stimson, *op. cit.*, p. 66.   [95] Lansing Warren, New York *Times*, Oct. 25.
[96] See above, p. 156.

have varied. On this occasion there is no anticipation on the part of my Government or myself that will be found necessary for me to attend the meetings of the Council.[97]

Thus at a time when the most pressing need was a common front of the Council and the United States against Japan's flouting of world opinion and of the efforts to achieve a peaceful settlement through moral pressure alone, the United States through the statements of its Secretary of State and its official representative insisted on placing the emphasis not on the common front and mutual concern but on its independent position and separate judgment.

Mr. Stimson has said it was left entirely to the Ambassador's discretion as to "whether and when he should attend in person the actual meetings of the Council" and Mr. Dawes confirms this.[98] League officials leaving Geneva for Paris on the eve of the sessions expressed themselves as hoping the Ambassador would eventually attend the sessions. They were not willing to believe he would remain absent from the meetings until the end of the sessions, although it was felt that the United States "had been acting on quite separate lines from the League." [99] The opinion was also voiced that the authorities in Washington must be waiting for another formal invitation to cooperate with the Council. This scarcely seems likely, but if either the Secretary of State or Mr. Dawes expected such action he was disappointed. Richard V. Oulahan, veteran correspondent of the New York *Times*, attributed the aloofness of Dawes to President Hoover's fear of the irreconcilable element in the Senate.[100] Other writers, not always so careful in their observations and comments, have placed the responsibility largely on Mr. Dawes's own shoulders, accusing him of being unwilling to play second fiddle, as it were, to Prentiss Gilbert, who had "stolen the headlines" as the first American to sit officially with the Council.[101] It is clear that a man of Mr. Dawes's position and outspoken nature could not have been asked to sit at the Council table and remain silent when questions of vital interest to the United States were being discussed. Mr. Dawes tells us he was thoroughly convinced from the outset that our influence

[97] Dawes, *op. cit.*, p. 414.   [98] *Ibid.*, p. 415. See also note 49, above.
[99] New York *Times*, Nov. 15.   [100] *Ibid.*   [101] Pearson and Brown, *op. cit.*, p. 320.

for peace could best be exerted through a "rigid maintenance of the independent right of judgment and action at all'times." He did not, however, close the door firmly and finally on any future attendance at the Council meetings because he realized that

in view of the importance of the critical situation in Manchuria my unexplained declination of a general invitation of the Council to attend its meetings would be regarded by many as lessening the influence of the United States toward a peaceful settlement and my right course there- fore was to hold a decision in this matter in abeyance until I could know better from contact with the situation where my duty lay.[102]

In a conference at the Quai d'Orsay on November 14, Briand urged Dawes to attend the meetings, insisting that his absence would inevitably be construed as evidence of a weakening of American sup- port and cooperation and would, therefore, be injurious to the prestige and influence of the League. Dawes's answer is reveal- ing:

I told him [Briand] that in my present judgment, if I did attend the Council meetings, it would lessen the helpfulness of the United States in the situation and that a parallel cooperation of the United States, re- serving its independence of action and decision, would be more effective in securing peace, than if, by attendance at the meetings, to the curiosity of the world press and the justified apprehensions of my Government, I became involved in the discussions of methods to be adopted by a body of which the United States was not a member. I told him, however, that I was holding in abeyance any final decision in this matter of attendance until contact with the situation in Paris for a time would enable me to settle the question wisely.

I said further that if in the future I came to believe that the greatest influence of the United States could be exercised by my attendance at the meetings of the Council I would not hesitate to attend them.[103]

Most observers, official or unofficial, agreed with M. Briand's view that the United States in remaining aloof was damaging an already bad situation, but there were those who were willing to give Mr. Dawes the benefit of the doubt and an opportunity to try out his plan of parallel cooperation. Writing to the New York *Times* on No- vember 15, P. J. Philip said:

[102] Dawes, *op. cit.*, p. 415.   [103] *Ibid.*, pp. 416–17.

Despite the withdrawal of the United States from the Council table the energetic action of Mr. Dawes in informing himself and establishing contacts with the delegations has done much to clear up the impression that Washington was dissociating itself from League action. It is admitted in some quarters that his presence as an outside negotiator may be even more useful than anything he might do in formal meetings, and further, it is now believed that a way may be found for him actually to participate if there should be any real need for it.[104]

Since a great deal of publicity had been given the question, little surprise was expressed that no place was set for the American representative when the Council met for its very brief opening session on November 16. What was surprising, however, was the fact that neither Mr. Dawes nor any of his aides nor any member of the American Embassy staff was present, although it had been customary in Geneva for American officials to be among the public observers at Council meetings. American diplomats who chanced to be in Geneva on official business, or otherwise, when the Council was in session had, of recent years, made it a point to be present at the public meetings whenever possible, so that their complete absence at such a time as this created something of a minor sensation.

However excellent the reasons, however sound the logic which determined Mr. Dawes's attitude or that of the Administration, as the case may be, it did not help the situation in Paris. Not only did the existence of two entirely separate centers of authority and negotiations, one at the Quai d'Orsay and the other at the Ritz, divide rather than concentrate the efforts to bring about a satisfactory settlement but it gave rise to all sorts of rumors as to the attitude of the United States, creating an atmosphere injurious to the prospects of a peaceful settlement and therefore helpful to the Japanese. Delegates were asking, in and out of meetings, what the United States would do, to what extent we would cooperate; gossip had it that we were withdrawing, that if urged to do so Mr. Dawes would sit with the Council, that we were working out a formula which would be submitted to the Council, that we were planning an entirely separate course of action based on the Nine Power Treaty and ignoring the

104 New York *Times*, Nov. 16; see also the dispatch of P. J. Philip from Paris in *ibid.*, Nov. 22.

League Council as a vital part of the world's peace machinery.[105] Mr. Dawes writes in his diary that he met the question everywhere he turned, and that Arthur Sweetser told him it was under considerable discussion in the Council meetings.[106] This seems to have made the Ambassador realize that the situation was getting out of hand and a final decision on his attendance at the meetings together with a statement on the attitude of his government must be announced. By this time he was convinced, he writes, that his greatest influence could be exerted by nonattendance. On November 19 he called Stimson by phone, told him how he felt, and asked the Secretary to announce from Washington that he was not to attend the Council meetings. Mr. Stimson, however, after discussing the situation at length, cabled a tentative statement to be made in Paris as emanating not from the State Department but from Mr. Dawes, this method of handling the situation having been approved by President Hoover. Accompanying this was a statement of the general position of the United States to be used in explaining the case to M. Briand. This was done in the latter's office at the Quai d'Orsay on the twentieth, after which the following statement was issued to the press:

I have been directed to come to Paris for the purpose of discussing with the representatives of the different nations assembled here the crisis which is taking place in Manchuria. As a signatory of the Pact of Paris and the so-called Nine Power Treaty, the United States is deeply interested with its fellow signatories in seeing that the lofty purpose of these treaties is fulfilled. It has been the hope of my Government that a settlement in accordance with the principles of those treaties would be arrived at through discussion and conciliation during the conference in Paris and that the presence here of a representative of the United States would contribute to bring about a solution through this method. The United States is, of course, not a member of the League of Nations, and it therefore cannot take part in the discussions bearing on the application of the machinery of the League Covenant. Since, in the crisis, it may be possible that such discussions may arise, it is obvious that my presence at the meetings of the Council would not only be inappropriate, but might even embarrass the efforts of the Council itself. But the position

[105] New York *Times*, various Paris dispatches of the period.
[106] Dawes, *op. cit.*, p. 419.

thus necessarily assumed by the United States in no way indicates that the United States is not wholly sympathetic with the efforts being made by the League to support the objective of peace in Manchuria. The United States must, however, preserve its full freedom of judgment as to its course.[107]

Mr. Stimson, commenting on this incident, implies that the opposition to attendance at the Council meeting was wholly Mr. Dawes's, and links that opposition to the question of sanctions which Mr. Dawes does not mention. The situation, writes the Secretary of State,

has been complicated by the insistence of some of the members of the Council that Mr. Dawes should take this precise time [November 19] to attend publicly a meeting of the Council and confer there with its members. Mr. Dawes was very much opposed to doing this at this particular time on account of the patent danger which would be involved of having his presence at such a meeting misconstrued as a commitment by our government on the question of sanctions which might be discussed.[108]

Far from considering that the presence of Mr. Dawes would be inappropriate or embarrassing, the Council members were anxious, even insistent, that he lend the weight of his personal prestige as well as that of his government to the public meeting then planned for the twentieth or twenty-first. Even the Foreign Office in Tokyo announced that the Japanese Government had no objections to his being seated at the Council table, although it reserved the right to examine the legal aspects of the case later.[109] Criticism by Council members of an official statement from the American representative would, of course, not be made public but there seems to have been considerable comment on several points. It was generally felt that the real significance and purpose of the announcement lay in the last sentence, "The United States must, however, preserve its full freedom of judgment as to its course." This, together with the reference to the Nine Power Treaty and the Kellogg Pact, gave rise to hopes among the Chinese that if League efforts failed they might still turn

[107] *Ibid.,* pp. 419–21.   [108] Stimson, *op. cit.,* p. 77.
[109] Hugh Byas, New York *Times,* Nov. 19.

to America for active intervention, although this would seem to be the exact opposite of Mr. Dawes's intentions.

This statement definitely closed the discussion of a seat at the Council table and it was not reopened until the contretemps of the last meeting when Mr. Dawes almost made a sensational appearance. It also threw away the last fruits of the victory which had been won at such cost of feelings and of questionable procedure at Geneva in October. The equally important question of the extent of American cooperation remained to plague the Council's efforts until the end of the session on December 10.

VI

THE PARIS MEETING

NOVEMBER 16 TO 21.—When the Council reconvened on November 16 it was with a sobering sense of the difficult task ahead. Nevertheless, there was present also the exhilaration and stimulus of a great dramatic situation. The second session had closed on October 24 with really high hopes that, in spite of Japan's adverse vote on the resolution of that day, the moral pressure of a united world public opinion would cause that government to accept it as it had accepted Mr. Gilbert's presence at the Council table. But in this, as we have seen, they were doubly disappointed. The United States had not followed up the Council resolution until so late that it failed to give the necessary moral support, and not even then did it associate itself with the demand for evacuation by November 16.[1] For her part Japan showed no signs of withdrawing or of accepting the spirit of the resolution in any way—quite the opposite in fact, for the exposition of the fundamental points [2] published on October 26 and Baron Shidehara's note of November 7 indicated quite plainly that the civilian element in the Japanese Cabinet was determined to retain the fruits of the several army advances in Manchuria even though it had not been responsible for or approved the means by which these had been obtained. Thus encouraged, the military leaders had pushed their advantage by extending the field of operations north along the Taonan-Anganchi line into the Nonni River region so that when the Council met they were at the very gates of Tsitsihar. Adding to the drama of the occasion was the absence of one of the principal characters, the United States of America.

At previous meetings of the Council it had been customary for the Chinese and Japanese representatives to present their views at great length, reading formal statements from their respective governments

---

[1] See Chap. IV, p. 124, above.
[2] *Official Journal*, Annex 1334, p. 2514; see also Chap. V, above.

and frequently wrangling over minute details, many of which were unimportant and served only to cloud the main issues. To the surprise, and disappointment, of the large audience crowded into the Salle d'Horloge of the Quai d'Orsay this opening session lasted about thirty minutes, after which the members went into closed meeting to discuss lines of procedure and compromise plans. In that short half-hour M. Briand welcomed the new members, particularly Sir John Simon and Herr von Bülow,[3] then summarized briefly the situation as it had developed since October 24. Both the Japanese and Chinese representatives were understood to have prepared long statements but were either induced beforehand not to present them or were given no opportunity to do so. According to Ambassador Dawes's *Journal* [4] this was one of the occasions on which his position as an outside negotiator was of great value. Learning that the Japanese statement was of such a nature that it would create an immediate deadlock if read in a public meeting he

promptly brought the situation to the attention of Sir John Simon, who had just arrived in Paris, of Sir Eric Drummond of the Council, and of Massigli who represented Briand. It was then arranged that at the first meeting of the Council there would be no speeches except the opening speech of Briand, followed by an adjournment subject to the call of the President. No opportunity was therefore given for a premature public precipitation of the serious impasse then existing between China and Japan.[5]

Neither the Chinese nor the Japanese liked this handling of the matter. The Chinese had from the beginning counted on public support of their case and in the open meetings of the Council had been able to gain the sympathy of a large section of the press, and through them of the reading public generally, as well as of the representatives of all of the small and most of the large powers. They were definitely afraid of a return to the old methods of secret diplomacy and bargaining behind closed doors, having suffered much from this in the past. The Japanese Foreign Office expressed great surprise that Yoshizawa

---

[3] *Ibid.*, pp. 2362–64.
[4] Dawes, *Journal as Ambassador to Great Britain* (New York, 1939), p. 419.
[5] *Ibid.* The whole account is worth reading, if only for the light that it sheds, unintentionally, on its author.

had not been given an opportunity to present his government's statement and was reported to have cabled instructions that he ask for an open meeting for that purpose on the following day. Two days later, however, it was announced that the request had been withdrawn,[6] perhaps because by that time Matsudaira and Yoshizawa had assured their government they could obtain the most satisfactory results by the very means China feared, secret diplomacy. For this is really the situation created by the independent and separate position of Ambassador Dawes in Paris—intermediaries rushing back and forth between the Ritz and the Quai d'Orsay, Matsudaira acting as liaison between Yoshizawa and Dawes,[7] Sweetser between the League and Dawes,[8] Dr. Sze coming to confer with the great man at his separate "office at the Ritz," [9] Dawes himself crossing the Seine to the French Foreign Office just three times in almost four weeks. Such an atmosphere bred rumors, doubts and suspicion; no one knew what anyone else was doing [10] and everyone feared the worst.

In the meantime the Council followed its opening meeting of the sixteenth with a series of private and secret sessions that continued until the twenty-first when the second public meeting was held. The chief subject of discussion at most of these was the scheme for simultaneous and parallel negotiations previously referred to. No official communique was issued giving details of the plan but the Associated Press reported them [11] to be substantially as follows:

1. Direct negotiations shall be opened between Japan and China on the first four of Japan's fundamental points.

2. Completion of evacuation shall not depend on these direct negotiations.

3. Direct negotiations on the fifth fundamental point—recognition by China of the validity of existing treaties with Japan—shall begin after, and only after, evacuation has been completed.

4. All of these activities shall be carried out as in pursuance of the

---

6 New York *Times*, Nov. 18, 19.   7 *Op. cit.*, p. 418.
8 See Chap. V, above.   9 Dawes, *op. cit.*, p. 418.
10 When told by correspondents that the representatives of other powers were giving out news as to developments, Dawes is reported to have said they were not telling anything about him for no one knew what he was doing. One caustic journalist commented that this was true, no one, certainly not Washington, and perhaps not even Dawes himself knew what he was doing.
11 New York *Times*, Nov. 17.

Council resolution, thereby leaving the problem still in the hands of the League.

This compromise, similar to the one proposed by Madariaga at the closing meeting in October [12] and definitely turned down at the time by Yoshizawa, seems to have had the approval of Briand, Simon, and Dawes.[13] The plan was to be carried out as follows. Negotiations for the evacuation of Manchuria were to be conducted on the spot, as rapidly as possible, and under the observation of a neutral body. It was felt, however, that the discussions on principles underlying the relations of the two countries should be undertaken in a different atmosphere; therefore negotiations were to take place somewhere in Europe on the first four points while the evacuation negotiations were going on in Manchuria, and on the fifth immediately after these had been completed.[14] Whether the parties to the dispute would accept this compromise was decidedly uncertain. China insisted she would not barter with Japan as to evacuation and rejected the idea of the legitimacy of treaties based on the infamous Twenty-one Demands, but maintained her offer, made in October, to refer this matter to the World Court. Japan refused this as tantamount to a repudiation of the treaties, insisted that an essential element of her security was the full right of railway operation in Manchuria according to the terms of existing treaties,[15] and demanded acceptance of all five points without further discussion or explanation.

At secret meetings of the seventeenth, "the Twelve" struggled with the question of how to reconcile these opposing views. The Nine-Power Treaty to which Ambassador Dawes had referred on his arrival in Paris [16] was studied to see whether its stipulations provided any guide to a settlement. This was not received with any

---

[12] *Official Journal*, p. 2353.   [13] New York *Times*, Nov. 14 and 17.

[14] Tokyo's interpretation of this compromise plan seems to have been quite different from that given out in Paris. Instead of the simultaneous and parallel negotiations outlined above it was reported there that the essential feature of the plan was "that the proceedings in Paris be adjourned and the decision be delayed until the Council has investigated the problem of holding special council meetings in Tokyo and Nanking or by sending out a very strong commission composed of statesmen and officials of Cabinet calibre." Hugh Byas, New York *Times*, Nov. 19.

[15] These include the secret protocols of 1905 whose legitimacy the Chinese refused to recognize and whose very existence, in treaty form at least, they questioned. See *Lytton Report*, pp. 44–45.

[16] Dawes, *op. cit.*, p. 421; New York *Times*, Nov. 21.

enthusiasm by the Japanese, and it is perhaps unfortunate that it was not followed up as it would have ended the complicated situation of the two centers of conferences and brought Mr. Dawes into immediate and direct consultation with the representatives of the other nine-power signatories, most of whom he did not see during his entire stay in Paris.[17] Some Council members, however, objected to making use of this treaty, as there seemed to be danger of taking the case out of the hands of the League, thereby lessening its influence as part of the world's peace machinery. As a result of the day's discussions M. Briand was authorized to act as negotiator to bring China and Japan to a point of agreement, and it was decided also to ask the Japanese delegate to state precisely what treaties were referred to in the fifth of the fundamental points. This request Mr. Yoshizawa agreed to transmit to his government.

For a short time there seemed reason for encouragement. Dr. Sze, after a conference with Ambassador Dawes, had withdrawn his demand for public meetings. The Japanese also seemed in a more conciliatory mood and it was understood that Tsuneo Matsudaira had assured Mr. Dawes that his government was willing to accept from China a general declaration of her recognition of treaties as a basis for discussions on security and evacuation. But unfortunately Mr. Matsudaira, on whose moderating influence our Ambassador counted so heavily, was not Japan's official representative and Mr. Yoshizawa, proving far more obdurate than his colleague, upset all calculations by announcing that the five fundamental points were not Japan's final requirements but section headings for a treaty regulating relations between Japan and China, including a specific reaffirmation of all existing treaties. Evacuation, he said, must be considered separately and only after an accord and a demonstration of good faith by China.[18] Once again, just as there was some hope for a solution Japan had increased her demands and once again this had coincided

[17] See Chap. VI, p. 213, below. It has been stated on good authority that when the Nine-Power Treaty was proposed as a basis for negotiations, Mr. Dawes refused to consider it.
[18] *The League and Manchuria, the Third Phase of the Chinese-Japanese Conflict* (Geneva Special Studies, Vol. II, No. 12, December, 1931), p. 40.

with a successful extension of her military operations, the advance of General Honjo's force on Tsitsihar.

According to reports, the full Council was in the midst of a discussion of the compromise proposals when this news came. Yoshizawa had again refused to give any satisfactory explanation of what was meant by "treaty obligations," maintaining that this was a matter for direct negotiations with China alone, without League or any other intervention,[19] while Dr. Sze pled for the immediate application of the antiwar treaties by the League and the United States on the ground that if the Japanese did occupy Tsitsihar they would be so strongly entrenched in Manchuria that there would be little possibility of displacing them. Matsudaira, apparently not so well informed as his colleague on what to expect from the militarist group at home, received the news with great agitation and rushed from the anteroom of the Salle d'Horloge to the Ritz for a long conference with Dawes. There can be little doubt that Yoshizawa's position before the Council was in contradiction to the assurances Matsudaira had given his American friend, and this serves to further emphasize the dangers inherent in the situation in Paris—divided centers of conference and authority; two sets of negotiations and negotiators; Matsudaira telling Dawes one thing, probably in good faith, while Yoshizawa told the Council something entirely different; Sweetser reporting the Council meetings accurately to the Ambassador, and the latter interpreting these according to his own preconceived ideas and in the light of the assurances given him by Matsudaira.

The immediate effect of the advance on Tsitsihar is plainly evident in the declarations of the representatives of the two powers concerned. Dr. Sze, according to press reports, raised the specter of sanctions by telling the Council that China was ready to invoke Article 15 [20] and would insist that the Council do its full duty under the

---

[19] "With a bow to the absent Mr. Dawes." Lansing Warren, New York *Times*, Nov. 19.

[20] Article 15 provides for publication of the facts of any dispute together with the Council's recommendation, also for referring it to the Assembly. Article 11 requires unanimous action, including the parties; under Article 15 the parties are barred. Article 15 leads to the use of economic and military sanctions of Article 16, as well as to action by the Assembly.

Covenant, while Yoshizawa gave notice that even if the security of Japanese lives and property appeared assured military occupation of Manchuria would be maintained until a new treaty had been negotiated.[21]

Because of the deadlock between the two disputants and the increased difficulty of the Council's task, the question of the method and extent to which this country would support the Council in its attempts to reach an amicable settlement became more and more important.[22] It was at this time that Mr. Dawes was faced with the necessity of making a decision in the matter of a seat at the Council table.[23] His announcement in the negative was a blow to League circles where it was felt that his absence would be looked upon as disapproval of Council action. An interpretation of our position which was far from anything the State Department or Mr. Dawes himself desired was reported by one observer as follows:

In many quarters the United States is considered as having played a considerable part in the League's originally undertaking a hearing of the dispute through the public announcement of support of the League's efforts. Throughout the Council's sittings the American attitude has held the greatest weight, both with the members of the Council and with the disputants in the affair, and should General Dawes dissociate himself from the resolution the Council adopts in Paris, it would, in the estimation of League members, not only deal a blow to the League, but the United States, in the eyes of the world, would be forced into the position of proclaiming itself as the League's successor in the mediation of the League conflict.

. . . Whether he [Dawes] desires it or not . . . his absence would be considered an indication that he feels a more tangible verdict could be obtained. If so, a natural act, on the part of China, at any rate, would be to turn to the United States with a demand that our government should

[21] In Washington, on the same day, Ambassador Debuchi told Secretary Stimson that Tsitsihar had been occupied by a "small body of troops and these would withdraw as soon as order was restored, if there were no untoward developments which interfered with the plan." *New York Times*, Nov. 20.

[22] This question evidently came up in the first private meetings on the 16th for the official communique reports Briand to have told the Council "he had reason to think he might rely on the entire cooperation of Mr. Dawes with the Council." *New York Times*, Nov. 17.

[23] See Chap. V.

champion the cause of the violated treaties, particularly as, since the days of General Grant, China has looked to the United States as an arbiter.[24]

Reports from Washington were as conflicting as usual. It was said there that some attempt would be made to get Japan to modify her course in Manchuria but no information could be obtained as to what steps might be taken, and administration spokesmen scoffed at the suggestion that the time had come to apply something stronger than moral pressure. On the nineteenth, Secretary Stimson told inquirers there was nothing to the report that the State Department was preparing a stiff note to Japan to remind her of her treaty obligations; two days later the Associated Press announced that this government had informed Japan (through Ambassador Debuchi) that it believed the occupation of Tsitsihar "in the Russian sphere of influence in Northern Manchuria" threatened dangerous complications. A dispatch from Tokyo indicates that the message was received on the twentieth by Baron Shidehara, who replied immediately that the advance on Tsitsihar was only the consummation of an operation of self-defense, not an extension of hostilities.[25]

That Secretary Stimson held an important conference with Ambassador Debuchi on the nineteenth we know from his own account in the *Far Eastern Crisis*. Having "finally concluded that the time had come when the cause of peace was no longer best served by a situation in which the normal methods of diplomacy left the public opinion of America practically unguided and voiceless in this controversy," [26] he called in the Japanese Ambassador and summed up his view of the situation to be reported to his chief:

. . . I told him that the picture presented to me by the occurrences of the autumn was concisely as follows: that on September 18th the regular organized Chinese government in Manchuria consisted of the government of the young Marshal, Chang Hsueh-liang; that this government had been recognized by the Central Government at Nanking and was the only regular government in Manchuria; that on that day and thereafter the Japanese army had attacked and destroyed the forces of Marshal Chang wherever they could find them and that instead of withdrawing

[24] Lansing Warren, New York *Times*, Nov. 20.   [25] *Ibid.*
[26] One wonders if a public servant of a democratic government has the right to leave public opinion thus "unguided and voiceless."

as promised by their own government, they only stopped attacking when there were no more Chinese forces left to attack; that in this latest instance they had penetrated to the extreme northern part of Manchuria many hundreds of miles beyond the Japanese railway zone in order to attack General Ma and to take Tsitsihar, and that I could not but regard this as a violation by the Japanese army of the provisions of the Kellogg-Briand Pact and of the Nine-Power Treaty.

I then told the Ambassador that under these circumstances I must ask him to tell his government that I must reserve full liberty to publish all papers and communications which had passed between our two governments on the subject; that I did not intend to publish them at once, necessarily, but that I must retain full liberty to do so. I told the Ambassador, that, as he knew, for two months I had been keeping these papers from publication in the hope of a settlement so that it might not embarrass the Japanese government on the chance of such a settlement. I reminded him that I had gone so far in such a hope as to urge our own press not to publish any matter that would influence American sentiment against Japan, but that now in the interest of my own government I must reserve full liberty of action to make public the whole matter.[27]

Although not literally "a stiff note" this was certainly a strong, plain-spoken statement, which did not mince words and which, according to Mr. Stimson's further account, greatly impressed Ambassador Debuchi. The latter replied to the Secretary that it was indeed a dark day for him but that he would report the whole matter to his government. This is the incident characterized by Whitney Griswold as Mr. Stimson's threat to invoke "the most potent sanction of publicity"[28] and right then was the time to put it into effect at least to the extent of releasing the substance of the Secretary's remarks to Mr. Debuchi and letting the American people know how matters stood. But the policy of silence was continued and in the press conference of that same day, the very day when the news of the occupation of Tsitsihar was received, Under Secretary Castle told reporters that Mr. Stimson did not want the Manchurian crisis discussed.[29]

Meanwhile in Paris the plan for parallel and simultaneous negotia-

[27] Stimson, *Far Eastern Crisis*, pp. 73–74.
[28] See Chap. V, above; also A. W. Griswold, *Far Eastern Policy of the United States* (New York, 1938), p. 420.
[29] New York *Times*, Nov. 20.

tions which had apparently engaged the entire attention of Council members since the meeting of November sixteenth was suddenly shelved in favor of a proposal for a suspension of hostilities in Manchuria and the sending of a strong international commission of enquiry to the scene of conflict. The announcement of this brought forth significant statements from several highly placed American citizens. Secretary Stimson himself rightly declined to comment, as he had received no official report from Ambassador Dawes, but it was widely rumored that American participation in such a commission was very uncertain—if it was to be a League Commission we probably would not be represented, if it was an impartial international body not under League auspices we might take part. Above all, said the rumor, we must maintain our independence of action.[30] Apparently this was far more important than stopping Japanese aggression.

Breaking the silence customary in a former Secretary of State when his successor in office is involved in difficulties, the co-author of the Kellogg-Briand Pact issued the following formal statement from St. Paul:

When I read press dispatches that China and Japan had in principle accepted an armistice in the Manchurian conflict and that they had also accepted in principle the proposal to send a commission of inquiry into Manchuria I was very pleased. Although later dispatches indicate that perhaps China has not accepted, as first announced, I very much hope that concessions by the two countries will speedily bring a settlement.

If they do not, all nations signatory to the Pact of Paris which have not done so, should send notes to China and Japan calling their attention to the obligations they assumed with all the other powers to renounce war as an instrument of national policy and to settle all their difficulties by pacific means, and the notes of all the nations should be published to mobilize the public opinion of the world.

Private conversations by ministers of foreign affairs with diplomatic representatives of China and Japan do not adequately meet the situation. The time for secret diplomacy in grave instances of this kind is past. Private conversations are apt to be misunderstood and misinterpreted.

No nation has a right to consider itself aggrieved by having its attention called to violation or threatened violations of treaties. War is no

[30] New York *Times*, Nov. 21.

longer the private affair of belligerent nations. The nations of the world should publicly acknowledge their own obligations and demand that the obligations of other signatories should be fulfilled if peace is to be maintained.[31]

Had this statesmanlike declaration of policy followed the publication of a strong statement from Mr. Stimson such as he tells us he made to Ambassador Debuchi, public opinion in this country, instead of being left "unguided and voiceless," would have been given a much needed lead in the right direction. But Mr. Stimson's voice was still unheard.

Very different in tone are the words of William E. Borah, then Chairman of the Senate Foreign Relations Committee:

The proposal made from Paris to intervene—in other words to employ force, for that is what it means, in the settlement of the Manchurian affair—seems incredible. In saying this I do not mean to approve what Japan is doing; far from it. But this talk of the use of force or intervention, implied from the very beginning, has had the effect of the very reverse of bringing about peace.

When the United States employs its good offices in every reasonable way to bring about peace, it has done all it can or should do. No treaty and no duty devolving upon peace-loving nations requires or permits the United States to go further.[32]

Failure to grasp the significant fact that peace is indivisible and strong measures may sometimes be required to maintain it—a truth which penetrated all too slowly the mind of the Western world—was not confined to Republican leaders. This is shown by a statement, only slightly less isolationist in sentiment from Senator Borah's, made the next day by the minority floor leader, Senator Joseph T. Robinson of Arkansas:

The latest developments in the war between China and Japan indicate a breakdown of efforts to restore peace. Both China and Japan have rejected suggestions for an armistice and it is to be feared that the conflict will continue with increasing vigor in spite of the good offices of peace makers.

The United States cannot decide the events of the controversy and enforce terms of peace. The wise and just policy for the United States,

[31] *Ibid.*   [32] *Ibid.*, Nov. 22.

in my opinion, is to indicate a strongly sympathetic attitude respecting proposals for peace and willingness to be helpful if the parties desire our impartial aid.

Any policy calculated to inject the United States into this Oriental controversy would be attended by far reaching and harmful consequences, and would be objectionable from every standpoint of justice and sound interest.[33]

Returning to the situation in Paris we find that the shift from the scheme for parallel and simultaneous negotiations to the proposal for a suspension of hostilities and a commission of enquiry was brought about by a number of factors, the most important of which were as follows:

1. The best efforts of Aristide Briand and Ambassador Dawes, working separately, had not succeeded in finding a basis for the former plan acceptable to both China and Japan.

2. The Japanese representative was understood to have received instructions to approve the appointment of an investigating commission without requiring China's prior recognition of all existing treaties.

3. Although most of the small powers considered any further delay to be dangerous, the great powers felt that the sending of a neutral commission was necessary not only to ascertain the facts and determine responsibility but to provide a cooling-off period for frayed tempers and taut nerves.

4. The United States, it seemed, was not ready to define its attitude regarding the use of measures stronger than moral pressure and insistence on the obligations of the Pact of Paris.

5. Finally, there was a strong preference for continuing the case under Article 11 in the hope of restoring unanimity in the Council and of avoiding the more drastic steps which would almost inevitably follow if recourse were had to Article 16 of the Covenant.[34]

Although not altogether satisfactory to anyone concerned, as it ended neither the Japanese occupation of Manchuria nor the Chinese boycott of Japanese goods [35] which had come to be one of Japan's

---

[33] *Ibid.*   [34] *The League and Manchuria, the Third Phase,* p. 45.
[35] Dealt with in the 4th of the fundamental points. See *Lytton Report,* Chap. VII, pp. 112 ff. for discussion of the boycott.

major complaints, the proposal was considered the most effective and feasible move that could be made at this time. High hopes were raised by a premature announcement that the two countries had agreed in principle to the plan, only to be immediately dashed by statements to the contrary from both China and Japan. The Chinese merely reserved their acceptance on the grounds that they had not yet received full details,[36] but in Tokyo it was characterized as "unthinkable" and the government declared that if its representative in Paris had committed himself to such a proposal he would be recalled. However, it was not the commission of enquiry to which the Japanese objected but the suspension of hostilities. An official spokesman told press representatives that the government could not consent thus to tie the army's hands in the face of the undisciplined Chinese forces in Manchuria and that, because the army would be rendered useless, the suggested truce would be equivalent to evacuation not only of the occupied areas but of the Chinese Eastern Railway zone. "Japan," continued this spokesman, "cannot agree to any conditions which restrict army activities in Manchuria, in view of the Japanese contention that these activities to date have been purely in self-defense and necessary to protect our interests."[37] The situation was not improved by a report from Mukden that General Honjo threatened to move on Chinchow if Chang Hsuehliang did not clear that city of his forces.[38]

There was no question of postponing the public meeting of the Council scheduled for the twenty-first, but there was general uneasiness as to the course it would take. Careful planning of the first meeting had prevented wrangling and mutual recriminations on the part of the disputants. Now, however, in the face of the unsuccessful negotiations of the intervening days and the heightened tension in the East there could be no thought of trying to prohibit the Chinese and Japanese representatives from making whatever statements their governments felt desirable, and there was no assurance that the underlying bitterness might not break out in violent

---

[36] *Official Journal*, Annex 1334, p. 2528; also Lansing Warren in New York *Times*, Nov. 21.
[37] Byas and AP dispatches, New York *Times*, Nov. 21. [38] Hallett Abend, in *ibid*.

words. That this was not the case was due again to the wise direction of Aristide Briand, who in his opening address set the tone of the meeting. Briefly he analyzed the existing situation: the Council was acting under Article 11 which required unanimous decision; the September 30 resolution, unanimously adopted, was still in force, and two of its important provisions were (1) Japan's declaration that it entertained no territorial designs in Manchuria and would "continue" the withdrawal of troops to within the railway zone as rapidly as the safety of the lives and property of Japanese nationals could be insured, and (2) China's assurance that it would assume responsibility for this safety as the withdrawal of Japanese forces took place and Chinese administrative authority was reestablished; the Council's present duty was to seek the means to enable the parties to carry out these undertakings as quickly as possible; the discussions of the preceding days had not been without value as they had cleared up certain points of view with regard to methods which might be used. Briand then addressed an urgent appeal to the Chinese and Japanese representatives "to confine themselves as far as possible during the present meeting to outlining the suggestions they desire to lay before the Council with a view to putting an end to the present situation in Manchuria." After emphasizing the fact that the Council shared the public emotion over the gravity of events he reminded the disputants of their promise to do everything in their power not to aggravate the situation and concluded with this caution:

The Council's efforts to settle the dispute peacefully might be rendered vain if military operations continued and if public opinion in the two countries could not recover the calm necessary to enable the two Governments to cooperate in full confidence with the Council for the maintenance of peace.[39]

To their credit both Mr. Yoshizawa and Dr. Sze responded wholeheartedly to the appeal of the President of the Council. The former reviewed briefly the now familiar Japanese version of the causes of the crisis, concluding with the statement "Japan's right to live and

[39] See *Official Journal*, pp. 2364-71, for an account of this meeting.

her very existence are at stake." He then made his proposal for the sending of a commission of enquiry. The scene, he said, was remote, the news received often inaccurate:

Accordingly, the Japanese Government concludes that the essential condition of a fundamental solution of the question is a real knowledge of the situation in Manchuria and in China itself. It is for this reason that it proposes that the League of Nations should send a Commission of Enquiry to the spot. I believe that the proposal cannot fail to obtain the approval of all Members of the Council. Of course this Commission would not be empowered to intervene in the negotiations which may be initiated between the two parties or to supervise the movements of the military forces of either. (Pp. 2365–66.)

The two restrictions on the commission's field of endeavor contained in the last sentence were highlighted by Mr. Yoshizawa's failure to mention the suspension of hostilities which had been a part of the original proposal and which had raised such a storm of protest in Tokyo.[40] This omission was not overlooked by Dr. Sze or by Lord Cecil, who, in the absence of Sir John Simon, once again represented Great Britain. The Chinese representative spoke briefly and to the point:

The military occupation of Chinese territory by Japanese forces in violation of solemn treaties and of the Covenant is the crux of the situation. No disposition which fails to provide for the immediate cessation of all military operations and the withdrawal of Japanese forces . . . can pretend to be a solution of the problem. (P. 2366.)

The Chinese Government, he reiterated, could not bargain for the withdrawal of Japanese forces or consent that this be dependent on anything but the safety of life and property in the evacuated area, responsibility for which China was ready to assume. His government would accept any reasonable arrangement involving mutual cooperation under the League, but the situation was rapidly going from bad to worse.

Further delay can only render more difficult the task which confronts us. In order to secure the prompt and complete evacuation of its territory China has the firm intention of demanding, as circumstances may

[40] Undoubtedly he had received rigid instructions on this score from Tokyo. See Byas, New York *Times*, Nov. 22.

require, every right and every remedy secured to it as a member of the League of Nations—by Article 11 and by any other articles of the Covenant. (P. 2366.)

Lord Cecil followed Dr. Sze with a pointed statement to the effect that "from the outset" of the discussions in September [41] he and his government had favored some such means of obtaining accurate information as to what was going on in Manchuria. Whereupon Mr. Yoshizawa drew attention to the fact that his proposal called for an inquiry not only in Manchuria but in China proper as well. Dr. Sze repeated his contention that "the matter before the Council is the immediate cessation of hostilities." Lord Cecil supported him in this, saying,

It would evidently be a complete failure of our duties—a complete failure of the whole object we have in view—if, during the progress of the work of this Commission, hostilities continued, as unhappily they have continued during the past weeks. (P. 2367.)

Other members of the Council then spoke in favor of accepting the proposal. Among these was Herr von Mutius, substituting for the German Foreign Minister Von Bülow. Herr von Mutius said:

The whole world is relying on the League of Nations to remove this danger to peace. The nations demand that we should find a satisfactory solution and that confidence in the League of Nations, which is the very foundation of its existence and the essential condition of the success of all its efforts, should in no way be impaired. Public opinion has told us again and again that the fate of the League of Nations—that is to say, the fate of all peoples—is now at stake.

We have, of course, no intention of asking two members of the League to surrender vital interests. The principal task of the League is to find just and equitable solutions. What we have to do is quite clear. The Council has not to solve all the questions at present at issue in Manchuria but to put an end to a situation which is very like war and which certainly presents a grave danger of war. (P. 2367.)

M. Briand thanked the Chinese and Japanese representatives for having kept their remarks within the bounds of "conciliatory and courteous discussion." He was glad that a concrete and definite

[41] In September, Yoshizawa had refused to consider a Commission of Enquiry, saying it was an insult to his country.

proposal had been made by the Japanese representative; the question of the character, powers, and composition of the commission was a matter for careful study. In closing he addressed a word to each of the disputants, to Japan a sharp warning, to China a kindly suggestion:

I would remind the Japanese representative that there can be no doubt that the despatch and labours of the Commission would occupy a certain time and it is unthinkable [42] that during this period acts of hostility could be committed which would lead to bloodshed and still further aggravate the situation. . . .

I hope the Chinese representative after obtaining all the explanations he very rightly desires will understand that here, too, he must make an effort to cooperate with a view to a peaceful situation. (P. 2370.)

Dr. Sze responded by assuring the President of his government's cooperation but made it a matter of record that China would not for a moment consent that the appointment of a commission should furnish an excuse for delaying the withdrawal of Japanese troops. Mr. Yoshizawa, inscrutable as usual, got in a last and somewhat disturbing remark to the effect that the particulars he had so far given were "only in the nature of general principles" and he was still in communication with his government on the subject.

The public session then closed with a statement from the President that as soon as a draft resolution could be laid before the parties and the other members of the Council another meeting would be held.

NOVEMBER 22 TO 25.—On its face the Japanese proposal for the appointment of a commission of enquiry seemed to be a move toward conciliation and amicable settlement, and as such it was generally received. It was expected that the draft resolution could be quickly worked out and the next meeting held within a few days. As a matter of fact a draft was ready by the twenty-fifth, supported by a statement of American approval "in principle" from Ambassador Dawes; but so many difficulties arose in the way of its acceptance by the parties to the dispute that it was not until December 9 that the Council was again called into public session. [43]

[42] M. Briand's use of the word "unthinkable" is perhaps a sly dig at the Japanese.
[43] See pp. 199–200, below, for draft resolution and statement of Mr. Dawes.

One major source of these difficulties was in the Japanese proposal itself. As has already been pointed out it omitted any reference to a cessation of hostilities and specifically excluded direct negotiations and military operations from the scope of the commission's authority. Although discussion of the proposal made it clear that Council members considered cessation of hostilities an essential to the commission's success, there was not the slightest yielding on this point by the inflexible Yoshizawa. Rather, his last statement regarding the general nature of his proposal, so reminiscent of his October stand on fundamental principles, opened wide the door for continued expansion of Japanese demands. Dr. Sze saw at once the possibility that the whole thing was a trap for him and his government: Japan had publicly proposed the sending of the commission and so put herself in the position of favoring League action; trusting to the probability that only the main proposal would receive much attention she then attached such conditions to it that China could not possibly accept it and would thus be put in the position of blocking the League; this would result in a complete reversal of the usual roles of the two parties before the Council. Danger of being misinterpreted did not, however, deter the Chinese statesman from maintaining his stand, and on November 22 he sent the Secretary-General a formal note summarizing his oral reservations of the previous day. China could not, he stated, consider the proposal made by the Japanese representative until adequate provision had been made for cessation of hostilities and withdrawal of Japanese forces, otherwise the proposal became a "mere device to condone and perpetuate for a more or less indefinite period the unjustifiable occupation of Chinese territory by an aggressor who has already attained his unlawful objective while these discussions have been going on."[44]

Another difficulty, directly connected with the above, was the continued activity of the Japanese army in Manchuria. Having destroyed Chinese military power and administrative authority in the northeastern province of Heilungkiang, thus bringing the last of the three provincial capitals, Mukden, Kirin and Tsitsihar, under their control, they had again turned their attention southwest toward

[44] *Official Journal*, Annex 1334, p. 2528.

Chinchow. On November 20, it will be recalled, it was reported from Mukden that Honjo was threatening to move on Chinchow unless Chang Hsueh-liang withdrew. There was no repudiation of this from Tokyo at the time, and rumors of troop movements in that direction continued. In Paris there was widespread suspicion that in proposing the commission the Japanese were merely trying to gain time for the extension of their authority to Chinchow,[45] the last real stronghold of China outside the Great Wall.[46] Also on November 20, a Rengo dispatch had reported that anti-Japanese disturbances had occurred in Shanhaikwan,[47] forcing Japanese women and children to take refuge in the Japanese barracks there, and that Chinese forces in the vicinity of Chinchow were increasing rapidly and were busily engaged in recruiting new troops. On the twenty-first a Reuters dispatch from Mukden told of increased activity in Honjo's headquarters, while Japanese troop movements toward Hsinmin were also reported. Dr. Sze brought all of these to the notice of the League Secretariat with the comment that Japanese reports of banditry and anti-Japanese disturbances in any area had come to indicate "that military activities in the regions concerned are under contemplation by the Japanese army"—tactics with which the world has since become all too familiar but then new and not quickly recognized. On the twenty-third, Sze again called attention to the rumors of concentration of Chinese forces at Chinchow and Shanhaikwan, all of which he branded as false. His contention was upheld by the official reports of British and French observers on the spot,[48] who, as late as November 24 to 26, found the situation at Chinchow entirely normal with no evidence of any increase in Chinese troops outside the Great Wall, no sign of any offensive preparations whatever, and, apparently, no arrangements being made for the defense of the city even though the authorities were expecting a hostile move by the Japanese. Both British and French observers

[45] Clarence Streit, New York *Times*, Nov. 23.
[46] Harbin on the Chinese Eastern Railway, still in Chinese hands, was within the Russian sphere of influence. See Chap. VII, below.
[47] Shanhaikwan is at the eastern terminal of the Great Wall. See p. 229, below.
[48] *Official Journal*, Annex 1334, pp. 2532, 2533, 2535–36, for the British notes, pp. 2536–37, for the French.

reported the occupation of Hsinmin by the Japanese advance guard on November 25. The French went further and urged that

the commander of the Japanese troops should receive instructions which would enable him to get into touch without delay with neutral observers so as to stop the forward movement of the Japanese troops and consider the fixing of a neutral zone.

Conflicting rumors coming from Tokyo did nothing to alleviate the situation: on the one hand, there was a United Press dispatch of the twenty-fifth declaring that the Japanese Government would not acquiesce in any agreement to stop hostilities until Chinese concentrations around Chinchow had been withdrawn or broken up, while on the twenty-sixth Baron Shidehara was said to have informed both the American and French Ambassadors in Tokyo that Japan had no intention of attacking Chinchow.[49] The report of the Lytton Commission shows very clearly, however, that whatever may have been the intentions of the Foreign Office or of the Cabinet at home the army in Manchuria was determined to carry out Honjo's threat of the twentieth. The disturbances in Tientsin were made the excuse for sending reinforcements to the small garrison there by way of Chinchow and Shanhaikwan. Of this the Lytton Report says: [50]

As a mere transport problem it would have been easier and quicker to despatch reinforcements by sea via Darien. But, considered strategically, the suggested route had this advantage, that it would enable the advancing troops to dispose en route of the very inconvenient Chinese concentration around Chinchow. It was assumed that the delay in taking this route would not be long, as little or no resistance from the Chinese was anticipated. The suggestion was approved [by Honjo] and one armored train, one troop train, and a couple of aeroplanes crossed the Liao River on November 27th.

At first the Chinese retreated, but a "shade of resistance" led the Japanese headquarters to send reinforcements of more armored trains, infantry trains, and artillery. Chinchow was bombed several times. Then, suddenly on November 29, to the great surprise of the Chinese the Japanese forces withdrew to Hsinmin.

[49] *The League and Manchuria, the Third Phase*, pp. 54, 55.
[50] *Lytton Report*, pp. 76–77.

The Japanese military had again thought to carry everything before them by the weight of a successful advance in Chinese territory, and there is every reason to believe that again they acted, if not against orders, at least, without them.[51] For once, however, they met with stubborn resistance in the field, and for the first and last time Shidehara summoned up his courage, ordered an immediate retreat, and was obeyed. Great Britain and the United States have each been credited with bringing this about, but it seems more likely that it was the happy combination of several well-timed actions: Aristide Briand's letter of the twenty-fifth to both parties urging that commanders in the field be given express orders to refrain from further engagements; his letter of the twenty-ninth to the Japanese alone urging consideration of the proposal for neutral observers in the Chinchow area; the joint publication on the twenty-fifth of the substance of the Council's draft resolution and of American approval of this measure; the strongly worded protest from the British Foreign Office that the advance toward Chinchow along the Peking-Mukden line endangered British interests,[52] and Secretary Stimson's indignation expressed in his message of the twenty-seventh [53] and in his press conference of the same day. No one of these by itself would have produced the desired result; together they had sufficient weight to make Shidehara act as he had never acted before.[54] For once the timing of all concerned was good, planned or not, and the results are evidence of what concerted action might have accomplished at other times.

The reasons for Mr. Stimson's indignation are clearly set forth in the second paragraph of his note of the twenty-seventh. In this he reminds the Japanese Foreign Minister that on the twenty-fourth the letter had assured him "with the concurrence of the Minister of War and the chief of staff" that there would be no movement of Japanese troops in the direction of Chinchow and that orders to that effect had been given. Relying on this, he had "urged con-

---

[51] Byas, in the New York *Times*, Nov. 27.   [52] Built through a British loan.
[53] *Conditions in Manchuria*, p. 42.
[54] Baron Shidehara is said to have gone to the Emperor with the result that the latter personally ordered the withdrawal. See Wilfrid Fleisher, *The Volcanic Isle* (Garden City, N.Y., 1941), p. 254.

ciliatory steps upon the Chinese Government and an acceptance of the proposal of the Council of the League of Nations." The note concludes: "I am quite unable to see how there can be any serious danger of a clash between Chinese and Japanese troops unless the latter troops should fail to observe the orders which your excellency assured me had been given."

Perhaps, however, in the last analysis, it was the press conference and its subsequent tempest-in-a-tea-pot which actually turned the trick. Mr. Stimson, thoroughly outraged at being hoodwinked, broke his silence and let the assembled correspondents know how he really felt about Japanese dual diplomacy. His words were strong, as were his feelings, but they were entirely proper for a Secretary of State to use in referring to a nation with which his government is still on friendly terms. But the Japanese press, getting its news second-hand and misinterpreting an agency report of the conference, quoted him as saying that the Japanese army was running amok in Manchuria. The jingo papers made the most of their opportunity, inveighing against the insult to their "noble army," the "best disciplined," the "most honorable army" in the world, and so on (this was before the rape of Nanking!), and the Foreign Office spokesman expressed himself quite discourteously, to say the least, on the subject of Mr. Stimson's ability and qualifications for his high office. The next day it was all explained away. Mr. Stimson issued a press release giving his exact words; the news agency published a statement showing how its report had been misinterpreted; and the spokesman for the Japanese Foreign Office said he had acted too hastily without waiting for official confirmation of the words attributed to Mr. Stimson.[55]

But the incident left its mark. The strain on American-Japanese relations was not entirely removed by the explanations, and the change already taking place in Mr. Stimson's point of view was un-

[55] For contemporary news reports of this "comedy of errors" as Hugh Byas calls it, see the Washington, Tokyo, and Paris dispatches in the New York *Times* of Nov. 27, 28, 29, and 30, and the "Weekly Summary" of news in the *Trans-Pacific* of Dec. 3. The AP explanation was published in the New York *Times* on Nov. 26. Probably the best account of the incident is that given by Wilfrid Fleisher (*op. cit.*, pp. 253 ff.). Fleisher says this is the only time Shiratori, the Foreign Office spokesman, ever made a retraction.

doubtedly accelerated. In Japan, too, it had its effect. The very violence of the press and of the Foreign Office spokesman indicates their extreme sensitiveness to criticism from this country and their anxiety as to the reaction of public opinion here. Moreover, Baron Shidehara acted quickly and effectively. The advance on Chinchow was halted, for the time being at least. It should be noted, however, that although the Japanese Government announced that their troops had withdrawn east of the Liao, the Lytton Report states that they moved back only to Hsinmin some miles west of that river, in keeping with their policy never to return completely to the point from which they started.[56]

Still another and more serious misunderstanding arose out of the advance on Chinchow. As has been said, sufficient progress had been made on the draft resolution for the Council to feel justified in issuing an official résumé of its substance, accompanied by a statement of American approval in principle. Coinciding as it did with M. Briand's note of the twenty-fifth to China and Japan, this action would seem to have been meant as a further step to prevent aggravation of the situation through a new outbreak of hostilities. Dr. Sze on the same day addressed a note to the Secretary General of the League in which he asked that the Council at once

take all necessary steps for the establishment of a neutral zone between the present stations of the Chinese and Japanese forces; such zone to be occupied by British, French, Italian and other neutral detachments under Council authority.

In such circumstances China could and would, if requested by the Council in the interests of peace, withdraw her forces within the Great Wall.[57]

There could be no mistaking the conditions of the Chinese offer as here made: she would withdraw her forces within the Great Wall if requested to do so by the Council, *provided* the council would establish a neutral zone occupied by neutral detachments under Council authority "between the present stations of the Chinese and Japanese forces." And yet a misunderstanding developed. About this time Dr. Wellington Koo, who had succeeded C. T. Wang as

[56] *Lytton Report*, p. 77. See also Chap. IV, above.
[57] *Official Journal*, Annex 1334, p. 2558.

Foreign Minister, seems to have made a similar proposal to the Japanese government through Count Damien de Martel, French Ambassador to Tokyo. This offer is not a matter of official record with the League, although there are references to it in the Japanese communications of the twenty-seventh and twenty-eighth,[58] therefore it cannot be said positively that the terms were the same as those set forth in Dr. Sze's letter to the Secretary General. It does not stand to reason, however, that the Chinese Government would attach such rigid requirements regarding neutral observers and forces within the neutral zone to her proposal to the League and at the same time make an unqualified offer of evacuation and neutralization to the Japanese Government. Nevertheless, Japan chose so to interpret the Chinese proposal, announced that she had accepted it and on that basis had agreed to the withdrawal of her forces from before Chinchow.[59]

The nature of the Japanese acceptance of China's proposal is found in the last two paragraphs of Tokyo's reply to Briand's appeal of the twenty-fifth in which he urged the two parties to take steps to prevent further hostilities:

[The Japanese Government] has no objection in principle to declaring that, should the Chinese forces be withdrawn from the Chinchow district to the West of Shan-hai-kwan, as the Chinese Government recently proposed through the Government of the French Republic, the Japanese forces will not enter the zone thus evacuated except in the event of a serious and urgent threat endangering the safety of the lives and property of Japanese nationals in Northern China and the safety of the Japanese troops stationed there.

The Japanese Government is prepared to instruct its authorities on the spot to conclude detailed arrangements in this connection with the Chinese local authorities.[60]

[58] *Ibid.,* pp. 2529–30, 2531–32. See also Ambassador Dawes's proposed statement on this subject quoted in full, pp. 215–16, below; and see William Martin, "The League and the Far Eastern Crisis," *Asia,* July–August, 1932, p. 407.
[59] Hugh Byas in his report to the New York *Times* on the 28th presents an interesting sidelight on the picture when he states that, although the government had on the previous day given a virtual promise not to seize the city and although the necessity for its occupation had disappeared with the acceptance of the Chinese offer, nevertheless "the army is apparently in full speed toward Chinchow."
[60] *Official Journal,* pp. 2529–30.

M. Briand followed this with a definite proposal to the two governments regarding the dispatch of neutral observers to the Chinchow area for the purpose of establishing the neutral zone, "or any other system calculated to prevent" further collision, and to act as liaison between the two forces in making the necessary arrangements.[61] This was, of course, a compromise between the Chinese request for neutral detachments to occupy the evacuated zone and the Japanese suggestion of direct negotiations with the Chinese authorities on the spot.

China accepted the proposal [62] unconditionally and without delay. Japan, on the other hand, just as definitely rejected "the interposition of third parties" but tried to smooth it over with suave words, restating her position as follows:

if China withdrew her troops entirely from the Chinchow district to Shan-hai-kwan and west of that place and only maintained the administration [including the policing] of the Chinchow district at Shan-hai-kwan, the Japanese Government would be prepared to undertake *in principle* that Japanese troops would not enter the zone thus evacuated except in the case of serious and urgent circumstances.[63]

Thus the Chinese were to evacuate "entirely" all of their own territory outside the Great Wall while the Japanese forces were to remain where they were before Chinchow with an extremely problematical neutral zone between, Japan undertaking only "in principle" [64] not to enter the evacuated district. In his answer [65] to this note, M. Briand pointed out the misunderstanding under which the Japanese Government seemed to be laboring as to the status of the neutral observers and made clear the nature of the original Chinese proposal, which "involved the despatch of international detachments" to the neutral zone. The members of the Council had compromised on neutral observers alone, and this proposal M. Briand again recommended to the attention of the Japanese Government.

[61] *Ibid.*, p. 2530. [62] *Ibid.*, p. 2531. [63] *Ibid.* Italics mine.
[64] Regarding the use of the phrase "in principle," W. W. Willoughby says that in international usage this phrase "carries as little commitment as the party using it may later desire." (*The Sino-Japanese Controversy and the League of Nations*, p. 167.)
[65] *Official Journal*, p. 2532.

No formal answer was made to this communication, as it was just at this time that Baron Shidehara ordered the withdrawal from before Chinchow. However, the situation continued tense and the need for establishing the neutral zone in the southwest remained and was to complicate the later discussions of the draft resolution. The entire incident recalls vividly the debate during the September meetings when Yoshizawa tried repeatedly to place a false interpretation on a similar compromise proposal made by Dr. Sze in hopes of facilitating the Council's action.[66] Now, as then, the Japanese failed to trap the wary Dr. Sze, ably seconded this time by the astute President of the Council; but it served well the purpose of the military group in that country since it involved all members of the Council in a futile discussion of the neutral zone and further postponed action on the Council resolution.

Finally there was the ever present uncertainty as to the extent of American cooperation. Neither Mr. Dawes's statement of the twenty-fifth nor Mr. Stimson's outburst of indignation on the next day banished this anxiety, for neither touched the crux of the question—would the United States actively and officially participate if the Council decided to appoint a commission of enquiry? In the light of the stand taken by Mr. Stimson in September,[67] our abstention now would be looked upon as disapproval of the Council's action and would serve only to strengthen the hands of the Japanese war lords. For this reason the Council could not act effectively until it knew what the United States would do.

Clarence Streit wrote from Paris on the twenty-third [68] that the enigma of the American attitude was one of the main excuses for inaction by the Council and he quoted a high League official as saying that one of their worst difficulties was that of coordinating American and League efforts to maintain peace despite the manifest desire of the two forces to pull together. From the outside, whether in Washington or in Paris, there was little evidence of such a desire on our part. Emphasis since October had been on independence of judgment and action, and the studied aloofness of Mr. Dawes had made

[66] See pp. 62–66, above.   [67] See pp. 47–49, above.
[68] New York *Times*, Nov. 24.

isolation a living reality to most of those in Paris.[69] The statements from Senators Borah and Robinson did not improve matters, and as yet there had been nothing from the State Department to indicate what, if any, action the United States might take. That the Council looked to this government for help seems clear, and at one point that aid was forthcoming—when Mr. Stimson, relying on Shidehara's promise that Chinchow would not be attacked, urged China to accept the Council's proposal notwithstanding the fact that it did not provide for immediate cessation of hostilities nor set a date for Japanese evacuation of the illegally occupied territories. But this was the exception and, generally speaking, there existed a deadlock between the Council and Washington—fully as critical as that between China and Japan—as to which one should take the lead in ending a situation which was permitting Japan to humiliate practically the entire world.[70] The American position, as viewed from Paris, was substantially this:

China has taken the case before the Council. Since the United States is not a member of the League and is free from the Covenant's obligations she is not called upon to tell those who have those responsibilities what to do. The United States, therefore, must leave the initiative to those who have the heaviest commitments and content herself with assuring them that the League has her support in the effort to keep peace.

This, Washington apparently believes, is sufficient to remove, in this case, the League's standing bogey that the United States might insist on the neutral rights of trading with an aggressor against whom the Council might be applying sanctions.

Members of the Council, however, note that the United States while promising general support, always declines to commit herself in advance to any specific action and hence the Council's doubts remain.[71]

In recent years the American public has been deluged with references by press and radio commentators, some shallow, some serious students of foreign affairs, to the effect that the United States is always left holding the bag whenever this government tries to co-

69 In the New York *Times* of Nov. 27, Streit writes: "Meanwhile the Council's silent partner, Ambassador Dawes, celebrated Thanksgiving day by leaving his room in the Hotel Ritz for the first time in seven days. He took a walk but was careful not to cross over to the Foreign Office side of the Seine." See also Streit's reports of Nov. 23 and Dec. 7.
70 *Ibid.*, Nov. 25.   71 *Ibid.*

operate with European powers in efforts to maintain peace or straighten out international difficulties. It is, therefore, interesting to note certain rather caustic comments in the European press imputing to us the very motives we are so given to discovering in others. From Paris comes the report that the Council was anxious lest it again be "left out on a limb" by Washington as was the case in October in the matter of setting a definite date for the withdrawal of Japanese forces. Europeans, this dispatch continues, felt that if, in spite of her vital interest in the Far East, the United States was not willing to play a strong role she might at least give an answer when a specific action was proposed, and the only explanation they could find for failure to do so was that the United States "wants the League to pull the American Chestnuts from the fire." [72] Similar interpretations are found in the editorials of two Spanish newspapers. *El Sol*, then Madrid's most important liberal paper, is quoted as saying the United States "is guiding the League Council and using it to pull its chestnuts out of the fire" [73] and *Crisol*, also liberal in policy, commented:

Despite surface indications that the League has the situation well in hand, the truth is the United States has created itself the final arbiter in the situation in which it is directly and considerably interested. The United States will dominate the Commission and try to get the maximum advantages out of its decisions, realizing this under the realistic and romantic camouflage of the League.[74]

To such unflattering misinterpretation had the vacillating policy of the Administration for the past two months laid this country open! This, then, was the situation on November 25 when the Council released the summary of the tentative draft resolution. According to press reports from both Washington and Paris the United States played a considerable part in drawing up the resolution and there is reason to believe that our lack of sympathy [75] with China's demand for the immediate evacuation of Manchurian territory by Japan was at least partially responsible for the weakness of the clause

[72] Streit, New York *Times*, Nov. 24.   [73] New York *Times*, Nov. 23.
[74] *Ibid.*
[75] Allan Nevins in his *America in World Affairs* (New York, 1942) says (p. 105):
"Apparently Dawes achieved his results by bringing pressure on the Chinese."

on this subject. This attitude on our part inevitably gave support
to the Japanese claim that their troops were the one force capable
of maintaining order in a chaotic Manchuria, although the Chinese
from the beginning had contended that the situation was being
brought about by the deliberate design of Japan to abolish all
Chinese administrations capable of maintaining order.[76] We know
from his own words that Ambassador Dawes was not in favor of
forcing Japanese withdrawal even from the Nonni River area [77] and
from all accounts he was very active behind the scenes, seeing both
the Chinese and Japanese representatives frequently.[78] His *Journal*
gives no information as to the drafting of the resolution but goes into
considerable detail as to the circumstances leading to the simultaneous release of the resolution and the statement of American approval.

Substantially the story is as follows. Aristide Briand, at a Council
meeting on the twenty-fourth, had indicated that it would help matters along if the United States would let its attitude be known and, if
it approved the proposed resolution, inform China and Japan to that
effect. Mr. Dawes thought it vitally important for the resolution and
the statement of approval to be published at the same time, for in
this way "not only the joint attitude of the Council of the League
and of the United States, but the parallel efforts and cooperation
which had led to it" would be made known. However, he thought
it equally important that no reference be made to this "cooperative
and parallel attitude" of the United States until the text of the resolution was published. Ordinarily this would not be done until it had
been presented at a full meeting of the Council, but Dawes wanted
to be sure that all the members (excepting the parties to the dispute) had agreed to its terms, and he therefore insisted on advance
publication of the main points in an official communique. He took
the matter up with the State Department and received permission to
proceed along that line. On the twenty-fifth he sent a copy of his
proposed statement to Sir Eric Drummond to be delivered confi-

---

[76] Note Prime Minister Churchill's warning statement to Parliament, July 27, 1943,
regarding Italy: that it would be a grave mistake for "the rescuing powers"—Britain
and the United States—"so to act as to break down the whole structure and expression of the Italian state" and cause anarchy there. Baltimore *Sun*, July 28, 1943.
[77] Dawes, *op. cit.*, p. 412. See also Chap. V, above.   [78] New York *Times*.

dentially to M. Briand. It was understood that Dawes himself would make the public announcement as soon as Briand notified him that the official communique of the Council had been released to the press. Receiving that notification on the afternoon of the twenty-fifth, Dawes immediately gave out the following statement:

The United States Government approves the general plan of settlement embodied in the proposed resolution of the Council of the League of Nations and has so informed both China and Japan. It has urged upon them acquiescence in the general plan of the proposed resolution.[79]

It seems strange that anyone could think that this statement of two sentences, of forty-one words, a statement, moreover, so general in its character that the old. question of what the United States proposed to do was still unanswered, could offset the cumulative effects of weeks of isolation and separate efforts. Yet both Mr. Dawes and the State Department assumed that to be the case. Concluding his story of the simultaneous publication of the two documents the Ambassador says, "Thus was the United States associated with the League before the world in this effort for a peaceful settlement between China and Japan." [80] Secretary Stimson told his press conference that he considered the introduction of the resolution and the approval given it by the United States as sufficient answer to unofficial complaints from Paris that this country was not co-operating with the League Council in its efforts for peace. Authoritative quarters in Washington were said to feel that this resolution was the last effort to be made to bring about a peaceful solution of the affair; should this fail, it was hinted, there would be an end to diplomatic negotiations so far as this country was concerned, since "officials entrusted with the conduct of American foreign relations tried not to handle lost causes too long," [81] a phrase whose significance could hardly have failed to impress the Japanese, whoever may have been its author. As to the Administration's opinion of the resolution itself, correspondents in Washington were told

[it] is drawn along broad lines and offers a wise course for adjusting the Manchurian crisis by providing for a cessation of hostilities coupled with

[79] Dawes, *op. cit.,* p. 423; New York *Times,* Nov. 26; *Conditions in Manchuria,* p. 41.
[80] Dawes, *op. cit.*   [81] New York *Times,* Nov. 26.

a gradual withdrawal of the Japanese forces to the railway zone, and an investigation by a neutral commission of the Manchurian problem.

The plan is felt here to possess high merit because it proposes application to the Manchurian crisis of the methods and principles that have long been utilized by nations for composing their differences by conciliation.[82]

Inasmuch as this was the same sort of commission proposed in September when the case was in its infancy and Japanese forces in Manchuria were still confined to a relatively small area outside the railway zone, and which Mr. Stimson then disapproved, one is impelled to ask why the difference now. Mr. Stimson's explanations fail to satisfy,[83] for the sooner conciliatory measures are taken the greater their chances of success, or conversely, the longer conciliatory measures are postponed, by so much are their chances of success lessened.

The tentative draft to which so many references have already been made was as follows:

The resolution of September 30th is recalled and reaffirmed. The two parties declare themselves solemnly bound by that resolution.

The two governments accordingly are invited to take all steps necessary to assure its execution so that withdrawal of Japanese troops within the railway zone—a *point to which the Council attaches the utmost importance*—may be effected as soon as possible.

The two parties undertake:

To give to the commanders of their respective forces strict orders to refrain from any initiative which may lead to further fighting and loss of life;

And to take all measures necessary to avoid any further aggravation of the situation.

Members of the Council are invited to furnish it with information received from their representatives on the spot.

It is proposed to appoint a commission to study on the spot and to report to the Council any circumstance which affects international relations, threatens to disturb the peace between China and Japan, or the good understanding between them on which peace depends.

China and Japan each would be represented by a member.

Appointment and deliberations of the Commission would not prejudice in any way the engagement taken by the Japanese Government and

[82] *Ibid.*   [83] Stimson, *op. cit.*, pp. 43–45.

embodied in the resolution of September 30th regarding withdrawal of Japanese troops within the railway zone.[84]

This was definitely a compromise resolution, an attempt to break the stalemate between China and Japan; but the greater concessions were to be made by China, the weaker power. Nevertheless, it was the best possible compromise when all effective measures had been ruled out. There is no mention in it of a date for the withdrawal of Japanese troops as in the October resolution and no reference to the immediate cessation of hostilities which China had made a *sine qua non* of her acceptance of a commission of enquiry. On the other hand there was no concession to the Japanese demand for direct negotiations with China or the exclusion of military operations from the scope of the commission's authority. The extent of such authority (under the euphemistic term "police powers to chase bandits"), together with a renewal of the conflict over the neutral zone before Chinchow, played a considerable part in the discussions of the succeeding days when all efforts were engaged in trying to persuade the two countries to accept the resolution as it stood.

Clarence Streit, writing from Paris on the twenty-fifth,[85] says informed quarters left no doubt that the publication of the resolution's contents and of the Dawes statement was meant to marshal public opinion and make it clear to Nanking that it had better accept the resolution as the best it could hope for, at least as far as the great powers were concerned. The small powers, on the other hand, agreed to publication for an entirely different reason. In almost open revolt over what they considered to be either the supineness of Great Britain, France, and the United States in the face of Japanese aggression, or their willingness to establish precedents more advantageous to the great than to the weak powers, the representatives of the small states refused to join in anything approaching pressure to force China to accept the resolution. They hoped that, when the vagueness of the clause on withdrawal was realized, public opinion would side with them and force the adoption of a stronger clause. In

[84] New York *Times*, Nov. 26. The italicized passages are not in the final resolution of Dec. 10.
[85] New York *Times*.

this they were disappointed. That there was a growing cleavage between the great and small powers was generally recognized by this time and in one of the best of the contemporary accounts it is analyzed as follows:

A difference of point of view and policy was developing in the Council itself between representatives of some of the Great Powers,[86] who did not desire to adopt a positive text which their nations would not be prepared to back up in action and representatives of some of the smaller countries, including Norway and Spain, who were refusing to adopt any resolution minimizing or sacrificing the principles of the Covenant and practically countenancing the invasion of the territory of a League member as a legitimate measure.[87]

Strenuous efforts on the part of Briand, Cecil and Madariaga prevented an open split and enabled the Council to reach a unanimous vote on the resolution of December 10 but the breach was not healed and the differences broke out afresh when the case was transferred to the Assembly under China's appeal to Article 15 of the Covenant.

NOVEMBER 26 TO DECEMBER 10.—At a private meeting of the Council on November 26 a committee was appointed with Lord Cecil as chairman to redraft the resolution in such a way as to reconcile, if possible, the conflicting views of the two parties and reach an agreement which could be adopted unanimously, thus keeping the procedure under Article 11. The work of this committee was undoubtedly facilitated by the temporary suspension of hostilities around Chinchow and the Japanese withdrawal, also temporary as later events proved, from the environs of that city.[88] On November 30 China further eased their still difficult task by agreeing not to insist on a definite time limit for Japanese evacuation. Provided the situation around Chinchow could be kept under control it was believed there was hope for a solution.

[86] Lord Cecil seems to have supported the small powers in their efforts, but apparently he was speaking more for himself than for the British Foreign Office and Sir John Simon, with whom he did not always see eye to eye. Streit, New York *Times*, Nov. 26.

[87] *The League and Manchuria, the Third Phase*, p. 52.

[88] Clarence Streit writing from Paris on the 29th says if the Council had been officially informed of the Japanese retirement it had failed to publish the good news. New York *Times*, Nov. 30.

By December 1, according to Mr. Dawes, only a few points of difference remained between Japan and China, "the principal one being the manner in which the declaration and resolution of the League would cover the point of protection of Japanese nationals against bandits." [89] But this optimistic view is not borne out by current news reports nor by the communications submitted to the Secretariat of the League by the Chinese and Japanese delegations.[90] Analysis of these shows that a number of obstacles to an agreement still existed. Some were, of course, less serious and more easily surmounted than others. One of the most difficult had already been removed by the Chinese concession of the thirtieth. There remained:

1. A difference of opinion as to the size of the Commission. China, supported by most of the small powers, wanted a large body made up of representatives of both the small and the great powers. The remainder of the Council wanted a small commission, assisted by experts—at one time a commission of three made up of representatives of Great Britain, France, and the United States had been seriously considered, but this was eventually increased to five to include Italy and Germany.

2. A three-cornered conflict as to the scope of the enquiry. Japan insisted it should cover conditions in China proper as well as Manchuria. China was equally insistent that domestic affairs should be excluded. The Council apparently agreed with China, but, as it would be difficult to define "domestic," thought it best to leave this point to the discretion of the commission.

3. A deadlock between Japan and China over the scope of the commission's authority. China insisted on the right of the investigating body to report with recommendations for Council action in the event that the terms of the September 30 resolution had not been met by the time of their arrival in Manchuria. Japan was equally opposed to the inclusion of such a clause.

4. Japanese resistance to the clause asking the governments of both countries to instruct their commanders in the field to refrain from

[89] Dawes, *op. cit.*, p. 424.
[90] *The League and Manchuria, the Third Phase*, pp. 64 ff.; *Official Journal*, pp. 2561–63, 2590–91; New York *Times*, daily through the last week in November.

any initiative which might lead to further fighting and loss of life. This was characterized in Tokyo as just an armistice in disguise and called forth more protests from the press than any other point.[91] More serious, however, from the point of view of the Council was

5. Japan's demand for the right to take "police measures against bandits." The Council was practically unanimous in its opposition to this as it involved approval of military action within the territory of another country. The Latin-Americans particularly opposed it as a dangerous precedent which might have serious consequences in this hemisphere, and the great powers felt the Council could not now countenance a state of affairs—Japanese military action in Chinese territory—which it had formally condemned in a previous resolution.

6. The Council therefore countered with the compromise suggestion that neutral observers might accompany Japanese expeditions against bandit irregulars, but Japan opposed this also and continued to delay Council action by determined opposition to any participation by neutral observers in the Chinchow situation. Regarding this as intervention by third parties in their troop movements, they stood fast on the old ground that they would deal only with the local Chinese authorities, at the same time insisting that there were no Chinese administrators who had the authority to negotiate or who could be trusted to carry out their obligations. For a time the Committee of Twelve also stood firm, declaring that there was no good reason why liaison between neutral observers and Japanese commanders in the field could not be effectively used in this way.

Finding Japan obdurate, the great powers in the Council together with Ambassador Dawes seem to have concentrated their efforts on obtaining further concessions from China. Not satisfied with the relinquishing of the vital demand for a fixed date for evacuation they tried to persuade China to withdraw most of her troops from Chinchow and the remaining territory outside the Great Wall. Japan, in the meantime, had followed her usual course of increasing her demands, this time asking that civil officials as well as the troops of Chang Hsueh-liang be withdrawn, the neutral zone established west

91 *Trans-Pacific*, Dec. 3; Hugh Byas, New York *Times*, Nov. 26.

of Chinchow, and that city placed under the new Japanese-controlled administration at Mukden.[92] But this time Dr. Sze refused to give way. "China will not evacuate Chinchow," he declared, adding that the city would be defended if attacked. Another compromise was then suggested: to freeze the armies as they were with a sort of twilight zone between them into which only the neutral observers were to go. No agreement was reached on this, and about all that could be hoped for was that no untoward incident would precipitate a new crisis while the Council was in session. Compromise was reached however on the two important points of evacuation and police measures: China had not only given up her demand for a fixed date for the withdrawal of Japanese forces to the railway zone but had consented that this question should be treated generally in the resolution, not emphasized as of vital importance;[93] the Japanese representative would make his own statement on police measures at the public meeting, that point being omitted both from the resolution and from the declaration to be made by the President of the Council.

The Japanese delegation in the meantime had suggested sending out the commission of enquiry without any specific powers and at the very last it was understood Tokyo would concur in the Council action provided the Commission was merely to furnish information concerning the fulfillment of the September 30 resolution. This viewpoint, that the commission was merely a fact-finding body, was strongly reflected in the Japanese press during the first week in December. An article by Dr. S. Washio which appeared in *Trans-Pacific* of December 3 commends the plan for an investigating commission but stresses the point that it should have no authority to intervene. In this same paper, in its day-by-day summary of developments in the Manchurian Crisis, we find the following under date of November 24:

[92] A high official of the League commented that it might not be a brilliant achievement to prevent a battle by getting the Chinese to withdraw from their own country, but what else could they do when no one would give them a single policeman or a single dollar? Would it be better to give up? Streit, New York *Times*, Nov. 30. See also correspondence of Nov. 25–30, *Official Journal*, pp. 2529–32.

[93] See pp. 208–9, below, for comparison of the Dec. 10 resolution with the draft of Nov. 25.

League leaders apparently took too much for granted when Japan proposed that a Commission of Inquiry be sent to China, it was stated in authoritative quarters yesterday, and have allowed themselves to be induced by China to modify the original proposal so much that it is now inacceptable to Japan. Observers added that it must be remembered Japan has always been opposed to intervention by the League and *intended the inquiry proposal as a gesture to help the League partially to save its own face and not as a measure towards a League of Nations solution of the problem,* which Japan still maintains can be solved only through direct negotiations between Japan and China.[94]

An editorial from the daily edition of December 2 (reprinted in the issue of December 10) concludes with these words:

> Too much must not be expected of the Commission of Enquiry. Its scope is limited and the League Council itself can expect little more of it than a report, which by the time it is made, it is hoped, may be superfluous. The Commission is to afford a palliative to China and a back door escape for all the rest.
>
> Japan will emerge from the League Council with her main thesis intact, free to negotiate directly with China whenever China is prepared to talk, without the intervention of a third party.[95]

The prediction, unfortunately, proved all too accurate. One comment from the nationalistic *Ji-Ji* is interesting, considering the stubborn opposition of Yoshizawa to a commission of enquiry in September:

> It is high time an inquiry were made into the true situation in Manchuria and other parts of China. It is unfortunate the League did not see fit to send an Enquiry to China when such an investigating body was suggested by Japan some time ago.[96]

The liberal *Asahi* is more reasonable, but even this paper takes exception to three clauses of the tentative resolution: to the clause asking for withdrawal of troops as soon as possible "because of course Japan will do this"; to the clause binding the parties to refrain from action causing further bloodshed, as this would prevent action against bandits and outlaws; and to the appointment of a commission to investigate the Manchurian question

---

[94] Italics mine.   [95] *Trans-Pacific,* Dec. 10.   [96] *Ibid.*

in order to contribute to a fundamental solution of the conflict. It is obvious that the Council, under the article of the Covenant on which its deliberations are based, has no power to solve the dispute. If it wishes to settle the dispute, it must act under Article 15 of the Covenant. This article has not been involved.[97]

Although the drafting committee, assisted by the parallel efforts of Ambassador Dawes, worked hard, it was not possible to iron out all the difficulties and up to a short time before the public meeting of December 9 there was no assurance that either of the parties would accept the resolution. Since no agreement could be reached on the question of the neutral zone around Chinchow that matter dropped entirely so far as formal action by the Council was concerned, but frequent references show it was not forgotten.

The third public meeting of the Council [98] was of short duration. The President read the draft resolution and his declaration concerning it. The meeting was then adjourned until the next day at the request of Mr. Yoshizawa who had not yet received final instructions from his government.

The draft resolution follows.

The Council,

(1) Reaffirms the resolution passed unanimously by it on September 30th, 1941, by which the two parties declare that they are solemnly bound; it therefore calls upon the Chinese and Japanese Governments to take all necessary steps to assure its execution, so that the withdrawal of the Japanese troops within the railway zone may be effected as soon as possible under the conditions set forth in the said resolution.

(2) Considering that events have assumed an even more serious aspect since the Council meeting of October 24th,

Notes that the two parties undertake to adopt all measures necessary to avoid any further aggravation of the situation and to refrain from any initiative which may lead to further fighting and loss of life.

(3) Invites the two parties to continue to keep the Council informed as to the developments of the situation.

(4) Invites the other members of the Council to furnish the Council with any information received from their representatives on the spot.

[97] *Ibid.*
[98] See *Official Journal*, pp. 2374–76, for full account of meeting and text of the resolution.

(5) Without prejudice to the carrying out of the above-mentioned measures,

Desiring, in view of the special circumstances of the case, to contribute towards a final and fundamental solution by the two Governments of the questions at issue between them;

Decides to appoint a Commission of five members to study on the spot and to report to the Council on any circumstance which, affecting international relations, threatens to disturb peace between China and Japan, or the good understanding between them upon which peace depends.

The Governments of China and Japan will each have the right to nominate one assessor to assist the Commission.

The two Governments will afford the Commission all facilities to obtain on the spot whatever information it may require.

It is understood that, should the two parties initiate any negotiations, these would not fall within the scope of the terms of reference of the Commission, nor would it be within the competence of the Commission to interfere with the military arrangements of either party.

The appointment and deliberations of the Commission shall not prejudice in any way the undertaking given by the Japanese Government in the resolution of September 30th as regards the withdrawal of the Japanese troops within the railway zone.

(6) Between now and its next ordinary session, which will be held on January 25th, 1932, the Council which remains seized of the matter invites its President to follow the question and to summon it afresh if necessary.

A comparison of this resolution with the tentative draft made public on November 25 and the points of difference remaining at that time [99] shows clearly that, contrary to the general opinion, the Japanese had won a significant diplomatic victory. China had given up her "vital demands" for immediate suspension of hostilities and a fixed date for the withdrawal of Japanese troops within the railway zone and was not even conceded the minor triumph of retaining in paragraph (1) the clause, "a point to which the Council attaches the utmost importance" in connection with that withdrawal. On the other hand, although Japan received no sanction for carrying out police measures, her remaining major demands were granted: the removal from paragraph (2) of the direction to the two governments

[99] See pp. 200–201, above.

to instruct their commanders in the field to refrain from any further hostilities, and the specific exclusion in paragraph (5) of direct negotiations and intervention in military arrangements from the scope of the commission's competence.

True, the President of the Council in his declaration stressed the point omitted from paragraph (1) of the resolution and added that it was indispensable for the parties to refrain from any further fighting. It had become customary in Council procedure to omit from the resolution any important point on which unanimity could not be reached but to emphasize that point in the accompanying statement by the President of the Council. This was supposed to carry great weight, and Willoughby refers to Aristide Briand's declarations in the open meetings of the ninth and tenth as authoritative.[100] Authoritative they were in the sense that they gave the Council's interpretation of the resolution, but binding from the standpoint of obligations assumed they were not. The procedure had been generally successful in the past but unfortunately, as was the case with all efforts depending for their effect on moral force alone, it simply did not work with Japan. The President's declaration had no more effect on Japanese policy than had the defeated resolution of October 24. In discussing this phase of the situation Clarence Streit once warned the present writer, "Forget the declarations. Keep your eye on the resolution itself: it is the only thing that really counts." That is exactly what Japan did. Beyond the letter of the unanimously adopted resolutions of September 30 and December 10 she refused to go, and the letter, moreover, she interpreted according to her own interests.[101] Following this line of reasoning it may be argued that Japan's reservation on police measures had no more binding effect than the President's declaration. Granted. But there is this all-important difference: Japan now had complete control of the situation in Manchuria and could make good her reservation whereas the Council was helpless and had tied the hands of the Commission by the ban on intervention in the military arrangements of either party.

[100] Willoughby, *The Sino-Japanese Controversy and the League of Nations* (Baltimore, 1935), p. 178.   [101] See pp. 229–30, below, and notes.

The President of the Council in his declaration also dwelt on the Commission's terms of reference, which, "subject to its purely advisory capacity," were wide. To the express provisions of the resolution he added another point which China had tried to have included in the text—that it was the duty of the Commission to report to the Council as speedily as possible, if on their arrival in Manchuria they found the resolution of September 30 had not been carried out. But there is nothing in either the resolution or the declarations authorizing the Commission to report with recommendations.

When members and observers assembled at the Quai d'Orsay on December 10 for the final meeting of the 65th Council.[102] Mr. Yoshizawa, in a brief address, accepted the resolution on behalf of his government with the reservation that it was not intended to

preclude the Japanese forces from taking such action as may be rendered necessary to provide directly for the protection of lives and property of Japanese subjects against the activities of bandits and lawless elements rampant in various parts of Manchuria.

Dr. Sze, having been forced to make the greater concessions in the drafting of the resolution, went to greater length in analyzing its text and in presenting the reservations of his government. There was a more important reason for this than the mere restatement, in a public meeting, of the Chinese views. China's juridical position was good, but her strategic position was bad. Therefore Dr. Sze felt that he must buttress the former, make it as strong as possible so that when the appeal was carried to the Assembly, as Dr. Sze intended it should be, he would not have compromised his country's case one whit. Only the more important of his reservations and comments need be summarized here.

China, he said, reserved all her rights under the Covenant of the League, which clearly pointed to the right of appeal under articles other than 11. He then analyzed the proposed settlement as having four essential and interdependent elements, the elimination of any one of which would destroy the integrity of the entire arrangement. These were: (1) immediate cessation of hostilities; (2) liquidation of the Japanese occupation of Manchuria within the shortest possible

[102] *Official Journal,* pp. 2376–83.

time; (3) the continuation of the system of reports by neutral observers; and (4) a comprehensive inquiry by the Commission. As to the Commission, he said China expected it to report "with its recommendations" if Japanese withdrawal had not been completed by the time it arrived in Manchuria. Very important was the reservation maintaining China's long-standing position with respect to the use of Japanese military forces *within* the railway zone.[103] Other reservations had to do with reparations and damages, police measures, and the artificial stimulation by Japan of so-called independence movements in Manchuria. No comment was made by other members on these reservations, but Lord Cecil and Salvador de Madariaga, who followed the Chinese representative, each attempted to offset the Japanese statement on police measures by pointing out that Japan would be bound by the terms of the resolution to use those measures only in extreme cases.

The resolution was then put to a vote and adopted unanimously, after which first the President of the Council and then other members expressed themselves regarding the action just taken. One thread runs through all the addresses: each speaker stressed the "exceptional" character of the situation in Manchuria and the "exceptional" nature of the settlement. No one of them was willing to accept the tacit recognition of military occupation of another country's territory on the grounds of self-defense or vital national interest—and this implication is inherent in the resolution—lest it set a precedent that might be used against his own country in some future case to come before the Council under Article XI. This "exceptional" quality is brought out in the resolution itself where the special circumstances in Manchuria are mentioned; it had been referred to by Cecil and Madariaga, and was emphasized by Briand in his survey of the situation and of the previous efforts of the Council which led to the adoption of this resolution.

The President followed the survey with a summary of the results so far obtained and those hoped for as an outcome of their work: The war which threatened had been averted, he said. Three months had been gained and this he thought was likely to bring about a

[103] While this was not an immediate issue it was almost sure to come up later.

calmer frame of mind and had already made it possible to create machinery for the local organization of peace. Both parties had agreed that neutral observers should be sent to the spot and this would supply the Council with valuable information which would be carefully examined. As to the future, if the Commission's work was to be effective it was "essential that no further incidents of any kind should take place." Briand closed by expressing confidence in the good faith and honor of the parties to the dispute, by thanking the members of the drafting committee for their valuable help and "the great Republic of the United States for having assisted . . . by means of parallel and incessant activities within the limits which it has itself determined."

Having listened with outward calm to the many references to the "exceptional character" of the situation and its settlement Dr. Sze rose and said quietly: "China cannot be expected to admit that the operation of treaties, covenants, and accepted principles of international law stops at the border of Manchuria."

The Council then went into brief private meeting after which the 65th session was declared closed by the President.[104]

AMERICAN COOPERATION.—As M. Briand's remark concerning "the parallel and incessant activities" of the United States would indicate, Mr. Dawes, during the first ten days of December, had emerged somewhat from his hermitlike isolation at the Ritz, and on the eighth had made his third and last trip across the Seine.[105]

[104] It is impossible to give a full account of the Council meetings here, but some of the comments are extremely interesting and informative. Lord Cecil, in his second speech at the final meeting, warned both China and Japan not to destroy by any untoward act the work of conciliation on which the Council had so long been engaged. Salvador de Madariaga pointed out a lesson to be learned from the tedious process of the recent months; this conflict, he said, had proved the need for recasting as quickly as possible the methods available for dealing with all international difficulties. Herr von Mutius again stressed the fact that his country was particularly interested in the maintenance of the principle that "the Pacific settlement of disputes is and must remain the principal task of the League of Nations." Concurring with the other speakers as to the "exceptional nature" of the case and its settlement, the Latin American representatives seemed more concerned with possible developments in the Western Hemisphere than with the Sino-Japanese controversy.

[105] His second visit had been on November 20, the day before the second public meeting of the Council when Yoshizawa proposed the Commission of Enquiry.

This time he stayed all of half an hour, in the course of which he consulted with Sir Eric Drummond as well as with the President of the Council. No information was released as to the subjects under discussion, but League officials expressed themselves well satisfied with the results and it was taken for granted that Dawes had conveyed the Administration's approval of the draft resolution.

The extreme to which our representative had carried his isolation from the Council is indicated by the numerous stories and quips which went the rounds in Paris. Some, though not many, were malicious; none were important except as straws in the wind, but certainly none of them increased our stature in Paris.[106] This last visit of the Ambassador is not without its story which, whether true or not, is so apt that it bears retelling here:

Entering the French Foreign Office Mr. Dawes passed a distinguished member of the Council.

"Who is that man?" said the latter to a friend.

"Why, that's Dawes," was the reply.

"Well, I thought I had seen that face somewhere," remarked the questioner.[107]

As a matter of fact Mr. Dawes had been more active than the public realized: the chief difficulty lay not in the limitation of his activities so much as in the manner and methods followed. As one critic expressed it, he seemed to be in Paris not so much to consult with the members of the Council as with certain of its members. With Matsudaira and Sir John Simon, when the latter was in Paris, he conferred frequently, as he did with Dr. Sze. Arthur Sweetser, his official liaison with the League, he saw daily. Three visits in four weeks comprised his contacts with Aristide Briand, French Foreign Minister and President of the Council. Other members of the Council, including the representatives of Germany and Italy, he saw not at all. Of his work Clarence Streit says:

Informed circles are aware that Mr. Dawes has worked very hard all the time and has sought to back up the Council whenever he thought he

---

[106] "The United States is not represented by an isolationist this time but by a hermit." "While Mr. Dawes hesitated to cross the Seine, General Honjo crossed the Nonni."

[107] New York *Times*, Dec. 9, AP dispatch.

could, and certainly he has never worked against the Council. The only criticism one hears of him personally is that having never been in contact with the League before and not realizing how active a role Ambassadors Gibson and Wilson and other American diplomats had come to play in it, he has interpreted his instructions much more literally than Secretary Stimson probably intended and has thus given an impression of aloofness from rather than collaboration with.

The main weakness in this collaboration, however, is traced to the vagueness of his instruction on the root question of what the United States will do to make treaties respected in the showdown, and that is traced to the Senate.[108]

On the morning of December 10 it seemed for a time as if Mr. Dawes intended to break completely out of his shell and come before the Council table, but fifteen minutes before the hour fixed for the meeting he telephoned that he had changed his plans and would not attend. At the time he gave no reason for the change but in his *Journal* he tells the following story.[109]

On the night of December 9 (actually 2:00 A.M. of the tenth), in the course of a telephone conversation Mr. Stimson told Dawes he had just discovered that the limits of the neutral zone proposed by Japan had been determined by geographical considerations, that this was understood by both countries,[110] and he thought the matter should be brought to the attention of the Council. Mr. Dawes immediately transmitted the information and then, feeling that a statement clarifying the situation might have a desirable effect upon public opinion generally, decided to make a personal appearance before the Council, "coming into the meeting after the resolution had been passed and its actual business concluded, but before its adjournment." Thereupon, he worked out a statement which he submitted to Briand, Matsudaira, Robert E. Olds (representing Sze), and Sir Eric Drummond, all of whom agreed to it. Apparently he did not think it necessary to submit it to the State Department since such matters had been left to his discretion. However, about half an hour

[108] New York *Times*, Dec. 8.
[109] *The League and Manchuria, the Third Phase*, p. 72; Dawes, *op. cit.*, pp. 428–29.
[110] This probably refers to Japan's new demand that the line of the neutral zone be drawn west instead of east of Chinchow. See pp. 204–5, above.

before the Council was to assemble Mr. Stimson called again to ask how things were going and Mr. Dawes then told him of his intended appearance and read him the prepared address. Mr. Stimson, he says, recognized its importance

but his time for consideration was of necessity limited to our short telephone conversation. The Secretary suggested that Briand read the statement which I told him was impracticable. He felt that he did not have sufficient time to consider the matter, and without argument, I told him I would not make it.

Another version [111] is that Dawes had informed Stimson of his prospective speech and the latter called him back to say it would be better not to make it as the Chinchow situation was somewhat easier. Mr. Stimson, according to the story, expected the Ambassador to attend the Council meeting and express to that body the cordial cooperation of the United States, but the latter interpreted his instructions as meaning he was not to attend and canceled the arrangements. Still a third version,[112] unflattering to both the Administration and the Ambassador, charges them with keeping a weather eye open to the American political scene. Mr. Dawes, they say, expected to use this sudden appearance, the publicity value of which he fully realized, to make a grandstand play which would further the infant Dawes-for-President boom.[113] Naturally such a move would not find favor with the Hoover Administration and just as naturally Mr. Stimson's suggestion that the statement be read by Briand would not be acceptable to Mr. Dawes.

The statement which was the cause of all this flurry is included in the Ambassador's *Journal* as an "interesting recollection." It reads:

The patient labor of the Council has now resulted in an agreement of China and Japan to refrain from future aggression and for the appointment of a Commission. This agreement, if faithfully observed by both parties, may well lead to a final and peaceful solution of this difficult problem.

For the moment, through a misunderstanding alone, the discussion of a most promising effort of bringing about a cessation of hostilities be-

[111] Russell M. Cooper, *American Consultation in World Affairs* (New York, 1934), p. 229.
[112] *Ibid.*, footnote.   [113] New York *Times*, Dec. 4, 5.

tween China and Japan is in abeyance. The misunderstanding arose as follows: Dr. Wellington Koo discussed tentatively with certain foreign ministers at Nanking the cessation of hostilities between the armies and the mutual withdrawal of forces around Chinchow. This suggestion was not intended as a proposal to the Japanese Government but was made merely for the purpose of sounding out on the subject the Powers represented by the Ministers. This tentative suggestion of Dr. Koo, which he did not intend should be made to the Japanese Government, was conveyed to it in such way that Japan regarded it as a definite proposition. The Japanese Government then made a definite proposition embodying the idea, agreeing to be responsible to the League for its observance of its arrangement,[114] if made, and this was a chief factor in causing orders to be given for a retreat of its troops which were already advancing. As matters stand at present, therefore, the Japanese public have the impression that Japan has been misled into troop withdrawal, and China, having made its suggestion only for discussion, is in a position where if she orders troops to withdraw, the public impression in China is created that China has been coerced. The situation is this:

China, in good faith, made a constructive suggestion for discussion, which having been presented to Japan as a proposition instead of a suggestion, Japan then, in good faith, ordered a troop withdrawal.

An understanding of this situation by the public of both nations should make possible the further exploration of the original idea of Dr. Wellington Koo, and the consequent proposition of Japan for a mutually satisfactory arrangement for a cessation of hostilities around Chinchow and a redisposition of the respective forces to avoid the risk of conflict. The continuance of such a discussion involves no humiliating concessions by either of the nations, and will only emphasize the earnest desire of both for honorable peace.[115]

Had Mr. Dawes ventured forth from the Ritz when the controversy over the neutral zone around Chinchow was at its height and attended one of the many private meetings then being held by the Council to make such a statement, later giving it to the press as his considered opinion in the matter, it might have had some value if only as an indication of the desire of the United States to help in bringing about a cessation of hostilities. Inasmuch as there

[114] There is nothing in the Japanese proposition, as recorded in the League documents, to confirm this.
[115] *Op. cit.*, p. 430.

was nothing new or startling in the statement,[116] it is difficult to see what practical purpose could have been served by its formal presentation to the Council at so late a date as December 10 just prior to final adjournment. Rather, it might seriously have belittled the prestige of this country if our Ambassador had put in a sensational appearance at the last moment only to make a statement of so little significance. One can readily understand Mr. Stimson's reluctance to approve it. On the other hand had Dawes attended this last meeting and responded to the President's expression of thanks with even a few words of American support for the Council action, a great deal of embarrassment would have been avoided for all concerned, and an impressive demonstration of solidarity given the world. As it was, tongues wagged freely when, at almost the last minute, a flunkey hurried into the Council room and removed the place arranged for our representative; nor were they quieted when it was observed that at this closing meeting, as at the opening one, no American official was present either in the diplomatic or public section.[117]

Dawes left Paris the following day, refusing to comment on the Council's action of the tenth, and on his arrival in London said only that he was tired and intended to get a good rest.[118]

In Washington the Manchurian crisis was not the center of attention during the first two weeks in December. There domestic problems, both political and economic, held the stage. On December 7, the Congress elected in November, 1930, met and organized. Democratic members wrested control of the House from the Republicans, who had held it since 1920, electing the Speaker by the slim margin of 218 out of 430 votes. In the Senate there was a practical deadlock between the two major parties, with two farmer-labor members holding the balance of power. On the same day, representa-

[116] As a matter of fact it gives a very inadequate picture of the situation and fails to mention the very point concerning which Mr. Stimson called him the previous night.

[117] Perhaps this is what Mr. Stimson had in mind when he told Hugh Wilson it would have been better to have sent him to Paris, that it would have made less of a sensation. Hugh Wilson, *Diplomat between Wars*, p. 263; see also Chap. V, above, note 84.

[118] New York *Times*, Dec. 12.

tives of hunger-marchers who had converged on Washington from
many parts of the country were refused admittance to the White
House, and the entire group was kept at a distance by police armed
with tear gas. As was natural under the circumstances the President's annual message regarding the state of the Union, delivered
on December 8, was devoted largely to the many urgent problems
growing out of the deepening depression. Foreign affairs, on which
he touched only lightly at this time, were the subject of a special message on December 10, when he discussed the Manchurian crisis quite
briefly, considering the seriousness of the situation. Since, with the
exception of a bare reference to it in his message of December 8, this
is President Hoover's sole public statement on the subject while in office, it deserves careful attention and that entire section of the message is quoted:

> We have been deeply concerned over the situation in Manchuria. As
> parties to the Kellogg-Briand Pact and to the Nine-Power treaty we have
> a responsibility in maintaining the integrity of China and a direct interest
> with other nations in maintaining peace there.
>
> When this controversy originated in September the League of Nations
> was in session and China appealed to the Council [119] of that body which
> at once undertook measures of conciliation between China and Japan.
> Both China and Japan have participated in these proceedings before the
> Council ever since. Under the Kellogg-Briand Pact all of the signatories,
> including China and Japan, have covenanted to seek none but pacific
> means in the settlement of their disputes. Thus the ultimate proceedings
> under this section of the Kellogg-Briand Pact and of conciliation pro-
> ceedings of the League Covenant coincide. It seemed, therefore, both
> wise and appropriate rather to aid and advise with the League and thus
> have unity of world effort to maintain peace than to take independent
> action. In all negotiations, however, the State Department has maintained
> complete freedom of judgment and action as to participation in any
> measure which the League might finally be determined upon.
>
> Immediately after the outbreak of the trouble this government advised
> both China and Japan of its serious interest. Subsequently it communi-
> cated its view to both governments regarding their obligations under the
> Kellogg-Briand Pact. In this action we were joined by other nations sig-
> natory of the pact. This government has consistently and repeatedly by
> diplomatic representations indicated its unremitting solicitude that these

---

[119] Again there is no mention of the fact that China appealed to the United States
as well as the League. See pp. 28–29, 258.

treaties be respected. In the recurring efforts of the nations to bring about a peaceful settlement this government has realized that the exercise of the utmost patience was desirable, and it is believed that public opinion in this country has appreciated the wisdom of this restraint.

At present a resolution is pending before the meeting at Paris with hopes of passage under which Japan and China will agree to take no initiative which might lead to conflict; in which Japan has reiterated its intention to withdraw the Japanese troops to the railway zone as soon as lives and property of Japanese nationals in Manchuria can be adequately protected; and under which both nations agree to a neutral commission to meet on the ground, to which commission all matters in dispute can be referred for investigation and report.[120]

As the final draft of the resolution had been submitted to the Council on December 9 and published before the President's message was delivered to Congress, there would seem to be little excuse for the inaccuracy of the last sentence. Two major subjects of dispute—direct negotiations and military arrangements—were, as the President must have known, expressly excluded from the matters with which the Commission could deal. In one other respect the statement is inaccurate, at least by implication. When the President says that in communicating our views regarding the Kellogg-Briand pact "we were joined by other nations signatory to the pact," the inference is that we initiated the action. Just the opposite was the case: we waited three days before following up the action of those signatories to the pact who were also members of the League Council.[121]

In his Armistice Day speech of 1929 President Hoover had said: "Peace is not a static thing. To maintain peace is as dynamic in its requirements as is the conduct of war."[122] Yet that dynamic quality is utterly lacking in this review of the situation which he submitted to the Congress of the United States when it assembled for the first time after the crisis originated. Nor is there any suggestion of approval and support for the use of force which he and his collaborator, Hugh Gibson, infer we gave the Council at this time.[123] In the light

[120] W. S. Myers, ed., *State Papers of Herbert Hoover* (New York, 1934), II, 76–77.
[121] See Chap. IV.
[122] R. L. Wilbur and A. M. Hyde, *The Hoover Policies* (New York, 1937), p. 580.
[123] Hoover and Gibson, *op. cit.* See also Chap. V, above.

of the continued Japanese military excesses, of which there is no mention, the President's message is mild, to say the least. The stress which he placed on our complete freedom of judgment as well as the evidence of a general lack of initiative on our part must have been reassuring to the isolationists, while anyone who feared the crisis was serious enough to involve the United States must have been lulled into a sense of false security by this presentation of the matter. As a report to the nation on an international crisis of vital concern, the President's message was wholly inadequate.

More suited to the occasion was Mr. Stimson's statement of the eleventh, expressing the gratification of this government at the unanimous adoption of the resolution. Now, when it was too late, the Secretary spoke quickly, in marked contrast to his fatal delays at the close of the September and October meetings when immediate American support might have helped to stem the tide of Japanese aggression. The resolution, he stated, "represents a definite step of progress in a long and difficult negotiation which M. Briand and his associates have conducted with great patience." Concerning the American relation to the case he said,

This Government has from the beginning endeavored to cooperate with and support those efforts of the council by representations through the diplomatic channels to both Japan and China. Not only are the American people interested in the same objectives sought by the league of preventing a disastrous war and securing a peaceful solution of the Manchurian controversy, but as a fellow signatory with Japan and China in the Kellogg-Briand pact and in the so-called 9-power treaty of February 6, 1922, this Government has a direct interest in and obligation under the undertakings of these treaties.

The statement continues:

The present resolution provides for the immediate cessation of hostilities. It reaffirms the solemn pledge of Japan to withdraw her troops within the railway zone as speedily as possible. It provides for the appointment of a commission of five members to study on the spot and report to the council on any circumstance which disturbs the peace or affects the good understandings between China and Japan. Such a provision for a neutral commission is in itself an important and constructive step towards an ultimate and fair solution of this intricate problem presented in Manchuria. It means the application with the consent of both China and Japan of modern and enlightened methods of conciliation to the solution of the problem. The principle which underlies it exists in many treaties of conciliation to which the United States is a party and which have played in recent years a prominent part in the constructive peace machinery of the world. The operation of such a commission gives time for the heat of controversy to subside and makes possible a careful study of the problem.

The ultimate solution of the Manchurian problem must be worked out by some process of agreement between China and Japan themselves. This country is concerned that the methods employed in this settlement shall, in harmony with the obligations of the treaties to which we are parties, be made in a way which shall not endanger the peace of the world and that the result shall not be the result of military pressure. These are the essential principles for which the United States and the nations represented on the council have been striving and it is in itself a signal accomplishment that there has been arrayed behind these principles in a harmonious cooperation such a solid alignment of the nations of the world.

On the other hand the adoption of this resolution in no way constitutes an indorsement of any action hitherto taken in Manchuria. This Government as one of the signatories of the Kellogg-Briand pact and the nine-power treaty, cannot disguise its concern over the events which have there transpired. The future efficacy of the resolution depends on the good faith with which the pledge against renewed hostilities is carried out by both parties and the spirit in which its provisions directed toward an ultimate solution are availed of. The American Government will continue to follow with solicitous interest all developments in this situation in the light of the obligations involved in the treaties to which this country is a party.[124]

Addressed primarily to the American people this statement may be construed as the first step in that process of educating public opinion which the Secretary at long last felt must be undertaken.[125] With this in mind several of Mr. Stimson's points must be carefully considered.

In one respect at least, the statement marks a step forward both in enlightening public opinion and in defining the State Department's attitude regarding our treaty commitments. In his opening paragraph the Secretary acknowledges for the first time that the

[124] *Conditions in Manchuria,* pp. 46–47.   [125] Stimson, *op. cit.,* pp. 73, 91 ff.

United States has not only an interest in the settlement of the Manchurian crisis but an *obligation* as a signatory of the Kellogg-Briand Pact and the Nine Power Treaty to assist in bringing about that settlement. Together with President Hoover's reference on December 10 to our "responsibility in maintaining the integrity of China" and our "direct interest in maintaining peace there" this constitutes the only public and official recognition by the Hoover Administration that we had any obligation whatever in this matter.

Summarizing the provisions of the resolution he again fails to point out, or perhaps to realize, the weakness of the clause on suspension of hostilities, for he says again, as he did in discussing the tentative draft published November 25, that it "provides for the immediate cessation of hostilities." Actually the resolution makes no reference to this. And "the solemn pledge of Japan to withdraw her troops as speedily as possible," if it can be called a pledge at all, is so qualified by the clause regarding the protection of lives and property as to give that country all the leeway necessary to do as she pleased in Manchuria. The whole course of events since September 30 when the "pledge" was first given should have made that abundantly clear to Mr. Stimson, and this knowledge he should have passed on to the American people. Likewise, in his last paragraph he refers to the "pledge against renewed hostilities." There may be some question as to whether the clause in question can be construed as a pledge but there can be no doubt that its strength was effectively vitiated by the Japanese reservation as to police measures.[126] Of this, however, Mr. Stimson takes no notice. Aside from misleading the American people into thinking the resolution stronger than it was, none of this matters very much. The real damage was already done—when the small powers and China failed in their attempt to arouse public opinion on these very points late in November.[127]

Discussing the appointment of the Commission, Secretary Stimson makes another mistake when he says, "It means the application with the consent of both China and Japan of modern and enlightened methods of conciliation to the solution of the problem." Unfortunately this was not a commission of conciliation and mediation but

[126] For text of the resolution see pp. 207-8, above.　　[127] See p. 201, above.

purely a fact-finding body, both in the literal meaning of the text of the resolution and so far as Japan was concerned. And Japan was determined that neither the Commission nor the League should have anything to do with the final settlement of the problem. That was to be between Japan and China alone without "the interposition of third parties."

The last two paragraphs are directed as much to Japan and China as to opinion in this country, and the last one, in particular, with its specific refusal to indorse what had already taken place in Manchuria points the way toward the famous declaration of January 7. Yet it was not until December 24 when there was again danger of a move on Chinchow that the Secretary of State addressed himself directly to the government of Japan. In this note [128] he expressed his apprehension over the situation in Manchuria where, according to reports from American military observers, there was no evidence that the Chinese were engaged in any offensive movement. He followed this with a formal statement of American approval "of the substance and the letter" of the resolution of December 10, concluding with this excerpt from his statement of the eleventh:

The future efficacy of the resolution depends upon the good faith with which the pledge against renewed hostilities is carried out by both parties and the spirit in which its provisions directed toward an amicable solution are availed of.

The Japanese answer [129] to this, received on December 27, defends the Japanese position, refers to the reservation made by Yoshizawa—now Foreign Minister in the new Cabinet—as to police measures against bandits, and justifies its action around Chinchow on this ground. At the same time it affirms the Japanese Government's loyalty to the League Covenant and other antiwar treaties to which it was a signatory. As neither of these communications was made public the process of informing American public opinion was not thereby advanced.

No more fitting words can be found to conclude this story of the efforts of the 65th Council of the League and of the United States than Mr. Stimson's own:

[128] *Conditions in Manchuria*, p. 48.   [129] *Ibid.*, p. 49.

Thus the efforts at conciliation faded away, leaving only two definite constructive accomplishments. One was the new clear precedent of frank outspoken American cooperation with the League in a case affecting the general peace of the world. The other was the appointment with Japan's consent of an international commission of inquiry upon a vital Far Eastern problem. Each of these was in its way an accomplishment of signal importance.[130]

Whether or not we can agree with Mr. Stimson's characterization of American cooperation with the League a brief review of the events after December 10 will prove the truth of his statement that efforts at conciliation had faded away.

[130] Stimson, *op. cit.*, p. 84.

VII

ANTICLIMAX

IT IS THE THESIS of this book that the final outcome of the Sino-Japanese controversy before the League Council was determined in the fall of 1931 and all that occurred thereafter was merely carrying the tragedy to its logical and inevitable conclusion. Even as late as December 10, however, there were still two possible turns the denouement might take: Japan could still be stopped by force—by war resulting either from an ultimatum on the part of the Western powers or from the joint imposition of sanctions by the League and the United States; or her aggression against China would be carried to a successful and unobstructed end. The possibility of a peaceful settlement based on the maintenance of treaty obligations and respect for China's territorial and administrative integrity no longer existed. There are those who think this possibility never had existed, that from the beginning Japan could have been stopped only by force. This may be a more accurate judgment than my own, but there are not many of these critics who would not now admit, to themselves at least, that war in 1931 would have been preferable to war in 1941, as it would have been fought with Japan alone and not at such terrific cost.

Be that as it may, since neither the Great Powers in the League nor the United States [1] had been willing to exercise anything more than moral suasion against Japan, the early months of 1932 saw this power sweep onward in her course to the complete flouting of her international obligations, to the final separation of Manchuria from China and to a new and more spectacular outbreak of violence at Shanghai. The last-named is outside the scope of this work; nevertheless, it brought Great Britain, the United States and others to act in concert for a time to stop Japan. And it should be pointed out

[1] This is equally true of Russia whose interest in the case has not been touched upon in this study.

that in the methods of mediation and conciliation used, particularly in the work of the commission of representatives set up on the spot to handle the affair, we have evidence of what might have been done with an equal degree of success in Manchuria had the same procedure been followed there from the beginning.

Indicative of the new conditions and problems with which Mr. Stimson says he was faced as the year ended [2] are the changes which took place in the governments of China and Japan within the week following the final session of the 65th Council. Significant also is the fact that within the same week came news of disorders between that Liao River and Chinchow, although that area had been quiet since the fiasco of November 30.[3] In the diplomatic field also there were important developments; the Commission of Enquiry slowly— very slowly—got under way; relations between the American State Department and the British Foreign Office were chilled by the unfortunate circumstances surrounding Mr. Stimson's nonrecognition note of January 7 and his subsequent letter to Senator Borah, Chairman of the Senate Foreign Relations Committee. China, convinced that the Council could, or would, do nothing more under Article 11, invoked Articles 10 and 15 and shortly after asked that her case be submitted to the Assembly, a special session of which was called for March 3, 1932.

The renewal of military activities in Manchuria may have waited until the Council members were safely out of Paris, but political developments in Tokyo did not. On December 11 the Minseito Cabinet fell and was replaced on the thirteenth by a Seiyukai Ministry with Takeshi Inukai as Prime Minister. To the Prime Minister's son-in-law, Kenkichi Yoshizawa, still in Paris, was entrusted the portfolio of Foreign Affairs [4] while General Araki became Minister of War. It is difficult to say just how greatly the Manchurian crisis contributed to this change of government. Certainly it played its part, but Mr. Inouye's inept handling of the financial situation was a de-

---

[2] Stimson, *Far Eastern Crisis* (New York, 1936), p. 87.   [3] Chap. VI, above.
[4] Hugh Byas expressed great surprise at the appointment of Yoshizawa, as the latter had been severely critized for his handling of matters in Geneva. Evidently his course had not been unsatisfactory to the military group. New York *Times*, Dec. 13; see also Introduction and Chap. IV, above.

termining factor and the attempt of Kenzo Adachi, Minister of Home Affairs, to form a super-party ministry added to the difficulties of Premier Wakatsuki and Foreign Minister Shidehara. Hugh Byas [5] attributes their fall to the financial set-up, and this is borne out by earlier accounts in both the Western and Japanese press.[6] *Trans-Pacific* in its December 17 issue says "the direct and apparently the only cause" was Adachi's insistence on forming a coalition government, but a contributed article in the same issue expresses the belief that an important factor was the Cabinet's "failure to exercise full control of and hearty cooperation with the younger element of the army." [7] Whatever the causes, the effect on the international situation was clear. Hallett Abend cabled from Mukden on the eleventh that the change would aid the army.[8] It also offers convincing evidence of the superficial effect of parliamentary procedure on political practice in Japan. The Minseito party still held in the Diet the majority they had won in the elections of May, 1930, and the Diet was not in session when the Cabinet fell. The Seiyukai, with its nucleus of financiers and industrialists, then came into power without a majority and without a Diet to give or withhold a vote of confidence. The lack of a majority was remedied by an election in February, 1932, but this did not prevent the Seiyukai from going the way of the Minseito three months later, nor did it save Mr. Inukai from assassination in May at the hands of the same group responsible for the death of Mr. Inouye in February. As a matter of fact the industrialists and financiers who made up the greater part of the Seiyukai did not wield the influence in the new regime which their numbers and wealth led them to expect, any more than did their counterparts in Germany in 1933; just as it was the young, radical, violent National Socialist element who furnished the driving power there, so in Japan this impetus was provided by the army and particularly by that group of younger officers [9] who had forwarded

[5] New York *Times*, Dec. 12.
[6] See articles and editorials in *Trans-Pacific*, Oct. 15, 29; Nov. 5, 26.
[7] *Ibid.*, Dec. 17. [8] New York *Times*, Dec. 12.
[9] Toynbee, ed., *Survey of International Affairs*, 1931 (London, 1932), Part V, pp. 408-32, furnishes material for further comparison of groups in Germany and Japan as well as an excellent discussion of National Socialist ideas in Japan.

the Manchurian outrage from the start,[10] who were largely responsible for the political murders of 1932, and who were now represented in the Cabinet by their champion, General Araki. It was clear from the beginning, as Mr. Stimson says,[11] that what the Minseito party could not do, the Seiyukai would not—that is, control the army.

The changes in China were neither so sudden, so disruptive, nor so lasting as those in Japan. The student riots and strikes which accompanied them and to which the Japanese pointed as proof of their contention that chaotic conditions and lack of control of her people deprived China of the right to be considered as a sovereign, independent power, were, it is true, violent symptoms of discontent and disorder, but not of any such deep-seated malady in the body politic as was evidenced by the long series of Japanese assassinations referred to above.[12] For some time negotiations had been in process between the rival Nanking and Canton governments, looking towards a consolidation of the nation and of the efforts to block Japanese aggression. Canton had insisted on the retirement of President Chiang Kai-shek as a prerequisite of collaboration. On December 14 the Nanking Government resigned, followed approximately a month later by the Cantonese, according to the agreement previously reached. In Nanking both Chiang and his brother-in-law, T. V. Soong, were out, but Wellington Koo, in spite of the student demonstrations against him, consented to remain in charge of the Foreign Office until a new government could be formed.[13] This was completed during the last week in December with both factions represented in important posts. Chiang Kai-shek, who had left Nanking on December 15 for his native village in Chekiang, did not, however, remain long out of power. The extension of Japanese military operations to Shanghai resulted in his return and on January 31, 1932, ap-

[10] Wilfrid Fleisher tells us that in September when the Cabinet sent Honjo instructions to withdraw his troops to the railway zone a group of these younger officers held up the message while another group forcibly detained the General until he agreed to pocket the instructions and proceed with the project.

[11] Stimson, *op. cit.*, p. 87.

[12] *Survey of International Affairs;* Stimson, *op. cit.*, pp. 87–88; Hishida, *Japan among the Great Powers*, pp. 281–82.

[13] Dr. Koo was succeeded by Eugene Chen of the Cantonese group, a bitter opponent of foreign privilege in China.

parently with the full consent of the Cantonese, he resumed his military authority. Even so early as this, "the China Incident" of Japanese expansion was pulling the Chinese people and rival political factions closer together, preparing them for the unbelievable efforts they were to put forth in the years after 1937.[14]

Even while the change of administration was taking place in Tokyo the Japanese began to lay the groundwork for their new military operations in Manchuria. On December 11 they submitted to the Secretary General of the League the first of a new series of statements protesting against the anti-Japanese boycotts throughout China and presenting evidence of widespread brigandage and disorders in Manchuria, Jehol, and Inner Mongolia.[15] On the twelfth, the Foreign Office issued a declaration on the Council Resolution, emphasizing Mr. Yoshizawa's insistence on the right to take "police measures" against bandits, the absence of a time limit for the withdrawal of troops, and the wide scope of the Commission of Enquiry. This was accompanied by comments in the Tokyo papers to the effect that the Council's action was a victory for Japan—as, indeed, it was.[16]

One week after the Council sessions closed there was ample evidence that a new offensive in southwestern Manchuria was in preparation, and, in spite of protests by the United States, Great Britain, France and the League Secretariat,[17] it was well under way by the closing days of the old year. On December 31 Chang Hsueh-liang announced his decision to withdraw within the Great Wall "in order to afford Japan no pretext for further aggression in North China," [18] and on January 3, after very slight resistance on the part of the Chinese forces, Chinchow was formally occupied by General Honjo's Manchurian army. The next day that part of Shanhaikwan which abutted on the outer face of the Great Wall fell into Japanese

[14] Political developments in China are well and thoroughly discussed in Part IV of *Survey of International Affairs,* 1931, and in Part V, 1932.
[15] *The League and Manchuria, the Third Phase* (Geneva Special Studies, Vol. II, No. 12, December, 1931, p. 81.
[16] Editorial from *Nichi Nichi* quoted in *Trans-Pacific,* Dec. 17.
[17] *The League and Manchuria, the Third Phase,* p. 86; *Survey of International Affairs,* 1931.
[18] *The League and Manchuria, the Third Phase,* p. 87.

hands and with it Shanhaikwan Pass. Since it was at this point that the Peking-Mukden Railway pierced the Wall, possession of the pass not only disrupted commercial traffic between China proper and the northern provinces but made it practically impossible for Nanking to send aid to Chinese forces in Jehol and Inner Mongolia.[19] Thus, as the new year began, Japan had found means and excuses for doing what the League and the United States had attempted to prevent—she had broken the last vestiges of resistance in the Eastern provinces and had compelled the Chinese forces to retire within the Great Wall, leaving all of Manchuria under the control either of the Japanese army or of officials subject to that army. Nor was this all. Japanese appetite improved with eating. As early as December 31, Hallett Abend reported Japanese officials in Mukden as saying openly that they would hold Manchuria, although Tokyo was still insisting Japan had no territorial ambitions there. Japanese newspapers like-wise had gone a step further and now contended that the Council Resolution amounted to a recognition of Japan's responsibility and right to keep order in Manchuria,[20] and some of them were begin-ning to talk of Japanese rights in Jehol and Mongolia, never a part of Manchuria and certainly far removed from the railway zone. By the middle of January there were reports of new military action under contemplation, this time to the north against Harbin, definitely within the Russian sphere of influence. Late in the month an expeditionary force was sent to the aid of their Manchu parti-san, General Hsi Hsia, and on February 5 Harbin was occupied, thereby putting a further strain on Japanese relations with the U.S.S.R.[21]

The swiftness with which the Japanese army moved to consolidate its position in Manchuria so that it was able to confront the Com-mission of Enquiry on its arrival there with a situation it was helpless to remedy was in marked contrast to the many delays with which that body started its work. On the 31st of December, three weeks after the resolution providing for it had been unanimously adopted

---

[19] *Survey of International Affairs*, 1932, p. 434.   [20] *Trans-Pacific*, January 7th.
[21] For discussion of Russo-Japanese relations see *Survey of International Affairs*, 1932, pp. 435–37.

by the Council, the British and American places were still vacant.[22] The French Government had announced the appointment of General Henri Claudel on December 20, followed two days later by that of Count Aldorovandi for Italy and Dr. Heinrich Schnee for Germany. It was rumored at this time that the Earl of Lytton would be the British member, but official announcement of his appointment was not made until January 7, two days later than that of Major-General Frank McCoy for the United States. Another week passed before the Commission was declared formally constituted by the President of the Council [23] and still another before the European members came together in Geneva.[24] There on the 21st of January, six weeks after the Council had adjourned, with Prentiss Gilbert substituting for General McCoy, they elected Lord Lytton President of the Commission and held preliminary discussions on their difficult problem, reviewing the data gathered for them by the Secretariat on treaties, railway rights, decisions of the Council, and so forth. It was decided, partly because of disturbed conditions on the Trans-Siberian, Chinese Eastern and South Manchuria railways and partly because of a desire to make some contact with American public opinion, to go East by way of the United States where General McCoy would join them. This meant a further delay and it was not until February 29, almost three months after the decision to send out the Commission and more than five since the case was taken before the Council, that the group reached Tokyo and began their investigations. By that time the fighting at Shanghai had reached alarm-

---

[22] And this in spite of the fact that both governments had expressed approval of the establishment of the commission some time before the resolution was finally adopted by the Council on December 10.

[23] *Official Journal*, February, 1932, p. 284; *The League and Manchuria, the Fourth Phase of the Chinese-Japanese Conflict* (Geneva Special Studies, Vol. III, No. 2, February, 1932), p. 11.

[24] *The League and Manchuria, the Fourth Phase*, p. 9; Willoughby, *op. cit.*, note 20, pp. 200, 201.

There was by this time considerable dissatisfaction among the small powers because of their omission from the investigating group. This feeling was ably expressed in a letter from the Polish delegation to the Secretary-General (Doc. C55 M.30. 1932. VII). The situation was recognized as unfortunate but it was thought to be the only possible course as Japan would not have accepted members who did not have considerable interests in the Pacific. The Netherlands, the only small power so placed, was not then a member of the Council.

ing proportions, the Chinese case had been appealed to the Assembly, which was about to meet in special session, and relations between the United States and Great Britain had been undergoing a most severe strain.

The now famous note of January 7 which caused this strain in British-American relations came more or less as a surprise to the outside world, but apparently it had been brewing in Mr. Stimson's mind for some time and was precipitated by the occupation of Chinchow on January 3. Although he gave no outward sign of it at the time, Mr. Stimson tells us that he suggested something along this line to his assistants as far back as November 9.[25] However, he seems still to have retained his trust in the right thinking of the Japanese people, in the Minseito Cabinet and its ability to control the army; for he says that after December 10 he was faced with new conditions and problems brought about largely by the change of government in Japan: hope of action within Japan on which American policy had been based throughout the autumn vanished when the moderate leaders were succeeded by men in sympathy with the military. "It was quite clear," he writes, "that a nation in Japan's present frame of mind must be left to dash her head against the hard, but slow-moving economic and social realities of the world." Nevertheless, while waiting for the realities to move [26] American interests were involved and must be protected.

There were three ways in which he thought our interests might be affected by trouble in the Far East:[27] by direct material damage to our trade and the less certain threat in the future to our own people and territorial possessions, by the blow to the cause of peace and prevention of war through permitting Japan to disregard and violate the post-war treaties she had ratified, and by immediate harm to American prestige in China and to our national interests there if we abandoned her to her fate when the covenants which we had helped to secure for her were violated. "The United States," said Mr. Stimson, "has made a good start in the development of China's friendship.

[25] Stimson, *op. cit.*, p. 93.
[26] But Mr. Stimson could not foresee that when they moved it would be at Pearl Harbor and that Japan and not the United States would set them in motion.
[27] See Stimson, *op. cit.*, pp. 87–91, for complete account.

It would have been the most short-sighted folly to turn our backs upon her at the time of her most dire need." But it must have looked to the Chinese very much as if we had done exactly that, when in September and October Mr. Stimson stressed our friendship and long cooperation with Japan on every possible occasion, never mentioning China or our interests there, and when for more than three weeks after the Mukden incident and China's subsequent appeals to the League and to the United States [28] Mr. Stimson did not personally receive the Chinese representative or hear his side of the case at first hand.[29] Mr. Stimson's words of 1936 and his actions of 1931 are scarcely compatible. He was right, however, when he characterized such an attitude as one of short-sighted folly. Folly it was, both as regards our prestige in the East, and the effect on Japan.

To meet the changed conditions and problems Mr. Stimson decided three steps were necessary:

First, the American people must be educated as to what it was all about.

Second, there must be an end to indecisive note-writing and at the same time Japan must be shown we had important rights involved and we proposed to stand on these without discussion.

Third, a way must be found to express the moral disapproval of the world, and, if possible, put behind it "a sanction which would bring pressure upon the party responsible to make amends." With every reason to know that economic and military sanctions would not be invoked he wanted to find a substitute which would carry the force and implication of a moral condemnation.[30]

As soon, therefore, as the Japanese army occupied Chinchow he "set to work upon the second step—the winding up of discussion by a final notice of our rights." [31] For this purpose he decided upon a restatement of the principle of nonrecognition used by William Jennings Bryan in 1915; but whereas with Bryan it had taken the form of an individual notification from the United States alone, Stimson saw the possibility of a much broader application if other nations would join us in the effort—the deterring influence of the doctrine

[28] See pp. 29, 85–86, 258.   [29] Chap. II, note 108.   [30] Stimson, *op. cit.*, pp. 91–92.
[31] *Ibid.*, p. 93.

would in this case be more powerful. The relations of the great powers with China had crystallized in the Nine Power Treaty "which placed the commercial rights of the signatory nations upon the far-sighted principle of respect for China's territorial and administrative integrity." This policy of "self-denial of aggression" had been reinforced by the Kellogg-Briand Pact and now

> if our warning should be so extended as to include non-recognition of the fruits of a violation not only of the treaties specifically relating to China, but also of the Kellogg-Briand Pact concerning the whole world, it would not only rest upon a more elevated and broader principle but it would appeal to a much larger number of nations in the world.[32]

It might even, Mr. Stimson thought, serve as a rallying point for the other nations and "as the substitute for sanctions for which we all had been groping." [33]

Having consulted his assistants in the Department and finding them in agreement with him, Mr. Stimson worked out two drafts, one along the narrower lines of the 1915 note, the other broad in principle and including the general obligations of the Kellogg Pact. These he laid before Mr. Hoover on the evening of January 4 and was delighted when the President without hesitation said, "I agree with you. Let us put it on the broad basis." [34]

The following day, January 5, the Secretary called in first the British, then the French Ambassador and to each in turn explained his position and read the draft note. Two days later, Thursday, January 7, he handed the identic notes to Ambassadors Debuchi and Yen,[35] after which copies were delivered to the representatives of the six other signatories of the Nine Power Treaty. The character and purpose of the note,[36] Mr. Stimson says, precluded any pre-

---

[32] *Ibid.*, p. 94.   [33] *Ibid.*, p. 95.   [34] See *ibid.*, pp. 93–97, for a full account.
[35] The latter had only recently arrived in this country, was received by President Hoover on the 8th and shortly after was instructed to proceed to Geneva to represent China on the 66th Council.
[36] Identic note sent by the American Government to the governments of China and Japan, January 7, 1932: *Conditions in Manchuria*, pp. 53–54; *War and Peace, United States Foreign Policy 1931–1941* (U.S. Dept. of State, 1945), pp. 159–60:
"With the recent military operations about Chinchow, the last remaining administrative authority of the Government of the Chinese Republic in South Manchuria, as it existed prior to September 18, 1931, has been destroyed. The American Government continues confident that the work of the neutral commission recently authorized by the Council of the League of Nations will facilitate an ultimate

liminary conference with other countries, but he hoped for their sympathetic understanding and perhaps immediate support. Particularly did he look for British cooperation, and as justification for this hope he points to that country's large commercial interests in China, to the close cooperation in naval and financial matters between the two governments in recent years, and to the Rapidan declaration of 1930 in which President Hoover and Prime Minister MacDonald had announced that their governments were resolved to accept the Kellogg-Briand Pact "as a positive obligation to direct their national policies according to its pledge." [37]

What Mr. Stimson apparently did not realize—and I know of no reason why he should have done so at that time—is that with the entrance of Sir John Simon into the British Foreign Office following the elections of October 27, 1931,[38] the whole picture was changed: the door was opened for appeasement and the support he might have received in the early weeks of the crisis could no longer be anticipated. Instead, he sustained one of the coldest public rebuffs it has ever been the lot of an American Secretary of State to receive at the hands of a friendly power. It was a stunning blow when on Monday, January 11, the London morning papers published the official communiqué of the British Foreign Office [39] backed

---

solution of the difficulties now existing between China and Japan. But in view of the present situation and of its own rights and obligations therein, the American Government deems it to be its duty to notify both the Government of the Chinese Republic and the Imperial Japanese Government that it can not admit the legality of any situation de facto nor does it intend to recognize any treaty or agreement entered into between these governments, or agents thereof, which may impair the treaty rights of the United States or its citizens in China, including those which relate to the sovereignty, the independence, or the territorial and administrative integrity of the Republic of China, or to the international policy relative to China, commonly known as the open-door policy; and that it does not intend to recognize any situation, treaty, or agreement which may be brought about by means contrary to the covenants and obligations of the pact of Paris of August 27, 1928, to which treaty both China and Japan as well as the United States are parties."

[37] Stimson, *op. cit.*, p. 100.   [38] See p. 7, above.

[39] This communiqué read as follows:

"His Majesty's Government stand by the policy of the open door for international trade in Manchuria, which was guaranteed by the Nine-Power Treaty at Washington.

"Since the recent events in Manchuria, the Japanese representatives at the Council of the League of Nations at Geneva stated on the 13th October that Japan was the champion in Manchuria of the principle of equal opportunity and the open door for the economic activities of all nations. Further, on the 28th December, the Japanese Prime Minister stated that Japan would adhere to the Open Door policy, and

by the even more specific editorial in the London *Times;* both the communiqué and the editorial [40] made plain a point of view radically different from that of the United States and offered encouragement to the Japanese to continue in their predetermined course of action.

Here, then, was tragedy. If Great Britain and the United States could not stand together to prevent aggression, particularly in a part of the world where the interests of both were involved, what possible combination of powers could be expected to do so? But the tragedy did not come like a bolt from the blue on January 11. Rather, the events of those days were a sort of delayed climax, the real crisis having occurred earlier, unnoticed by all but a few close observers. Like so many of the mishaps in international affairs of recent years, it was largely a matter of timing, of doing the right thing too late. If the United States or, to be more specific, Mr. Stimson had gone along with the Council at a time when the liberal elements in Great Britain were still strong, when the voice of Lord Cecil could still be heard and his influence felt in Geneva and London, if, on September 23 when the Council seriously considered setting up an investigating commission even against the wishes of Japan, he had pushed them on instead of pulling them back, there would have been at least a chance of effecting a peaceful settlement. Perhaps the British would have held back even then. Lord Cecil is reported to have told an American friend of the League that they were glad the United States had not pushed them. There can be little doubt that Simon and many of the permanent officials in the Foreign Office thought Cecil and Reading [41] had gone too far in support of the League and of China in October. But the implication is that if they

---

would welcome participation and co-operation in Manchurian enterprise.

"In view of these statements his Majesty's Government have not considered it necessary to address any formal note to the Japanese Government on the lines of the American Government's note, but the Japanese Ambassador in London has been requested to obtain confirmation of these assurances from his Government." (From *Survey of International Affairs,* 1932, pp. 541–42.)

[40] The theme of the editorial was that "in declining to address a communication to the Chinese and Japanese Governments on the lines of Mr. Stimson's note, the British Government have acted wisely." A pertinent passage which undoubtedly encouraged the Japanese was as follows: "Nor does it seem to be the immediate business of the Foreign Office to defend the 'administrative integrity' of China until that integrity is something more than an ideal. It did not exist in 1922, and it does not exist to-day." *The Times,* London, Jan. 11, 1931.

[41] Lord Reading's attitude is well described in an article by "Augur" in the New York *Times* of Oct. 26.

had been pushed they would have gone ahead. It was too late for this on January 7. All the moral support Great Britain could have given us then would not have been sufficient to persuade Japan to evacuate the vast spaces of Manchuria which her armies had overrun and retire to the narrow cramped zone on either side of the South Manchuria Railway. More than that she could not so retire and face her own people or the world; she had gone too far and could not now draw back except at the cost of the greatest national humiliation and, rightly or wrongly, any nation, any people worth its salt goes to war rather than eat such humble pie. No, the time had passed for peaceful settlement. British moral support of Mr. Stimson would have meant only so many more words—and there had been too many of these already—or it would have meant war.

None of what has just been written is intended as an excuse for the action of the British Foreign Office; the tone of the communiqué and of the *Times* editorial is not to be excused. The simple fact is that as we failed the Council—and Britain, since she was a member of that body—in September, so Britain failed us now. If Britain left us out on a limb in January, 1932,[42] we just as surely left the forces of conciliation and peace out on a limb in the fall of 1931.[43] But our offense, if offense there was on either occasion—shall we call it, rather, our mistake?—was the more serious, for in September and even in October of 1931 there was still, I believe, a chance to stop Japan without a great war resulting. In January, 1932, there was no such chance. And the road from Manchuria lead directly through Ethiopia to Spain, to Munich and Warsaw, and back across the Pacific to Pearl Harbor.

Mr. Stimson writes that the contents of the British communiqué "were such as to be taken by most readers, including—what was most important—the Japanese, as a rebuff to the United States," [44] that Japan was quick to take advantage of this assurance of divided counsels, and that the tone of the Japanese note of January 16 gave evidence of this reinforcement to the Japanese cause and seemed to paraphrase the very words of the *Times* editorial. He gives no sign, however, that he ever realized that Japan had followed a similar

[42] Actually we had no business going out on that limb without assurance of support.
[43] For our failure in these cases see pp. 45 ff., 122 ff., above.
[44] Stimson, *op. cit.*, p. 101.

course throughout the previous autumn. Then it was Mr. Stimson's sympathetic attitude which stiffened Yoshizawa's defiance of the Council [45] and Mr. Stimson's words which the Japanese representative at Geneva, now the Foreign Minister and author of the note of January 16, seemed to paraphrase. Undoubtedly the British rebuff did lead Japan to believe the United States was without support in advancing the nonrecognition doctrine as a sanction against aggression. It also destroyed much of the effect of previous Anglo-American cooperation in the Orient, and subsequent collaboration at Shanghai could not undo this damage. But the responsibility for the failure to stop Japan must be divided between the United States and Great Britain.[46] It was the hesitation of both governments which led to the success of this attack against the system of pacific settlement of disputes set up by the post-war treaties. Equally, the greatest possible hope for preventing aggression in the future is for these two great powers to stand together, preferably within the framework of an international organization which will eventually include all other peoples, but, whatever comes, together. The most portentous result, therefore, of this drama of errors lay not in the failure to stop Japan—that crime had already been committed—but in the misunderstanding, the strained relations between the two governments and, more serious still, in the seeds of distrust, suspicion, and misinterpretation sowed in the minds of the people of the two countries. These bore bitter fruit in later years when we and the British failed to work together in the Orient. Japan, always quick to learn her lessons at the hands of her Western tutors, had lost no time in taking advantage of the divided counsels which existed almost from the start, playing up first to the United States and then to Great Britain. From this time on she played her game more openly and more brazenly, as evidenced by the almost incredible incident which took place in Mukden early in January, the beating of an American Consular official by Japanese sentries, and by the thinly veiled insolence of Mr. Yoshizawa's reply to the note of January 7.[47]

[45] See p. 47, above. [46] R. L. Buell, *Isolated America*, p. 61.
[47] For a caustic British comment on both the Foreign Office communiqué and the Japanese note see *Survey of International Affairs*, 1932, pp. 542–46.

It is not our intention to make a study of the note as an important document in international affairs—that has already been done by acknowledged experts in the field of international law—but to put it in its proper perspective as one phase of American participation in the case and to show that it was not at this point—that is, in the British failure to go along with us either in January or in February when Mr. Stimson made another attempt along the same lines—that the case was lost. We believe we have done this. There is, however, something more to be said on the subject, some bits of information which have been brought to the surface recently, some things which Mr. Stimson fails to tell us in his *Far Eastern Crisis*. None of these are particularly startling, none of them excuse the actions of the British Foreign Office, but they should mitigate the severity of our judgment and, above all, make us realize that the mistakes were not confined to one side.

In the first place Mr. Stimson acted hastily without giving the British government sufficient time for considering the matter. In the second place, the British Foreign Office did answer Mr. Stimson other than through the medium of the press.

According to Mr. Stimson's own account the note, which had been lying in his mind for so long, came with little advance notice to the British Government. The draft, it is recalled, was read to Sir Ronald Lindsay on the fifth and a copy handed to him for transmission to his government on the seventh, *after* the notes had been delivered to the Chinese and Japanese representatives. There seems to have been no delay on Sir Ronald's part, for a message was transmitted to the Foreign Office the same day explaining Mr. Stimson's idea and his desire to obtain British cooperation in this step.[48] While this was still being studied in London the note was delivered to the governments of China and Japan through their representatives in Washington and made public.[49] This action seems to have come as a surprise to the British Foreign Office. After all, from the fifth to the seventh is not a very long time for consideration of the many angles involved in any departure from traditional policy. Non-

[48] Letter from Sir John T. Pratt, formerly of the British Foreign Office, the London *Times*, Nov. 30, 1938.
[49] *Ibid.*

recognition was more or less in the tradition of American policy in the Far East but it certainly was not in that of Great Britain. Was it not somewhat unreasonable then to expect the British to fall in immediately with our ideas? Since September we had been insisting, almost *ad nauseam*, on our own independence of judgment and action. Now we wanted others to follow us practically overnight and without prior consultation. Moreover, was it wise to put ourselves in a position to be caught out on a limb? Even though the note was to be regarded primarily as a statement of American policy would it not have been better to hold off long enough to sound out thoroughly the attitude of the other signatories of the Nine Power Treaty? This was the first time the treaty had been invoked, even by inference,[50] and we were not the only ones concerned. What reason had we to complain if, in our earnest desire to rebuke Japan immediately after her occupation of the last truly Chinese stronghold in Manchuria, we acted so quickly that others had not had time to decide on their course of action? As a matter of fact, it has not been Mr. Stimson who complained so much as some of our self-appointed interpreters, journalists, and radio commentators, who have lost no opportunity to play up British failure to cooperate at this point until it is the one thing the vast majority of Americans remember about the whole affair.

This misinterpretation is perhaps due in part to another basic misunderstanding which Sir John Pratt attempted to clear up in his letter of November 30, 1938. In the British Foreign office, he explains

the note was interpreted as an attempt to circumscribe any advantage that Japan might gain—but only so far as these advantages might trespass on American interests. The note had not at that time become invested with the significance which, because of its subsequent history, became attached to it.[51]

Then, after discussing in some detail the reasons for their decision, he states flatly that: "An official reply was accordingly sent to Mr. Stimson on January 9th [52] explaining that her position as a member of the

---

[50] Although Mr. Stimson does not specify the Nine Power Treaty there has never been any doubt that this was the treaty concerned.   [51] The London *Times*.
[52] This was Saturday and government offices in both London and Washington customarily closed for the afternoon.

League precluded Great Britain from sending a note on the lines suggested." Neither at the time nor in his *Far Eastern Crisis* did Mr. Stimson give any hint that he was informed of the British position other than through the official communiqué published on the eleventh. Because of the customary week-end closing of government offices both in London and Washington it is very likely that he did learn of it first through the medium of the press, but much of the sting could have been taken from the blow had he let it be known that the British Government had informed him of its decision in advance; better still would it have been to publish the British reply, which in all probability held less encouragement for Japan than the unfortunate communiqué.[53]

Concerning the latter Sir John Pratt writes:

> Mr. Stimson does not complain of the British refusal to write a similar note. . . .
>
> What he does complain of—and with good reason, is the Foreign Office Communique of January 9th published in the Press of January 11th. I am not revealing any very closely kept secret when I say that the Foreign Office have never attempted to defend the communiqué and have always regretted that a slip was made which has, it would seem, proved a real obstacle in Anglo-American relations. The communiqué was drafted and approved in haste by permanent officials at 1 o'clock on Saturday and it was not realized until it appeared in the press on the following Monday that it read like a rebuff to America.[54]

British failure to support the note was followed by similar lack of action on the part of France and the other signatory powers but on the 28th of January and again on February 16 the neutral members of the Council—the Twelve—expressed themselves in a declara-

---

[53] It is worth noting here that the State Department's construction of the note as given in the New York *Times* of January 8 is quite in line with Pratt's statement of the British Foreign Office interpretation. Also it may be said that the Secretary should have been forewarned as to the British position by a dispatch from London in the same paper on January 9. The latter said in part:

"It is generally felt in the British capital that the United States cannot expect the co-operation of the National Government in the sense that Great Britain will take independent action similar to that of the United States. . . .

"At the same time messages from Washington late to-day showed that what had at first appeared to the British to be a direct challenge to Japan was merely an action assertive of American rights to the maintenance of the Open Door in China."
[54] *Op. cit.*

tion along the lines of Mr. Stimson's note,[55] while on March 11 the Assembly unanimously [56] adopted the nonrecognition resolution introduced by Sir John Simon.

In Shanghai, meanwhile, events had followed their violent course and in February Mr. Stimson was again constrained to seek cooperative action. Briefly, it came about in this fashion.[57] On January 31 the Japanese, alarmed by the situation into which they had been thrown by Admiral Shiozawa's indiscreet attack on Chapei, requested the United States, together with other powers, "to use its good offices to induce the Chinese troops not to bring up reinforcements and to withdraw the troops now in Shanghai to a safe distance to avoid clashes." [58] In concert with the British and with the concurrence of the French and Italian governments, a plan for the cessation of hostilities [59] was drawn up and presented to both parties to the conflict on February 2. This tender of good offices was promptly accepted by the Chinese. The Japanese, however, "curtly rejected" two of the five points and so qualified their acceptance of the other three as "to deprive them of any substantial value." [60] President Hoover thought the Japanese note should be answered but Mr. Stimson decided against this. The Secretary of State felt that it was useless to reopen "the note-writing contest" unless he had "some new and constructive rejoinder to make." Things took a slightly different turn, however, on February 8, when the Japanese came out with "feelers" looking toward the establishment of demilitarized zones around the principal Chinese ports [61] as well as the demilitarization of Manchuria. Demilitarization to the Japanese meant, of course, no Chinese arms or fortifications. The Foreign Office spokesman,

[55] The statement of Jan. 28 was presented to the Council on the 29th in somewhat modified form by its President, M. Joseph Paul-Boncour, while that of February 16 was a formal appeal addressed to Japan alone.
[56] China and Japan abstained from voting.   [57] Stimson, *op. cit.*, pp. 145–50.
[58] *War and Peace*, Document 6 (793, 94/3902d), pp. 160–61. Ambassador Matsudaira remarked to Hugh Wilson that the action of the Chinese in bringing reinforcements into South Station, Shanghai, by armored train was "indiscreet, very indiscreet." Wilson, *Diplomat between Wars*, p. 149.
[59] *War and Peace*, loc. cit.
[60] Stimson, *op. cit.*, p. 149. The Japanese reply is quoted from Willoughby, *op. cit.*, pp. 320–21. It seems entirely in keeping with Mr. Stimson's policy of not letting one's right hand know what the left was doing that he should cite Willoughby for a state paper received when he was in office.
[61] Reuters dispatch quoted in Stimson, *op. cit.*, p. 157.

says Mr. Stimson, was reported to have admitted "that such a proposal was contrary to the Nine Power Treaty but that ten years' trial had proved the ineffectiveness of the policy which it laid down and that the only policy that could result in benefit to China as well as to foreigners was a policy of intervention." [62] This gave Mr. Stimson his "something constructive" on which to work, the idea that now the Nine Power Treaty might be formally invoked by the United States and Great Britain and Japan brought to a conference table with the signatory powers.[63] On February 9, having broached the matter to the President, who agreed, he consulted with the British Ambassador. On the eleventh, at Mr. Hoover's suggestion, he called Sir John Simon in Geneva [64] and explained his idea fully and at length. On February 12 he talked with Simon again, and at the latter's request cabled him the tentative draft of a statement which he proposed they jointly send Japan.[65] Sir John was returning to London on the 13th and would take the matter up with the Prime Minister. The obstacles did not seem insuperable to the Secretary but the same train of mishaps which had beset his course in January again dogged his steps. He talked with the British Foreign Minister in London on the thirteenth and again on the fifteenth, apparently getting no satisfaction from him for he tells us that

while no explicit refusal to my suggestion was ever made, I finally became convinced from his attitude in those conversations that for reasons satisfactory to it, and which I certainly had no desire to inquire into or to criticize, the British government felt reluctant to join in such a demarche. I therefore pressed it no further.[66]

It is at this point that misunderstanding seems to center. Hugh Wilson, who had returned to his post as Minister to Switzerland and was then in Geneva for the Disarmament Conference, has this to say:

. . . It was at this period that the incident occurred which has been so much publicized and on account of which the American public is so

---

[62] Stimson, *op. cit.*, p. 158.   [63] *Ibid.*, pp. 160–61.
[64] He was there for the meeting of the Disarmament Conference, the opening session of which on February 2 had had to be postponed for two hours, so that the Council could meet and discuss the Shanghai situation.
[65] *War and Peace*, Doc. 8, pp. 164–68.   [66] Stimson, *op. cit.*, p. 164.

ready to accuse the British Government of having been unwilling to act vigorously. . . . Mr. Stimson and Sir John Simon were in constant telephone communication; and in my frequent encounters with Sir John he would tell me what had taken place on the telephone. . . .

One day Sir John told me of the talk which he had with the Secretary of State in Washington. Sir John was perturbed. Mr. Stimson had suggested taking such vigorous action that Sir John felt it might lead to the use of the American and British fleets to enforce it. He added that the British public was in no state of mind to support a war in such a remote region . . . [and] he questioned whether the American public would not also be reluctant to assume such a risk.

It became clear subsequently that the Secretary of State in Washington understood that he had met with a definite refusal, or rather with such dilatory cooperation as to constitute a refusal in fact, and considerable acrimony developed later in the press of the two countries on the failure of the British Government to give thorough going assistance to the American Government in a matter of such importance to the peace of the world.[67]

Mr. Wilson concludes his account with this observation regarding telephone diplomacy:

However, it seemed to me then as now that the telephone between two responsible statesmen is a method of communication which is fraught with danger. Few men in the world are able to think rapidly enough and accurately enough in matters involving war and peace to take the immediate decisions that a telephone conversation calls for. Messages of this importance should be carefully drafted, experts in both Foreign Offices should go over them thoroughly, they should be so formulated that their meaning is precise and clear and offers no basis for subsequent misunderstanding. The danger of a few hours delay in sending a written message is incomparably less than the risk of a misunderstanding arising between the Foreign Ministers of two great nations.[68]

In this instance also Sir John Pratt refutes the charge that no answer was made to Mr. Stimson and denies that the British Government failed to "go along" with the Secretary of State in his proposal for a joint invocation of the Nine Power Treaty. His story is that

on receiving the draft of Mr. Stimson's proposed joint invocation the Foreign Office telephoned to Geneva a paragraph containing the non-

---

[67] Wilson, *op. cit.*, p. 277.
[68] *Ibid.*, pp. 277–78. Mr. Stimson, as we have seen (p. 243), did prepare a draft which he sent to Mr. Wilson in Geneva for delivery to Sir John Simon.

recognition doctrine and this paragraph was embodied in the declaration issued by the twelve members of the Council on Feb. 16th, 1932. At the same time a written answer was handed to the American Embassy for transmission to Mr. Stimson stating that the British Government was most anxious to cooperate with America in this matter and that in view of their adherence to this declaration it was hoped that those League powers who were signatories of the Nine Power Treaty might also associate themselves with the proposed joint invocation. The Foreign Office so far from refusing to go along with Mr. Stimson did all they could to further his proposal. To obtain the concurrence of several Governments in a particular draft, is, however, always a cumbersome and sometimes a lengthy process. It is not in general the kind of procedure which commends itself to the State Department and Mr. Stimson preferred to drop the idea of a joint invocation and turn his draft into the letter from himself to Mr. Borah of Feb. 24, 1932.[69]

Several points in this account deserve comment and emphasis. In the first place it would appear, as Pratt indicates, that Mr. Stimson's memory deceived him when he implied that he received no definite answer from the British Foreign Office. Mr. Stimson's words, quoted above,[70] are that he received no explicit refusal but the reader unquestionably infers that there was no answer other than that given over the telephone. Second, granting that the action the British felt themselves able to take fell far short of what Mr. Stimson desired, there was certainly no delay in putting their decision into effect. Four days after Secretary Stimson had cabled his draft proposal to Hugh Wilson for delivery to Sir John Simon, the declaration of views and principles addressed to Japan alone[71] was adopted by the Committee of Twelve. During those four days, February 12 to 16, Sir John Simon had made the trip to London, presumably taking the draft with him, talked to Mr. Stimson from London on the thirteenth and again on the fifteenth, talked the matter over with the Prime Minister, drafted, either personally or through the permanent officials of his office, the paragraph on nonrecognition which was then telephoned to Geneva, where it was incorporated in the declaration of the sixteenth. In the third place, there is no good reason why Great Britain should not have insisted on action within the Council,

---

[69] Letter to the London *Times*, Nov. 10, 1938.   [70] See p. 243, above.
[71] See Stimson, *op. cit.*, pp. 145–50.

rather than apart from it. In fact, there would seem to be every reason why she should. Great Britain was, in the very nature of things, one of the mainstays of the League; she was a permanent member of the Council and the case was still in the hands of that body, to whose responsibility for initiating action Mr. Stimson had pointed again and again. Moreover, it was the constant fear of the smaller nations whose safety lay in the preservation of collective security through the League that the case might be taken out of its hands and a fatal blow struck at its prestige and its ability to function against a great power. Refusing to act at all through the earlier stages except in tardy recognition or lukewarm support of Council action [72] our State Department now appeared to be trying to hurry Great Britain into acting with us alone. However suspect the motives of Sir John Simon may be, the position of the British Foreign Office as regards its relations to the League was at least technically correct. Whitney Griswold says that Simon "would not step out from behind the constitutional shield which English membership in the League afforded him." [73] It can be said with equal truth that in the fall of 1931 Mr. Stimson would not push aside the screen provided by our nonmembership in that organization. Finally, as regards the propriety of the suggestion of the Foreign Office that the League powers who were also signatories of the Nine Power Treaty associate themselves with Great Britain and the United States in the invocation of that treaty, it should be recalled that this is exactly the procedure followed by our State Department when, in answer to M. Briand's suggestion for a treaty between the United States and France, Secretary Kellogg countered with the proposals which eventuated in the adoption and ratification of the Pact of Paris.

Mr. Stimson, however, was deeply discouraged over the outcome of his efforts and writes that he seemed doomed to inaction while a great tragedy took its course. On February 21 a solution occurred to him by which he might state his views on the Nine Power Treaty

[72] Mr. Stimson's words to the Council were always cordial and enthusiastic but his actions lacked the wholehearted support of that body necessary to make Japan feel the full force of the world's moral opinion. Great Britain's "backing" of Mr. Stimson now lacked the same element.

[73] Griswold, *Far Eastern Policy of the United States,* p. 431.

"without having them nullified by the doubts and fears of others": [74] following the example of Theodore Roosevelt he would write an open letter on the subject to Senator Borah. Directed to the Chairman of the Senate Foreign Relations Committee, the letter [75] was really intended for five unnamed addressees: to China it was meant to be a message of encouragement; to the American people an explanation of policy—inadequate and long overdue in this writer's opinion; to the members of the League, a suggestion of possible action the Assembly might take in the future; to the Conservative Party in Great Britain, a gentle reminder that they, through Salisbury and Balfour, were joint authors with us of the Open Door Policy and the Nine Power Treaty; and finally, to Japan a reminder that "if she chose to break down one of the Washington treaties" other nations might feel themselves released from some of those treaties which were as important to her as the Nine Power Treaty was to us.[76]

The suggestion [77] that the 1922 treaties were an interrelated, interdependent group was, of course, Mr. Stimson's "constructive rejoinder" [78] to the Japanese feeler of the eighth to the effect that it was time to do something about the Nine Power Treaty. As was to be expected, the reaction of the press and the Foreign Office in that country was immediate and violent.[79] The confidence of the Japanese Militarists in their ability to get away with the aggression against China and the violation of the Nine Power Treaty was based on the practical naval superiority in Asiatic waters conferred on them

[74] Stimson, *op. cit.*, p. 165.
[75] *War and Peace*, Document 9 (500A4D/203), pp. 168–73; also Stimson, *op. cit.*, pp. 166–67.
[76] See the *Survey of International Affairs*, 1932, pp. 548–51, for analysis of and favorable comment on the letter; and see Hishida, *op. cit.*, p. 307, for unfavorable comment.
[77] The statement referred to here reads: "The willingness of the American Government to surrender its then commanding lead in battleship construction and to leave its positions at Guam and in the Philippines without further fortifications, was predicated upon, among other things, the self-denying covenants contained in the Nine Power Treaty, which assured the nations of the world not only of equal opportunity for their Eastern trade but also against the military aggrandizement of any other power at the expense of China. One cannot discuss the possibility of modifying or abrogating those provisions of the Nine Power Treaty without considering at the same time other promises upon which they were really dependent." (Stimson, *op. cit.*, p. 171.)
[78] *Ibid.*, p. 161.   [79] New York *Times*, Feb. 26, 1932.

by the 5–5–3 ratio of the Washington treaty together with the agreement of the United States and Great Britain not to erect additional fortifications in their Far Eastern possessions. If these agreements should be modified by the other parties concerned, even by the United States alone, Japan's course would not look so bright, nor her course so easy. In the words of the naval spokesman in Tokyo, "it would be extremely serious for Japan if Mr. Stimson's note could be interpreted as meaning that the United States had resumed its right to fortify Guam." [80]

As to the motives and reasons back of Sir John Simon's introduction on March 7 of the nonrecognition resolution unanimously adopted by the Assembly of the League on March 11, Mr. Stimson suggests an explanation quite at variance with that of Sir John Pratt, but probably more in keeping with the general opinion of that astute politician who was the Foreign Minister of Great Britain. The story as Mr. Stimson tells it is substantially as follows: On March 4 he became greatly disturbed over reports indicating that the British government might not support such a resolution in the Assembly. Leadership in Geneva on matters of world-wide importance seemed confused and he decided that until this situation cleared up it would be just as well for us to "go a little slowly in our cooperation as to matters which seem" of much less general importance. Fighting at Shanghai had stopped on March 3. On March 4 our representatives there were instructed not to attend any more meetings of the Conference of Ministers until further notice. Mr. Stimson then informed Sir John Simon of what he had done and why. The latter replied to the message "with a cordial reassurance as to Britain's intentions in the Assembly and there was thereafter no further trouble." [81]

The incident which so upset Mr. Stimson seems to have been that of March 2, when Anthony Eden, then Under-Secretary of State

[80] *Ibid.* Arnold Toynbee, in the *Survey of International Affairs,* 1932 (p. 551), makes this pertinent comment: "Thus in Japanese minds and hearts, the sting went home and the question now presented itself whether the ultimate outcome of the Far Eastern Crisis would really be a liquidation of the whole settlement that had been achieved at Washington and a resumption of naval competition in the Pacific between the principal naval powers of the world."

[81] Stimson, *op. cit.,* pp. 177–78.

for Foreign Affairs, in reply to a question in the House of Commons as to whether the government approved the principles laid down in Mr. Stimson's letter, said it would be safer to assume that "we approve the statement to which we set our name with the other members of the Council." The statement to which Mr. Eden here refers is that of February 16 and the paragraph, which Pratt says was telephoned to Geneva by the British Foreign Office,[82] is as follows:

The Twelve Members of the Council recall the terms of Article 10 of the Covenant by which all members of the League have undertaken to respect and preserve the territorial integrity and existing political independence of all other members. It is their friendly right to direct attention to this provision, particularly as it appears to them to follow that no infringement of the territorial integrity and no change in the political independence of any member of the League brought about in disregard of this article, ought to be recognized as valid and effectual by the members of the League of Nations.[83]

On the same day that Mr. Eden in London was putting the government stamp of approval on the Council declaration, the Council itself heard an unexpectedly vigorous statement on the Shanghai situation from the British Secretary of State for the Dominions, substituting for Sir John Simon who was in London. The meeting had been called at the request of the British representative for the purpose of notifying the Council of the action taken by his government, "in concert with the Government of the United States of America," in response to the Japanese request for the use of their good offices; [84] and his statement stressed both the cooperation of the United States and the fact that the views of this government regarding violations of the Covenant, the Pact of Paris and the Nine Power Treaty were the same as those held by members of the League. Since both of these speeches—Mr. Eden's in London and Mr. Thomas's in Geneva—are more, rather than less, in support of Mr. Stimson's position it is a little difficult to understand just why he was perturbed at this particular time. It may be, however, that although it is the Under-Secretary whom he mentions [85] it was the

---

[82] See pp. 242, 245, above.
[83] *Official Journal*, March, 1932, pp. 383–84; *The League and Manchuria, the Fourth Phase*, pp. 51–52.
[84] See p. 242, above.   [85] Stimson, *op. cit.*, p. 177.

Minister whose words disturbed him, for Sir John also made an address in the House of Commons, on the same day and on the same subject as Mr. Thomas's in Geneva. The Foreign Minister's speech was nothing like so vigorous as that of Mr. Thomas, and although he did state that the proposals addressed to Japan and China "have been concerted with the United States Government" he made no mention of the violation of principles or provisions of the post-war treaties. It was, of course, well known even then that Simon had little more than lip service to pay to the League and the cause of collective security. Whatever the source of Mr. Stimson's depression his action was timely and brought the desired result—the incorporation of the principle of nonrecognition in the Assembly Resolution of March 11. The paragraph containing this statement is substantially as Sir John proposed it to the General Commission [86] on March 7. When the resolution was submitted to that body by the Drafting Committee on the morning of the eleventh reference to the Pact of Paris was omitted and it was Simon, supported by Politis of Greece, who insisted on its inclusion, and the draft was so amended before it went to the Plenary session of the Assembly late that afternoon.[87]

So far as this study is concerned, Mr. Stimson's letter to Senator Borah completes our story. Subsequent events are outside our province and only a few of these are needed to bring the loose ends together.[88] The United States continued its cooperation to the end: at

[86] This General Commission was set up by the Assembly at its second meeting on March 3 (*Official Journal*, Special Supplement 101, p. 25), and was in the nature of a committee of the whole since every state was or could be represented by one member. Its conclusions were, of course, not final. See Willoughby, *The Sino-Japanese Controversy and the League of Nations*, p. 284.

[87] The paragraph referred to reads: The Assembly "Proclaims the binding nature of the promises and provisions referred to above and declares that it is incumbent upon the Members of the League of Nations not to recognize any situation, treaty, or agreement which may be brought about by means contrary to the Covenant of the League or to the Pact of Paris."

[88] For a more detailed discussion of the case before the Assembly see Margaret Burton, *The Assembly of the League of Nations* (Chicago, 1941). Excellent shorter discussions are found in Cooper and in Fleming, both referred to elsewhere in this work. W. W. Willoughby's *Sino-Japanese Controversy* remains the most detailed and most thoroughly documented history of the entire case as dealt with by the League of Nations, while the six issues of the Geneva Special Studies (*The League and Manchuria*) devoted to the crisis furnish an invaluable contemporary record.

Shanghai, where a settlement was reached in May; with the Committee of Nineteen set up by the Assembly of the League for the handling of both the Shanghai and the Manchurian crisis,[89] and in the work of the Lytton Commission.

The Commission spent approximately five months in the Far East and submitted its report to the Council late in September. At the second meeting of the 68th Council on September 24, Japan requested that consideration of the document be postponed for six weeks in order that she might have time to study it and prepare her answer, so that it was not until the fifth meeting of the 69th Council on November 21 that it actually came before that body. After hearing detailed statements from Yosuke Matsuoka and Wellington Koo, Lord Lytton was asked to appear before the Council in order that it might be ascertained whether the Commission had anything to add to its report or wished to make any changes in the light of the statements made by the representatives of the parties to the conflict.[90] There being no changes and no additions, it was decided to send the Report together with the Minutes of the Council meetings to the Assembly in accordance with the resolution of March 11, without any general discussion in the Council. The latter seemed unnecessary since Council members would participate in the debates in the Assembly, where their votes, with the exception of the parties to the conflict, were necessary for the adoption of any resolution under Article 15.[91] Moreover, the statements of the Chinese and Japanese representatives [92] showed their governments to be so far apart that there was no prospect of the adoption of a resolution in the Council where unanimity, including the parties, was required.

The report came before the Assembly on December 6. After seven plenary sessions during which the small states participated in the debate more fully than previously, the matter was referred to the Committee of Nineteen for study and for the drafting of proposals

---

[89] Resolution of March 11, Sec. III. See *Official Journal*, Special Supplement 101, p. 98.
[90] This was done over the protests of Matsuoka who insisted that the work and the life of the committee ended when its report was submitted.
[91] Article 15, Sec. 10.
[92] *Official Journal*, December, 1932, No. 12, Part I, pp. 1870–90.

"with a view to the settlement of the dispute." [93] The report [94] of the Committee of Nineteen, the recommendations of which follow closely those of the Lytton Commission, was circulated to League Members on February 17, 1933, and was unanimously adopted by the Assembly on February 24.[95]

As W. W. Willoughby has said, the Lytton Report is, in spite of its length, "so concise in its language, that justice can be done to it only by a complete reading of it," and without a very careful examination of this important international document no one can fully understand the Sino-Japanese controversy.[96] It is, in truth, a masterly arraignment of Japanese acts in Manchuria, sound in its reasoning, convincing in its conclusions, impartial in its judgments, but, together with the subsequent action of the Assembly, it came too late. Had it been possible in September to set up a commission on the spot with such authority as was later conferred on the Consular Committee in Shanghai, some constructive settlement might have been achieved. Now, however, when Japan had victories galore to the army's credit and the inflamed nationalism of her people for support, the inevitable and tragic conclusion of this arraignment was Japan's withdrawal from the League of Nations.[97] Nevertheless, the Lytton Report, like Mr. Stimson's note of January 7, which also came too late, became a great historic milestone on the path to the organization of peace. Despite its failure to achieve results, it was an evidence of progress in that it was a forthright condemnation of a great power for its illegal actions against a weak state on the basis of evidence impartially secured, a verdict, moreover, by a jury which Japan was forced to acknowledge as her peers since it was composed of representatives of great powers alone. If moral suasion could have had any effect at

[93] *Official Journal*, Special Supplement 111, p. 75.
[94] *Ibid.*, Special Supplement 112, pp. 65–76.
[95] Forty-two out of 44 votes were cast for adoption. Siam, the only independent Far Eastern State besides China and Japan, abstained from voting. As the consent of the parties to the dispute is not necessary under Article 15, M. Hymans, President of the Assembly, declared the report unanimously adopted. *Lytton Report*, p. 22.
[96] Willoughby, *op. cit.*, p. 384.
[97] The Japanese delegation withdrew from the Assembly on February 24, 1933. On March 27 the Japanese government gave formal notice of its intention to withdraw from the League (*Official Journal*, May, 1933, p. 657) and this withdrawal became effective March 27, 1935.

that late date, the report of the Lytton Commission and the unanimous adoption of the recommendations of the Committee of Nineteen by the Assembly would surely have put an end to Japanese aggression in eastern Asia.

The action of the Assembly, says Denna Frank Fleming, saved its soul:

If it could not persuade or control an unruly member, it at least refused to bow to her. Instead, she was virtually expelled from the League by a temperate judgment which was also so firm that Japan had either to accept it or to leave the League. That it is enough to pass judgment and do nothing more would not be alleged by this writer. But the League did look to the future and the future belongs to the League. The Japanese militarists may trade upon the slender resources of Japan until she sinks suddenly back into the ranks of the small nations. A few militarist nations may be able to plunge the world into another war which will hurl other peoples down with them into a common ruin. But when the destruction of civilization has again been halted, the need for the League, in all its original strength, will be piteously greater, not less. The experience gained by the League up to that time will also be infinitely larger than that which existed in the year 1931.[98]

The feelings of Hugh Wilson, our Minister to Switzerland, as he watched Matsuoka summon his assistants and brusquely leave the Assembly on the 24th of February, 1933, were very different. Concerning the wisdom of the course followed by the League and the United States he writes:

The final session of the Assembly remains indelibly printed on my mind. . . . Matsuoka's speech on that day in the Assembly was delivered with a passionate conviction far removed from his usual business-like manner. He pointed out the danger of pillorying a great nation. He warned that the Assembly was driving Japan from its friendship with the West toward an inevitable development of a self-sustaining, uniquely Eastern position. . . .

. . . For the first time the gravest doubts arose as to the wisdom of the course which the Assembly and my country were pursuing. I began to have a conception of the rancor and resentment that public condemnation could bring upon a proud and powerful people, and I began to question, and still do question whether such treatment is wise.

[98] Denna Frank Fleming, *The United States and World Organization* (New York, 1938), p. 454.

If the nations of the world feel strongly enough to condemn, they should feel strongly enough to use force, if necessary, to rectify a situation which they find deplorable. To condemn only merely intensifies the heat. Condemnation creates a community of the damned who are forced outside the pale, who have nothing to lose by the violation of all laws of order and international good faith. It is exasperating without being efficacious. If it were only exasperating that would be bad enough, but it is worse, it is profoundly dangerous. The community of the damned can bring together unnatural allies, allies who in their hearts despise one another but who can unite in their hatred of the smug and respectable nations.

Japan was the first great nation to be condemned; it was followed by other instances, and in no single case has the condemnation brought forth good fruit; in every case deplorable consequences have flowed forth from it. A domestic court may arraign and castigate a prisoner because it has the power to inflict punishment and because the laws of domestic society have provided sanctions which may restrain the bitterness arising from the arraignment. Not so in international law; there is no force other than war, or risk of war through economic sanctions, which can be brought to bear, hence the arraignment leaves a sullen resentment which no sanction of society yet invented can curb.

. . . Not only did such doubts regarding arraignment arise in me, but for the first time I began to question the non-recognition policy. More and more as I thought it over I became conscious that we had entered a dead end street. I could see no way out of this situation with dignity for either side. A declaration of non-recognition means that eventually one side or another will find itself in a situation where it must "eat crow." If it were in any way a deterrent to the use of force, one could, of course, admit its value. I doubted then if it would prove such a deterrent, and the past few years have more than justified such a doubt.[99]

In the light of later events it is easy enough to criticize the Secretary of State for not following up the "reminder" in his letter to Senator Borah with a more direct warning to Japan that unless she abandoned her violation of the Nine Power Treaty we would on our part abrogate the remaining agreements entered into in 1922. But public opinion in the United States would not at that time have supported Mr. Stimson in so drastic a step. If there is any doubt on that score one has only to consider the outcry in certain quarters when it was announced that the entire fleet, then on maneuvers in the

[99] Wilson, *op. cit.,* pp. 279–81. Italics mine.

Pacific, would for the time being remain based on Hawaii, and to recall that when the next Administration wanted to fortify Guam, following Japan's renunciation of the naval treaties, Congress refused to grant the necessary appropriations and failed even to provide sufficient money for the improvement of harbor and air facilities. This was, in part at least, Mr. Stimson's fault. Public opinion would not have supported him because throughout the fall of 1931 it had been confused by the State Department's constant reiteration that Japan was our friend, that her intentions were honest, her statesmen were to be trusted, and there was absolutely nothing to be concerned about. As Mr. Stimson himself points out,[100] there had always been in this country a greater spirit of friendliness, a greater sympathy for China than for Japan. Intelligently directed and in full possession of the facts—those which favored China as well as those derogatory to her, those derogatory to Japan as well as those in her favor—public opinion would have been in better case to respond in Mr. Stimson's time of need.

The first step, it will be recalled,[101] which Mr. Stimson felt necessary under the changed conditions of 1932 was that of popular education, a process which, he says, was begun in November when he warned Ambassador Debuchi—privately—that he must retain the right to publish the communications between this country and Japan.[102] The Secretary's reasoning shows clearly why there was need for "popular education" and why we were left "unguided and voiceless" for so long. He writes:

The long discouraging negotiations of the autumn had necessarily been conducted behind the veil of diplomatic procedure. If they had been successful in accomplishing a fair settlement between the two countries in controversy that would have been sufficient. No further enlightenment as to the facts of the controversy would have been necessary for the people of our country. They would have been satisfied with the result and would have let it go at that. But now when we were confronted with the indefinite continuance of a dangerous strife which might at any time flare up and involve our own national interests or even

[100] Stimson, *op. cit.*, pp. 153 ff.   [101] P. 233 above, this chapter.
[102] For the very meager results of this decision so far as publicity is concerned see Chap. VI, above

safety it was important that the American people should know what it was all about to a much fuller and more accurate extent than they actually did.[103]

It is always important that the American people know "what it is all about." Intelligence does not function within a vacuum and it is only through the proper functioning of public intelligence [104] that democracy attains its ends. Mr. Stimson's point of view seems to be directly contrary to the policy the State Department should follow as regards public interest in and right to information on foreign affairs and the formulation of foreign policy. Granted that there are many negotiations which cannot be exposed prematurely to the public view, it is nevertheless true that no State Department can afford to keep a free people in ignorance of what is going on in the world. Munich and "peace in our time" are the inevitable result.[105]

Apparently the Foreign Relations Committee of the Senate had

---

[103] Stimson, *op. cit.*, p. 91.

[104] Cynics of the extreme right and left to the contrary notwithstanding, there is such a thing.

[105] Lord Cecil in his *Great Experiment* discusses at considerable length the uses and value of publicity in diplomacy. Much of what he says has a very definite application to our case. Writing of the insistence of Austen Chamberlain and the French on holding secret meetings of the Locarno powers at Geneva in 1926, when the question of German membership in the League was under discussion, with the "usual result," unreasonable statements and misinterpretation to the public, he says: "The Germans . . . rejected every kind of compromise and then told their papers that all the difficulty was caused by Sweden. Secrecy in such a case merely means a facility for misinterpretation."

This was certainly the case as regards the State Department policy on publicity: Mr. Stimson's failure to publish his notes to Japan permitted misinterpretation of our position in both the American and Japanese press, with very bad results.

At another point Lord Cecil makes these equally pertinent comments:

"It is surely the case that the sooner and more clearly the intentions of each important Power are laid before the world, the less chance there is of the misunderstandings which are among the chief causes of international unrest. . . . It is my profound conviction that, though in certain cases really private conversations may be useful, publicity is an immensely powerful guarantee against injustice and misunderstanding.

"I am aware that diplomatic opinion is largely against me at this point. . . . All the same, I maintain that one of the merits of the Geneva system was its publicity, that it was possible to say things openly in the Assembly which it was very desirable to say and which could not have been said under the old diplomatic conditions, that frequently agreement has been reached under pressure of publicity which could not have been reached otherwise, that when the Council sat in private, it very often failed to reach any conclusion, and that I cannot myself recollect any occasion on which publicity did or would have done any harm except where the qualifications of some individual for an appointment or the like was to be discussed."

been given little more information than the general public for on December 17th—"quite without my previous knowledge," writes the Secretary—a resolution reported by that committee requesting the Secretary of State to transmit to the Senate "notes, correspondence, and communications" relating to the conditions in Manchuria, was introduced by Senator Johnson of California and, after some discussion as to its propriety, adopted without dissent.[106] A month later—January 19, to be exact—the following colloquy took place in the Senate chamber:

Mr. Johnson: . . . I desire to say that on the 17th of December the Senate adopted a resolution calling upon the Secretary of State for the papers relating to the Manchurian controversy and asking that they be transmitted to the Senate of the United States. I inquire of the chair has any response been made to that resolution of the Senate.

The Presiding Officer: There is no record of it.

Mr. Johnson: More than a month has passed and no response of any kind or character has been made to the Senate resolution.[107]

On January 27 the Vice-President laid before the Senate the documents selected by Mr. Stimson; these were referred to the Committee on Foreign Relations and ordered to be printed.[108] They were accompanied by the following laconic statement from President Hoover:

To the Senate of the United States:

In response to Senate Resolution 87 of December 17th.

I transmit herewith a report by the Secretary of State including copies of documents referred to therein.[109]

Mr. Stimson writes that there being no reason for longer withholding them from publication they were sent to the Senate on January 26. He continues:

Fortune played into our hands in that the time when they were published by the Senate coincided with the attack by the Japanese on Shanghai.[110] This was arousing nationwide excitement. Therefore the correspondence was given the most earnest attention by both Congress

---

[106] *Congressional Record*, LXXV, Part I, 671–73. [107] *Ibid.*, Part II, p. 2283.
[108] *Conditions in Manchuria*, Senate Document 55, 72d Cong., 1st Sess.
[109] *Congressional Record*, LXXV, Part III, 2769.
[110] This occurred on January 28–29.

and the people and it helped powerfully towards clarifying the issues involved.[111]

The Senate did not ask Mr. Stimson for all the correspondence, nor did the resolution specify communications between the Secretary of State and our representatives abroad, except where the League, the Nine Power Treaty, or the Kellogg Pact was concerned. It is disappointing, however, to find no reference to the information obtained by Messrs. Salisbury and Hanson on their mission to southern Manchuria in September and October of 1931.[112] In *War and Peace, 1931–1941*, the volume of documents published by the State Department, we find one communication withheld by Mr. Stimson in January, 1932, which would certainly have "helped powerfully towards clarifying the issues involved." This is Nelson Johnson's telegram [113] dated September 22, 1931, in which he gave his "personal reaction to events described in my telegram above referred to." Our Minister to China had, it appears, already sent two messages on the subject to Mr. Stimson, one of these "referring to Nanking's appeal to us under the Kellogg Pact." [114] These have not yet been published, but it is easy to see why Mr. Stimson makes no reference to this communication for it denies the whole concept on which he says he based the State Department policy during 1931.[115] What is difficult to understand is how it could have been passed over so lightly, how it could have been so completely ignored in the formation of that policy. Excerpts from Mr. Johnson's telegram follow:

According to all information available to me here I am driven to the conclusion that the forceful occupation of all strategic points in South Manchuria . . . is an aggressive act by Japan apparently long planned and when decided upon most carefully and systematically put into effect. *I find no evidence that these events were the result of accident nor were they the acts of minor and irresponsible officials.* . . .

It is my conviction that the steps taken by Japan in Manchuria must fall within any definition of war and certainly may not be considered as a pacific means of settling a dispute with China, a national also adherent to the treaty.[116] . . .

[111] Stimson, *op. cit.*, p. 93.
[112] *Ibid.*, p. 45. See also pp. 70–71, 88 ff., above.
[113] *War and Peace*, Doc. I (793–94/1838), pp. 155–56.   [114] See pp. 28 ff., above.
[115] See Stimson, *op. cit.*, pp. 34 ff., also Chap. II, pp. 31 ff., above.
[116] That is, the Kellogg-Briand Pact. Italics mine.

It seems to me necessary that the powers signatory to the Kellogg treaty owe it to themselves and to the world to pronounce themselves in regard to this Japanese act of aggression which I consider to have been deliberately accomplished in utter and cynical disregard of signatories of that pact.

This telegram was received at 9:30 A.M. September 23,[117] the very day on which the fatal decision not to send an investigating committee to the scene of the conflict was taken in Geneva, and in this decision Mr. Stimson played a determining part.[118] Although Mr. Johnson's vigorous statement regarding Japan's aggressive intentions seems to have had no influence whatever on Mr. Stimson's view of the situation, public understanding thereof would have been considerably advanced had it been known that at least one of our Far Eastern representatives [119] thought the action was deliberate.

The publicity which the Secretary of State gave to his note of January 7 and to his letter to Senator Borah apparently completed the formal campaign of educating the general public—a task which to a man of Mr. Stimson's mold must have been rather distasteful. It should be said, however, that press conferences were a little more fruitful of information during 1932 than they had been in 1931.

In Conclusion.—And so our story ends on a note of frustration and confusion. The first great attack by a ruthless power on the post-war attempt to organize the world for peace instead of war was carried through to a successful finish. Seeing Japan violate her international obligations with impunity, Italy and Germany were encouraged to put their aggressive designs to the test with results all too well known.

Where were the mistakes made? Why, with the United States supporting the League as never before, was Japan not checked?

So far as the collaboration of the United States with the League is concerned the outstanding causes of failure may be summarized as follows:

Whatever the causes may have been, whose the responsibility, whether President Hoover's, Mr. Castle's or Mr. Stimson's, the fun-

---

[117] *War and Peace.*   [118] See Chap. II, also Stimson, *op. cit.*, pp. 42–44.
[119] The only one on the spot, for that matter, as Cameron Forbes, Ambassador to Japan, was on his way home when the Mukden incident occurred.

damental reasoning, the basic concept on which our original policy was based was wrong. The initial mistake was the failure to recognize that the Mukden incident was an act of aggression on the part of Japan and therefore raised a question which could be answered only by international action.

The failure of Mr. Stimson's attempts to cooperate with the League was, I believe, due to no lack of sincerity on his part, but was occasioned in large part by the fact that he promised support to the League one day, yet seemingly withheld it the next, a kind of policy which kept the Council in constant suspense as to the extent to which they could count on American cooperation. This derived apparently from three factors: discord in the department, which the Secretary denies but which unquestionably existed—Dr. Hornbeck pulling for China with the aid, we now know, of Nelson Johnson, Mr. Castle rooting for Japan; the restraining hand of President Hoover, who would have nothing to do with sanctions; and fear of the isolationists who were very strong in the 72d Congress. Still another deterrent to cooperation was our insistence on independent judgment and action. Our extreme care to preserve this was the source of most of our delayed actions, for instance, in support of the September 30 and October 24 resolutions and in the matter of the Kellogg Pact, October 20.[120] The whole story of Ambassador Dawes and his separate office at the Ritz is, of course, the most glaring example of the extremes to which this was carried. But perhaps the chief cause of Mr. Stimson's failure to cooperate successfully, for it would have been disastrous even if the other factors had not existed, was the complete lack of a technique of collaboration,[121] a technique just as necessary for peace as we have found it to be in war, the perfecting of which in North Africa and Sicily in preparation for the final test against Germany brought such great success to the Allied cause in World War II.

One of Mr. Stimson's greatest mistakes lay in keeping the American people in ignorance of the true state of affairs. It is recognized that the State Department itself does not always have all the facts in its possession, nor can all the facts be published in some cases. As a

[120] See Chaps. II and IV.   [121] See Chap. II, pp. 53–54.

general proposition, however, we, the people, do have a right to know the essential facts in any situation affecting our welfare. It was this right which Mr. Stimson by implication denied. It was a tactical error as well. Mr. Stimson and the President staked their whole cause on the force of moral opinion, but made it impossible to mobilize that opinion against Japan by consistently minimizing that country's faults and displaying quite prominently its sometimes nonexistent virtues.

Lack of harmony between the United States and Great Britain contributed to the general debacle. As has already been pointed out, the fault was on both sides, the results disastrous.

Mr. Stimson puts great stress on the confused leadership in Geneva in March of 1932. This had been the case almost from the start and Mr. Stimson himself was partly to blame. The simple fact is there was no one to take the lead. The United States would not do so and, lacking assurance of what this government would do in case League pressure on Japan precipitated action which would have to be supported by sea power in the Far East, Great Britain felt she could not run the risk. That statement could be reversed with equal truth—the result would be the same.

Poor timing and faulty judgment at crucial moments combined with all the other causes and helped to bring on the final catastrophe. The gap between the United States on the one hand and the League on the other was never closed and it was through this that Japan made her thrust.

There are, in addition, certain general conclusions looking towards the future, lessons we must learn if the present tragedy is not to be repeated. We must recognize that the only time to stop a war is before it begins, before a nation, or a group of nations, becomes so involved that it cannot draw back without humiliating loss of face. Japan might have been stopped in September when the blame and the disgrace could still have been laid on a few hot-headed junior officers of the Manchurian army, but not after the prestige of the entire army, to say nothing of the nation itself, was at stake. We must recognize also that there is no chance of success in a major crisis involving one or more of the great powers so long as any great power remains outside the international organization. And, finally, implicit in what we have just said, there must be an international organization of some sort with power to act and which will eventually include all the nations of the world.

The only justification for this study is if it points the way to a better understanding for the future, if it makes clear the necessity of a full and wholehearted participation by the United States in the affairs of the world, which are our affairs, and if it destroys the myth that *we* did everything in our power to stop Japan and only other nations are to blame for this first tragic step toward World War II.

INDEX

Abend, Hallett, 227, 230; quoted, 61
Adachi, Kenzo, attempt to form a coalition government, 227
Aldorovandi, Count, 231
Anganchi, Japanese moved towards, 126
Anglo-Japanese alliance, compensation to Japan for renunciation of, 16
Araki, General, 226, 228
Asaki, Tokyo, 103; excerpt, 60; view of international police for Manchuria, 139n; exception to three clauses in tentative resolution of Nov. 25, 206
Associated Press, report on Japan's intention re fundamental points, 137, 139; on plan for simultaneous and parallel negotiations, 172; on U.S. message to Japan on occupation of Tsitsihar, 177
Astor, Lord, 7n
Austria, financial collapse, 5

Baldwin, Stanley, attitude toward League, 8
Balfour, Arthur James, Lord, 8
Baruch, Bernard, 142n
"Bases of American Foreign Policy . . ." (Stimson), excerpt, 153
Beaverbrook papers, attacks on Council, 138, 141
Benes, Eduard, on sanctions, 154
Bolivia-Paraguay case, 52
Borah, William E., on duty of U.S. in Manchurian affair, 180; isolationist sentiments, 180, 196; Stimson's open letter to, 245, 247, 250
Bowman, Isaiah, 142n
Boycott of Japanese goods by China, 181
Briand, Aristide, 22; personal prestige: lacked support of staff at Quai d'Orsay, 8; quoted, 40; as President of Council, 95 ff.; disappointment re unrealized hopes of Sept. 30, 97; masterly handling of proceedings, 99; attempt to break deadlock between China and Japan, 103, 121; prestige, courage, 104; drafted invitation to U.S., 107; on proposed invitation to U.S., 108; appeal to

generosity of Japanese, 109; welcome to Gilbert, 111; idea of American participation, 112; to notify signatories of Pact of Paris re notes to China and Japan, 114; report on action taken under Pact, 115; on positions taken by China and Japan, 116; attempt to obtain explanation of fundamental principles, 119, 120; warning to Yoshizawa, 120, 186; re Council meeting in Paris, 131; urgent appeals to China and Japan, 132 f., 183, 190, 192; urged Japan to conform to terms of Sept. 30 resolution, 135; and to withdraw troops into railway zone, 136; belief that aloofness of U.S. was damaging bad situation, 165; approved plan for simultaneous and parallel negotiations, 173; as negotiator to bring China and Japan to agreement, 174; relied on cooperation of Dawes, 176n; wise direction of meeting, 183; suggestion to Sze, 186; Japan's reply to appeal of Nov. 25, 193; proposal re dispatch of neutral observers to Chinchow area, 194; re position of U.S. on proposed resolution of Nov. 25, 198; declared point omitted from resolution had no effect on Japanese policy, 209; emphasis on exceptional quality of crisis, 211; on parallel and incessant activities of U.S., 212; Dawes's contacts with, 213; agreed to statement submitted by Dawes, 214
Brown, Constantine, D. Pearson and, 31n
Bruening, German Chancellor, 95
Bryan, William Jennings, 233
Buell, Raymond Leslie, 142, 143; quoted, 146
Bülow, Prince von, 171, 185
Byas, Hugh, 124, 137n; quoted, 26, 27, 83, 133, 137; on Tsitsihar affair, 131; on Japan's advance on Chinchow, 193n; surprised at Yoshizawa's Cabinet appointment, 226n; on cause of fall of Minseito Cabinet, 227

Castle, William R., Jr., 69; U.S. Under Secretary of State, knowledge of Far East, 11; influence with Hoover, 12, 13, 86; friendship for Japan, 12, 47, 260; difference of opinion between Hornbeck and, 31*n*

Catt, Carrie Chapman, 142*n*

Cecil, Lord, 184; quoted, 5, 8; as head of British delegation at Geneva, 7, 22, 46; cause of shifts in position re China and Japan, 7; advocate of collective security, worker for world peace, 8; speech outlining League procedure, 39; re withdrawal of troops occupying territory of other party, 40, 41; support of Chinese delegate: on cooperation and support of U.S., 41; appeal to Yoshizawa, 43; answer to Yoshizawa's proposal for a commission of enquiry, 49, 185; sharp rejoinder to Sze's reference to Article 15, 57, 113; change in attitude, 57, 66; on duty of Council under Article 11, 58; Japan's criticism of, 59; restatement of Sze's proposal, 64; version corrected by Sze, 65; demand for clarification of "fundamental points," 92; prestige, courage, 104; idea of American participation, 112; attempt to obtain explanation of fundamental principles, 119, 120; apparent bias toward China, 138; supported Sze's demand for cessation of hostilities, 185; appointed to redraft resolution, 202; support of small powers, 202*n*; re police measures, 211; reference to exceptional quality in crisis, 211; warning to China and Japan, 212*n*; Foreign Office believed had gone too far in support of League and China, 236; on value of publicity in diplomacy, 256*n*

Chamberlain, Sir Austen, 8, 256*n*

Chang Hai-peng, trouble with Ma Chanshan, 129

Chang Hsueh-liang (the "Young Marshal"), 20; Japan's effort to frustrate, 13; Manchuria under, growing closer to China, 13, 14, 17; authority of, no longer recognized by Japan, 83, 84; arrangements for troops to maintain order as Japanese withdrew, 87; army's purpose to put end to administration of, 95, 128; civil administration of, destroyed, 126; Honjo's threat to, 182, 188; withdrawal of troops of, demanded by Japan, 204;

decision to withdraw within Great Wall, 229

Chang Tso-lin (the "Old Marshal"), 14*n*

Chapei, attack on, 242

Chen, Eugene, 228*n*

Chiang Kai-shek, Japan's effort to frustrate, 13; China drawing closer together under, 14, 17; out of office: reinstated, 228

China, appeal to Council of League, 6, 22, 28; A. S. Sze delegate to 65th Council, 9; at time of Manchurian crisis, 14; Twenty-one Demands forced upon, 16; strong independent, essential to peace in East, 16; political conditions of the twenties, 17; anti-Chinese riots in Korea: death of Nakamura, 17; appeal to U.S., 22, 28; elected to seat on Council, 22; three things asked of Council, 29; U.S. made no answer to appeal, 29; hostilities between Russia and, in Manchuria, 33; note to U.S. Government, 34; friendship of U.S. for, 35, 255; first public session for consideration of appeal to Council, 35 ff.; disclaimed any part in precipitating Mukden affair, 36; claimed redress, 36, 67; would not agree to direct negotiations while part of its territory under military occupation by Japan, 37, 50, 103, 173; left case in hands of Council, 39, 103; Stimson's note to, 54; reply to Council's note, 54, 56; might shift appeal to Article 15, 57, 113; amazed at policy of U.S., 61; belief that Japan's militarists were arousing warlike spirit of people, 61; deadlock with Japan, 62, 103; attempt to compromise, 62 ff., 71; insistence on neutral aid in arrangements for evacuation, 67, 71; reply to Stimson's note, 67, 69; demand that Japan withdraw all troops immediately, 67, 71, 184, 185, 187; committed to protection of Japanese lives and property, 75, 87, 183, 184; warned U.S. and League that Japan was up to no good, 82; request that U.S. and Council send representatives to Manchuria, 88; compliance considered unnecessary by U.S., 89; asked League to send commission to Chinchow: U.S. requested to participate, 90; recommendations to, in draft resolution of the "Twelve," 116 ff.; Sze's discussion of bases of acceptance of resolution, 118; scheme for simultaneous and parallel negotiations, 120, 139, 172, 178; turned down by Japanese, 120, 173; salt and other public revenues seized, 128; offer to submit interpretation of treaties to arbitration, 137, 173; compromise settlement made impossible by military events, 139; did not insist upon sanctions, 145; delegation feared return to old methods of secret diplomacy, 171; has long looked to U.S. as arbiter, 177; acceptance in principle of armistice and proposal to send commission of enquiry to Manchuria, 179; boycott of Japanese goods, 181; denied acceptance of new plan, 182; Yoshizawa's proposal to send a commission of enquiry to, 184, 185; demanded every right secured to it as member of League, 184 f.; Japan's trap for, 187; proposal for neutral zone, occupied by neutral observers, in Chinchow area, 192 ff.; accepted Briand's compromise proposal, 194; asked to evacuate all territory outside Great Wall, 194; tentative draft resolution released Nov. 25, 197; *text*, 200; greater concessions to be made by, 201; small powers refuse to join in pressure to force acceptance of resolution, 201; concession on time limit for Japanese evacuation, 202, 204, 205, 208; obstacles to agreement still existing, 203; efforts of Council and Dawes to obtain further concessions from, 204; not conceded even a minor triumph in draft resolution, 208; judicial position good, strategic, bad, 210; invoked Articles 10 and 15, asked that case be submitted to Assembly, 226; discontent and disorder: efforts of Nanking and Canton governments to block Japanese aggression: both governments resigned, 228; rival factions pulling closer together, 229; forces compelled to retire within Great Wall, 229, 230; commercial traffic with northern provinces disrupted, 230; American prestige at stake, 232; London *Times* on nonexistence of administrative integrity in, 236*n*; plan for cessation of hostilities accepted by, 242; Japanese desire to establish demilitarized zones around principal ports, 242; *see also* Chang Hsueh-liang; Chiang Kai-shek; Koo,

Wellington; Soong, T. V.; Sze, A. S.
Chinchow, bombing of, 77 f., 82 ff., 126, 189; chosen seat of provincial government, 83; bombing shattered Stimson's confidence in Debuchi, 85; last stronghold of China outside Great Wall, 188; rumors of concentration of Chinese forces at, 188, 189; advance halted: withdrawal of Japanese forces to Hsinmin, 189, 192; serious misunderstanding arose out of advance on, 191, 192; proposal to dispatch observers to area to establish neutral zone, 192 ff.; Briand's compromise proposal: accepted by China, rejected by Japan, 194; Japan's demand that neutral zone be established west of, 204 f.; demand that, be placed under Japanese administration: China's refusal to evacuate, 205; matter of neutral zone dropped, 207; disorders between Liao River and, 226; occupied by Honjo, 229; strain in British-American relations precipitated by, 232
Chinese Eastern Railway, Japanese move toward, 126
Churchill, Winston, on break down of Italian state, 198
Claudel, Henri, 231
Commission of Enquiry, proposed by Sze, 38, 42, 46, 56, 75; his proposal for local arrangements, a committee "on the spot," 46, 65, 74, 75; Yoshizawa defiant and obstinate: report that U.S. would not approve, 47; Stimson's part in affair, 47 ff., 67; Yoshizawa's proposal to send, to Manchuria and China, 49, 143, 184, 185; Minseito Cabinet would have consented to, 51; sent too late for any possible peaceful settlement, 51; suggestion abandoned, 60; refused by Japan, 62; why, at Paris meeting, Yoshizawa proposed sending, 127; proposal for an international, 179, 181; Yoshizawa's restrictions on field of endeavor, 184, 187; question as to participation of U.S., 195; conflict as to size, scope, and authority, 203; Japanese suggested sending without specific powers, 205; hands tied by Council, 209; major subjects of dispute excluded from matters with which, could deal, 219; not an instrument of conciliation and mediation but a fact-finding body, 222; Japanese swift move to consolidate position before

Commission of Enquiry (*Continued*) arrival of, 230; members, 231; delay in beginning investigations, 231

Commission of neutral observers, sending of, to Manchuria suggested by Sze, 63; Yoshizawa's misinterpretation of proposal, 66

Committee of Five, 49, 71, 105; personnel, 46; reply to Stimson's message, 52; bid for closer cooperation than diplomatic support, 53; importance of, 106; Gilbert at meetings, 122

Committee of Nineteen, 251, 252

Committee of Twelve, *see* "Twelve, The"

Condemnation, deplorable consequences have always flowed from, 254

Conditions in Manchuria, 29; excerpt, 156

Conference of Ministers, U.S. representatives instructed not to attend any more meetings, 248

Crisol, excerpt, 197

Curtius, Julius, head of German delegation, 9, 42, 46

Curzon, George N. C., Lord, 8

Czechoslovakia, Hitler's occupation of, 82

Davis, John W., 142*n*

Dawes, Charles G., 102*n*, 143; questioned re imposition of sanctions, 144; authorized to make known position of U.S. to Briand, 144, 145, 146; conference with Briand, 145; would probably have discouraged use of sanctions, 155; appointed to go to Paris for meetings of Council, 156-69; instructions, 156; not instructed to sit with Council, 157; liaison with Council, 158; selection indicated that peak of cooperation with League had passed, 159; refused to confer with Gilbert, 160; isolationist sentiments, 160, 213; lack of interest in crisis, 160; friendship with Matsudaira: definite bias toward Japan, 161; quoted, 161, 163; began separate set of negotiations: inaccessible to other Council members, 163; attendance at meetings left to his discretion, 164; aloofness, 164, 195; emphasis on independent position and separate judgment of, 164, 165, 168, 195; urged by Briand to attend Council meetings: plan of parallel cooperation, 165; attitude did not help

situation in Paris, 166; as an outside negotiator, 166, 171; explanation of his nonattendance, 167; statement closed discussion: threw away last fruits of victory, 169; situation created by independent and separate position of, 172; approved plan for simultaneous and parallel negotiations, 173; refused to consider Nine Power Treaty as basis for negotiations, 174*n*; interpretation of reports of Sweetser and of Matsudaira, 175; decision not to take seat at Council table a blow to League circles, 176; not in favor of forcing Japanese withdrawal, 198; attitude on proposed resolution of Nov. 25, 198; public announcement of U.S. approval of plan, 199; emerged from his isolation, 212; activities: sought to back up Council, 213; vagueness of his instruction on root question traced to Senate, 214; why he did not come before Council table, Dec. 10, 214 ff.; *text* of statement, 215; if he had attended last meeting, 217

Debuchi, Katsuji, Japanese Ambassador to U.S., 13, 61, 69; asked to defer leave, 24; words taken at face value, 25; re sending a commission of enquiry to Manchuria, 47, 143; received by Stimson, 77; Stimson's confidence in assurances of, shattered, 85; loyal to Shidehara, 85*n*; re Nonni River affair and advance upon Tsitsihar, 131; reflected stiffening attitude of Japan, 138; told that U.S. would not participate in sanctions, 142; report to Stimson on Tsitsihar, 176*n*; conference with Stimson, 177; warned that Stimson reserved liberty to publish communications with Japan, 178, 255

Diplomat between Wars (Wilson), excerpt, 157*n*

Disarmament, collapse of movement threatened, 98

Dooman, Eugene, 158

Drummond, Sir Eric (Earl of Perth), head of permanent staff of League, 10, 11, 171; Japanese believed unfriendly to them, 24; message to Stimson re Kellogg Pact and Mukden incident, 30, 34; circulation of Stimson's note, 84; trip for consultation re Disarmament Conference postponed, 123; agreed to statement submitted by Dawes, 214

Eden, Anthony, 248, 249
Edge, Walter E., 156
Ethiopia, 145, 237

Far East, U.S. prestige in, at stake, 35, 232; effect of British rebuff to U.S. upon Anglo-American cooperation in, 238; U.S. and Great Britain agreed not to erect additional fortifications in their possessions, 247n, 248
Far Eastern Crisis, The (Stimson), excerpts, 25, 30, 31 ff., 70, 71, 78, 100, 143, 152, 177; does not mention China's appeal to U.S., 29
Far Eastern Policy of the United States, The (Griswold), 143
Fleisher, Wilfrid, 14, 228n; quoted, 14n
Fleming, Denna Frank, 253
Forbes, Cameron, 12, 124
Foreign Policies of the Hoover Administration, The (Myers), 143
Foreign Policy Association, petition to Hoover, 142
Four Power Consultative pact, 16
France, delegates to 65th Council of League, 8; conservative sentiment adverse to Japan, 95; notes to China and Japan, 114; Paris considered pro-Japanese, 132; hostility toward nationalistic movement in Orient and to Soviet Union, 132n; attitude toward sanctions, 154; unofficial complaints that U.S. was not cooperating with Council, 196; insistence on secret meetings of Locarno powers, 256n
Fundamental points, Japan prepared to open negotiations on, 90, 91; Cecil's demand for clarification, 92; statement re, read into minutes, 99; Japan's effort to force China to accept direct negotiations, 118; futile efforts to persuade Yoshizawa to clarify meaning, 119, 120, 126; basis of settlement prerequisite to evacuation, 126; why not made public, 127; Japan's summary of, 135; Shidehara insists on recognition of, 136; Japan's intention to secure signed agreement witnessed by League, 137; demanded recognition of treaties which China never considered legitimate: offered to refer matter to arbitration, 137, 173; compromise proposal, 172; Japan demanded acceptance without further discussion, 173; Yoshizawa asked to state what treaties

referred to in fifth, 174; not Japan's final requirements, 174

Gannett, Frank E., 142n
Germany, financial collapse, 5; head of delegation to 65th Council, 9; voted with Japan, 109; driving power provided by young officers, 227; effect of secret meetings of Locarno powers, 256n; encouraged to put her aggressive designs to test, 259
Gibson, Hugh, U.S. Ambassador to Belgium, 101, 160; delegate to London Naval Conference, 158; active role, 214
—— Herbert Hoover and, 219; quoted, 152
Gilbert, Prentiss, U.S. Consul in Geneva, an observer at Council meetings, 11, 101, 164; role assigned to, 102; privilege of attending secret meetings, 105, 106; participated in discussions under Pact of Paris, 110, 114; Briand's welcome to, 111; statement as to part U.S. would take in deliberations of Council, 111 f.; results of presence at Council table, 114; enforced silence during debate on resolution, 121; role at secret sessions, 122; directed to retire from seat at Council table and resume position as observer, 122n, 163; those who thought he had gone too far in cooperation with League, 158; not permitted to go to Paris, 160; substitute member of Commission of Enquiry, 231
Grandi, Dino, head of Italian delegation, 9, 42, 46, 95
Great Britain, propaganda for those who would divide U.S. and, 4; debacle of Labour Party, 5, 128; internal crises of 1931, 5; Conservatives dominant, 6; gold standard abandoned, 6, 28; new attitude toward Geneva, 6, 7; delegation to 65th Council of League, 7; policy determined by Simon, 7; bias toward Japan, 66, 162n; Conservative opinion more adverse to Japan, 95; notes to China and Japan, 114; National government became arch-conservative, 129; Conciliatory attitude, 138; attitude toward sanctions, 154; strain in British-American relations, 226, 232, 235 ff.; door opened for appeasement of Japan, 235; stunning rebuff to Stimson, 235 ff.; official com-

Great Britain (*Continued*)
munique of Foreign Office, Jan. 9, 1932, *text*, 235*n*; not business of Foreign Office to defend administrative integrity of China, 236*n*; rebuff convinced Japan that nonrecognition doctrine was without support, 238; responsibility for failure to stop Japan divided between U.S. and, 238; nonrecognition not in tradition of policy in Far East, 240; Pratt's explanation of communiqué of Jan. 9, 240, 241; official reply to Stimson, 240; attitude toward Stimson's proposed joint invocation of Nine Power Treaty, 243 ff.; relations Foreign Office to League, 246; agreed not to erect additional fortifications in Far Eastern possessions, 248

Great Experiment (Cecil), excerpt, 256*n*

Greco-Bulgarian case of 1925, 36, 48, 97

Grew, Joseph C., 45

Griswold, A. Whitney, 143, 178, 246; interpretation of Stimson's policy re sanctions, 146 ff.

Guam, U.S. left position in, without further fortifications, 247*n*; appropriations to fortify refused by Congress, 255

Halifax, Edward Wood, Lord, 8

Hamaguchi, Yuko, Japanese Premier, assassinated, succeeded by Wakatsuki, 13; ratification of London Naval Treaty, 32

Hanson, George C., *see* Salisbury-Hanson Mission to Southern Manchuria

Harbin, 230

Hayes, Carlton J. H., 142*n*

Heilungkiang, trouble in province, 129; under Japanese control, 187

Hibbens, John Grier, 142*n*

Hitler, Adolf, occupation of Czechoslovakia, 82

Hokutaiei, 27

Honjo, General, commander in Manchuria, 14; abolished government and authority of Chang Hsueh-liang, 83, 84; demanded repair of Nonni River bridge, 129; ignored orders from Tokyo, 130, 131; ultimatum to Ma, 131, 162; would not withdraw from Nonni River, 162; advance on Tsitsihar, 175; threat to move on Chinchow,

182, 188; army determined to carry out threat, 189; Chinchow occupied by, 229

Hoover, Herbert, 243, 257; effort to prevent financial crises in Europe, 5; effect of elections of 1930 on, 6; knowledge of Far East, 11; restraining influence on U.S. policy of collaboration with League, 85; attention occupied with financial crisis, 86; consented to Council's request that U.S. sit jointly with them: condition, 87; did he choose Kellogg Pact as agency for collaboration with League, and why? 102; foresaw use of force if Japan were to be stopped, 113; decision as to capacity in which representative should act, 113; embittered by lame-duck Congress, 129; petitions urging him to support League and to have representative at Nov. session, 142, 142*n*; authoritative discussions of policies of, 143; analysis of situation, 149; opposed application of sanctions by U.S., 150 ff., 260; assumed more active direction of foreign affairs: position in re nonrecognition, 151; attitude toward international cooperation, 153; fear of irreconcilables in Senate, 164; method of handling Dawes's nonattendance at Council meetings approved by, 167; special message on Manchurian crisis, 218, 222; *text*, 218 f.; inadequacy of message, 220; approved Stimson's note of Jan. 7, 234; Rapidan declaration, 235

—— and Hugh Gibson, 219; quoted, 152

Hoover Policies, The (Wilbur and Hyde), 143

Hornbeck, Stanley, 77*n*; U.S. Chief of the Division of Far Eastern Affairs, 11; knowledge of Far East, 12; checkmated by Castle, 13; effort to aid China, 260

Howard, Roy W., 142*n*

Howland, Chester P., on sanctions, 154

Hsi Hsia, General, 230

Hsinmin, Japanese troop movements toward, 188 ,189, 192

Hyde, Arthur M., R. L. Wilbur and, 143; quoted, 149, 150

Hymans, M., 252*n*

Immigration, Japanese: treatment of subject by Congress of U.S., 32

Inouye, Japanese Finance Minister, in-

ability to stabilize situation, 128, 226; assassinated, 227
"In principle," use of phrase, 194n
International law, no force other than war on economic sanctions, 254
International organization which will include all nations imperative, 262
International security contingent upon success of League, 98
Inukai, Takeshi, 94; Prime Minister of Japan, 226; assassinated, 227
Invasion of one state by another on grounds of legitimate defense and protection, 97
Invergordon, insubordination in fleet at, 6
Ishii, Viscount, re withdrawal of troops from Mukden, 60
Isolated America (Buell), 143
Isolationists, seek goals by secret and devious means, 4; Hoover's hesitancy about offending, 7; sentiment of Stimson's political party, 53; would have relished slap at League, 102n; opposed cooperation with League, 129, 155; sentiments of a few important Senators, 155, 180, 196; should have felt reassured by appointment of Dawes, 159; sentiments of Dawes, 160; very strong in 72d Congress, 260
Italy, 145; head of delegation to 65th Council, 9; encouraged by Japan's success to put her aggressive designs to test, 259

Japan, world's failure to stop, 4; head of delegation to League, 9 (*see also* Yoshizawa, K.); plans for expansion of control in Manchuria, 12; Foreign Office made agency for undermining policies of liberals, 13 (*see also* Shiratori, T.); officer group or army took bit between its teeth, 14; internal political struggle, 17, 82); army and navy face loss of control, 17; anti-Chinese riots in Korea, 17; parliamentary setup, 25; policy directed by military group, 26, 34, 127; initiative in Manchuria held by army, 27, 134; Foreign Office attitude toward Mukden incident, 27 f.; army attitude, 28; army had independent access to Emperor, 30; violent nationalism inflamed by victories in Manchuria, 34, 134; effort to keep U.S. out of League, 43, 45; public opinion uninformed, 45; played

upon by military group, 45, 127; way open to separate Manchuria from China, 54; possibility of withdrawing from League, 54, 137; Stimson's note to, *text*, 54; reply to Council's note: official statement re situation in Manchuria, 54; opposed intervention by League, 55, 206; appeal to, to withdraw troops to railway zone, 59, 63, 117, 136; defied League and U.S.: Council's effort to save face, 59; deadlock with China, 62, 103; reply to Stimson's note, 68; assertion that troops acted only to protect railway, and lives and property of its nationals, 68; alleged bombing of trains by Japanese, 69; committed to speedy withdrawal, 75, 183; burden of responsibility placed upon, 76; bombing of Chinchow, 77 f., 82 ff. (*see also* Chinchow); army in possession of all Southern Manchuria, 79; disregard of treaty obligations or world opinion, 79, 137, 164, 225; impact of American policy, 82; practice of shifting forces without withdrawing: excuses, 87; insistence upon direct negotiations, 36, 37, 39, 55, 67, 90, 91, 103, 206; reference to "fundamental points" of settlement, 90, 91, 118, 119, 120 (*see also* Fundamental points); reply to Lerroux's appeal, 91; need for strong pressure on militarists, 92; effort to prevent a rapprochement between U.S. and League, or U.S. and Great Britain, 93; efforts to dominate China, 93; tactics used to cloud issues and confuse minds of delegates, 93, 94, 99; conservative opinion in Britain and France more adverse to, 95; appeasement of, 100; recommendations to, in draft resolution of the "Twelve," 116; counterproposal which would have given her diplomatic victory, 118; refusal to fix date for withdrawal of troops, 119; scheme for simultaneous and parallel negotiations, 120, 139, 172, 178; turned down by Yoshizawa, 120, 173; counterproposal rejected, 121; broadened field of military operations and of political and diplomatic relationships, 126; Foreign Office mystified by Yoshizawa's refusal to discuss "fundamental points" with Council, 126; control of foreign policy the objective of War office, 127; serious financial and economic

Japan (*Continued*)
situation, 128; attitude of France toward, 132; pleased with prospect of Paris meeting of Council, 132; shift in position from Sept. to Oct., 134; summary of statement re fundamental principles, 135; urged by Briand to conform to terms of Sept. 30 resolution, 135; rejection of Briand's arguments, 136; hardening attitude, 137, 138; military events made compromise settlement impossible, 139; opinion not uniformly behind military, 139n; exercise of diplomatic pressure suggested, 141, 147, 148; U.S. trade with, 145; satisfaction re appointment of Dawes, 160; Dawes's bias toward, 161; willing that he be seated at Council table, 165; insisted on full right of railway operation in Manchuria, 173; interpretation of compromise plan, 173n; increasing demands, 174, 204; denied acceptance of truce, 182; declared it had no territorial designs, 183; "right to live and very existence at stake," 183 f.; door for continued expansion of demands opened wide, 75, 187, 222; playing for time for extension of authority to Chinchow, 188; military acted without orders, 190; relations with U.S. strained, 191; policy of troops in retreat, 192; proposal to, for a neutral zone, occupied by neutral observers in Chinchow area, 192 ff.; nature of acceptance of proposal, 193; rejected interposition of third parties, 194; tentative draft resolution released Nov. 25, 197; *text*, 200; a compromise resolution, 201; obstacles to agreement still existing, 203; significant diplomatic victory, 208; answer to Stimson justifying action around Chinchow, 223; could have been stopped by force or sanctions, 225; extension of military operations to Shanghai, 225, 228; driving power provided by young officers, 227; long series of assassinations, 228; plans laid for new military operations: protest to League against boycotts and brigandage, 229; army moved swiftly to consolidate position before arrival of Commission, 230; could draw back only at cost of national humiliation, 237; quick to take advantage of British rebuff to U.S., 237; responsibility

for failure to stop, divided between U.S. and Great Britain, 238; alarmed by indiscreet attack on Chapei: requested U.S. and other powers to induce Chinese to withdraw from Shanghai, 242; rejected plan for cessation of hostilities, 242; withdrawal from League, 252; virtually expelled from League, 253; first great nation to be condemned, 254; Johnson's telegram re aggression of, 258
—— Minseito Cabinet, cause of downfall, 50, 226 f.; would have consented to Commission of Enquiry, 51; army's struggle with civilian element in, 127; party still held majority in Diet, 227
—— Minseito party, 13; demand for withdrawal of Minami, 26; situation that gave *coup de grâce* to, 128
—— Seiyukai Ministry, in power, 128, 226; belief that Japan should withdraw from League, 137; fall, 227
—— Tanaka Cabinet, 33
—— Wakatsuki Cabinet, 13; ratification of London Naval Treaty, 32; played into army's hands, 91, 95; tenuous hold weakening, 128; *see also* Shidehara; Yoshizawa
Japan Advertiser, 50
"Japanese Dual Diplomacy" (Byas), excerpt, 26
Jehol, brigandage in, 229; aid to Chinese forces cut off, 230
Ji-Ji, excerpts, 103, 206
Johnson, Nelson T., 29n, 34; reply to China's request that U.S. and Council send representatives to Manchuria, 88; request for data on Manchuria, 257; excerpt from telegram of Sept. 22 re Japan's aggression, 258; desire to help China, 260
Journal as Ambassador to Great Britain (Dawes), 143, 146; excerpts, 171, 214, 215
Journal de Genève, 122
Journal des Debats, 96

Kanaya, General, 26
Kawamoto, Lieutenant, 19
Kawashima, Captain, 20
Kellogg, Frank Billings, 246; on obligations of signatories of Pact, 179
Kellogg-Briand Pact (Pact of Paris), 49; China's appeal to U.S. under, 22, 28; U.S. saw no reason for invoking, in Mukden incident, 25; involved in

Mukden incident? 30; endangered at moment of birth, 32; U.S. a sponsor and signatory, 35; Japan's departure from spirit of, 96; cornerstone of peace threatened, 97; chosen as agency for U.S. collaboration with League, 102; invitation to U.S. based on, 107; U.S., acting on principles of, sat with nations acting on Covenant of League, 110; Gilbert participated in discussions under, 110, 115; question of invoking, 114; Briand reported on action taken, 115; Japan's deliberate flouting of, 137; solely a moral instrument, 149; territory obtained in violation of, 151; effect of Dawes's reference to, 168; violated by Japan, 178; responsibility of U.S. under, 218, 220, 221, 222; self-denial of aggression reinforced by, 234; Rapidan declaration of British and American resolution to accept, 235

Kirin under Japanese control, 187

Koo, Wellington, 251; proposal to Japan re neutral zone, 192; tentative suggestion to foreign ministers at Nanking, 216; in charge of China's foreign office, 228

Korea, anti-Chinese riots, 17

Kuan Yuheng, 18

Labour Party, British, smashed, 5, 128

Latin America, opposed Japan's demand for right to take police measures against bandits, 204; chief concern of delegates, 212*n*

League and Manchuria, The, 46, 85; excerpt, 51

League of Nations, Britain's attitude toward, 6, 7; decision on course of action, the work of States Members, 10; effects of estrangement between U.S. and, 15; liaison in China, 24; first case of world-wide importance, 35; criticisms against, unjustified, 40; skeptics felt that it had failed completely, 81; covenant, cornerstone of peace, threatened, 97; influence of isolationists in weakening American cooperation with, 129 (*see also* Isolationists); accusation of Japanese press against, 134; ability to exert economic pressure doubted, 141; Hoover and Gibson on failure to use force, 152

—— Assembly: gratification over American cooperation with Council, 52; China asked that case be submitted to: special session called, 226; adopted nonrecognition resolution introduced by Simon, 242; principle of nonrecognition incorporated in resolution of Mar. 11, 250; Committee of Nineteen, 251, 252; publicity one of merits of its system, 256*n*

—— Council, 65th meeting: crucial period, 3; British delegation, 7; French delegation, 8; *Sept. meetings*, 22-80; Mukden incident: case important in League history, 22; China's appeal to, 22, 28; mistakes and delay, 25; formal consideration of China's appeal, 35 ff.; warned by Yoshizawa to keep hands off controversy, 38, 39, 44; question of American cooperation, 41, 99, 129, 176, 195, 212-24; notes to China, Japan, and U.S.: quick action toward peaceful settlement, 44; Committee of Five: personnel, 46 (*see also* Committee of Five); cast in gloom by attitude of U.S., 49; attempt to keep door open for U.S. to participate directly in action, 53; competence to undertake settlement not recognized by Japan, 55; Sze on Article 15 of Covenant, 57; Cecil on duty of, under Article 11, 58; deadlocked between China and Japan, 62, 103; opinion that in following advice of U.S. it abdicated its duty, 67; draft resolution of Sept. 30, 72 ff., 200, 207; adopted, 75; *first interlude, Oct. 1-12*, 81-92; preparation for Oct. meeting, 82, 90; assumed that Japan was carrying out her obligations, 82; impact of American policy on, 82; request that U.S. sit jointly with them in discussion of controversy, 87; first mention of "fundamental points," 90 (*see also* Fundamental points); convened Oct. 13, 91; *Oct. meetings*, 93-127; faced with whole Manchurian problem, 93; Briand as President, 95 ff.; re invitation to U.S. to send representative, 99, 104, 107; Gilbert authorized to accept, 101; decision to keep in communication with U.S., 104; Oct. meetings provide illustration of actions of, 105; real advantage of American presence at table, 105; important work of special committees, 105; Yoshizawa's proposal to appoint a committee of jurists to settle constitutional question, 108, 109; rejected, 109; state of tension, 110; abnormality of U.S. position vis-à-vis, 110; representative of U.S. received, 110; U.S., acting on principles of Kellogg Pact, sat with nations acting on Covenant, 110; tension sagged as import of Gilbert's instructions were grasped, 111; delegates' idea of American participation, 112; idea of force abhorrent to majority of governments represented, 113; results of Gilbert's presence, 114; draft resolution of the "Twelve," 116 ff. (*see also* Twelve); suggestion that conciliation committee be set up by China and Japan, 117; Briand's warning to Yoshizawa, 120; attempt at compromise, 121; Gilbert's silence during debate, 121; his role at secret sessions, 122; resolution demanding complete evacuation of Chinese territory, 122; disturbed by changed attitude of U.S., and by Stimson's silence, 123; *second interlude: Oct. 24-Nov. 16*, 128-69; military and diplomatic developments, 128-39; Paris meeting suggested by Briand, 131; opposed by Sze and League Secretariat, 132; Japan's deliberate flouting of Covenant, 137; question of sanctions brought before, 139-55 (*see also* Sanction); consideration of parallel and simultaneous negotiations, 139, 172, 178; tragic history of Wilson and the Covenant not forgotten, 140; possible action under Articles xv and xvi considered, 145; would it have consented to sanctions? 154; appointment of Dawes to go to Paris meetings, 156-69; dismay at appointment of Dawes, 160; Dawes and Simon advocated cessation of hostilities without change in location of troops, 162; belief that withdrawal of U.S. representative would do serious injury to cause of peace, 163; Dawes's attendance left to own discretion, 164; absence of American officials from opening session, Nov. 16, 166; members insistent that Dawes attend next public meeting, 168; *Paris meeting, 170-224; Nov. 16-21*, 170-86; exhilaration of a great dramatic situation, 170; dangers inherent in situation in Paris, 171 f., 175; private and secret sessions, 171, 172; use of Nine-Power Treaty objected to, 174; provisions of Articles 11 and 15, 175*n*; proposal for suspension of hostilities and sending Commission of Enquiry to Manchuria 179 (*see also* Commission of Enquiry); factors that brought about change of plan, 181; uneasiness as to course meeting of Nov. 21 would take, 182; Briand's wise direction of meeting, 183; Sept. 30 resolution still in force: two important provisions, 183; *Nov. 22-25*, 186-202; difficulty of coordinating American and League efforts, 195; tentative draft resolution of Nov. 25, 197, *text* 200; attitude of U.S. toward resolution, 198 ff.; *Nov. 26-Dec. 10*, 202-12; committee appointed to redraft resolution, 202; drafting committee and Dawes unable to iron out all difficulties, 207; draft resolution of Dec. 10, *text*, 207 f.; diplomatic victory for Japan, 208; Council helpless, had tied hands of Commission, 209; final meeting, 210; resolution unanimously adopted, 211; turns denouément might have taken, 225; deterrents to U.S. cooperation with, 260; confused leadership, 261

—— Secretariat: opposed meeting in Paris, 132; accused of uncritical acceptance of Sze's statement, 137; study of Article 16 with view of diplomatic break with Japan, 141

League of Nations Association, The, 142*n*

Leger, Alexis, 95

Lerroux, Alejandro, as president in 65th Council, 9, 46; quoted, 23; proposal re Mukden incident, 42; appeal to Japan to withdraw troops to railway zone, 59, 77; on essential points of problem, 72; appeal to China and Japan, 91; compelled to remain in Madrid, 95

Lewis, Sir Wilmot, quoted, 132*n*

Liao River, disorders between Chinchow and, 226

Lindsay, Sir Ronald, transmitted Stimson's nonrecognition note to his government, 239

Locarno powers, result of secret meetings, 256*n*

London Naval Conference, American delegation, 157 f.

London Naval Treaty ratified by Minseito Cabinet, 32

Lyttleton, Mrs. Alfred, 7*n*

Lytton, Lord, 7*n*, 251; President of Commission of Enquiry, 231

Lytton Commission, 51; Report, excerpts, 17-18, 19-21; on bombing of Chinchow, 83; on Nonni River affair, 130; on Honjo's threat to Chinchow, 189; on retreat of troops from Chinchow to Hsinmin, 192; Report submitted to Council, sent to Assembly, 251; careful examination of Report necessary to understand Sino-Japanese controversy, 252

Ma Chan-shan, trouble with Chang Haipeng, 129; resignation demanded, 130; Honjo's ultimatum to, 131, 162; ultimatum rejected: defeat, 131; excitement in Paris caused by news of defeat, 144

McCoy, Frank, 231

MacDonald, James Ramsay, repudiated by Labour Party, 5; as Prime Minister, 5, 129; Rapidan declaration, 235

Madariaga, Salvador de, Spanish delegate to League, 9; influence, personality, courage, 10, 95, 104; active in bringing Mukden incident before Council, 24; on Committee of Five, 106; re invitation to U.S., 108; warning against delay in collaboration, 114; compromise proposal turned down by Yoshizawa, 120, 173; on police measures, 211; on need for recasting methods for dealing with international difficulties, 212*n*

Manchuria, time ripe for trouble, 12; drawing closer to China, 13, 14, 17; common back yard of Japan and Asiatic Russia, 16; strategically important to Japan, 26

—— crisis of 1929: hostilities between Russia and China, 33

—— crisis of 1931: precipitated into lap of world: two myths concerning, 3; Mukden incident, 16-21 (*see also* Mukden incident); factors which precipitated, 17; confusion on Mukden incident, 25; seizure by Japanese of wires and wireless, 37; Sze's requests for a Commission of Enquiry or for local arrangements, a neutral committee "on the spot," 38, 42, 46, 56, 74, 75 (*see also* Commission of Enquiry); territory under occupation being extended, 42; Japan disclaimed aggressive designs in, 44, 117; Yoshizawa's proposal to send a commission of enquiry, 49, 143, 184, 185; door opened wide for continued expansion of Japanese demands, 75, 187, 222; bombing of Chinchow, 77 f., 82 ff. (*see also* Chinchow); Japanese army in possession of all Southern, 79; army officers took matters in own hands, 81; first discussion of, by U.S. Cabinet, 85; hope of peaceful settlement vanished, 85; conciliation committee suggested by Council, 117; field of military operations broadened, 126; military and diplomatic developments: Oct. 24–Nov. 16, 128-39; events in Northern, fraught with disaster, 129; quarrel the result of Twenty-one Demands, 133; army wagered its existence and control of policy on outcome, 134; consideration of parallel and simultaneous negotiations, 139, 172, 178; international police force suggested to replace Japanese troops, 139*n*; impossible for a western nation to intervene by military force: area of possible action, 147; negotiations for evacuation, 173; Japan insisted on right of railway operation, 173; maintenance of military occupation threatened until new treaty negotiated, 176; penetrated far beyond railway zone, 178; proposal for suspension of hostilities and sending international commission of enquiry, 179, 181; Japan's refusal to restrict army activities, 182; Sze's demand for cessation of hostilities, 184, 185, 187; Yoshizawa unyielding on cessation of hostilities, 187; provincial capitals under Japanese control, 187; tentative draft resolution of Nov. 25, 197; *text*, 200; proposed zone between armies where only neutral observers were to go, 205; draft resolution of Dec. 10, *text*, 207; Japan in complete control of situation, 209, 230; essential elements in proposed settlement, 210; independence movements stimulated by Japan, 211; exceptional character of situation and of settlement, 211; group of young officers responsible for outrage, 227 f.; new offensive underway, 229; protest against Chinese brigandage, 229; road from, led to Pearl Harbor, 237; Japanese desire to demilitarize, 242; Lytton Report a

Manchuria (*Continued*)
masterly arraignment of Japanese acts in, 252
Manning, William, 142*n*
Martel, Damien de, 193
Martin, William, 122
Massigli, René, delegate to League, 8, 46, 95, 171
Matsudaira, Tsuneo, Dawes's friendship with, 161; liaison between Yoshizawa and Dawes, 172; moderating influence counted on by Dawes, 174; disturbed by news of advance on Tsitsihar, 175; Dawes's contacts with, 213; agreed statement submitted by Dawes, 214; quoted, 242
Matsuoka, Yosuke, 251; left Assembly, 252*n*, 253; speech in Assembly, 253
Military Commission of Inquiry, *see* Commission of Enquiry
Minami, General, Japan's Minister of War: illiberal diplomatic position, 13; in agreement with army group: denounced Shidehara, 26; criticized by press: withdrawal demanded: declined, 26; a follower of Tanaka, 33
Minseito Cabinet and party, *see* Japan, Minseito
Misunderstandings among chief causes of international unrest, 256*n*
Mitsubishi clan, effort to swing, into reactionary column, 17
Mitsui clan, effort to swing, into reactionary column, 17
Mongolia, strategically important to Japan, 26
Mongolia, Inner: brigandage, 229; aid to Chinese forces cut off, 230
Moral opinion, *see* Sanctions, moral
Morrow, Dwight, 158
Mukden, beating of American consular official, 238
Mukden incident, 3, 16-21; report of Lytton Commission, 17 ff., Japanese version, 19; Chinese version, 20; Commission's conclusions, 21; brought to attention of League: an important case in League history, 22; situation confused, 25; made little impression outside of Japan, 27; representatives in Geneva swayed by own interests, 29; Council's formal consideration of case, 35 ff.; argument between Sze and Yoshizawa, 35 ff., 43; question of direct negotiations as opposed to League action, 36, 37, 39; Council warned to keep hands off controversy, 38, 39, 44; Lerroux's proposal, 42; expansion into crisis involving whole of Manchuria, 82
Munich, 237
Mutius, von, German representative, 95; quoted, 185; on principle task of League, 212*n*
Myers, William Starr, 143; quoted, 149, 151

Nakamura, Shintaro, death at hands of Chinese, 17, 127; army plans to obtain satisfaction for murder, 28
Nanking, *see* China
National Council for Prevention of War, 142*n*
Negotiation under military occupation, contrary to new diplomacy, 138*n*
Neutral zone, proposal for establishment of, in Chinchow area, 192 ff.; Briand's compromise proposal: accepted by China, rejected by Japan, 194
Neville, Edwin L., 69
News-Chronicle, excerpt, 159
Nichi Nichi, view of international police for Manchuria, 139*n*
Nine Power Treaty, 16, 49, 247; involved in Mukden incident? 30; U.S. a signatory of, 35; shift from, to Kellogg Pact as agency for U.S. collaboration with League, 102; solely a moral instrument, 149; effect of Dawes's reference to, 167, 168; studied by the "Twelve," 173; use of, objected to by some Council members, 174; violated by Japanese, 178; responsibility of U.S. under, 218, 220, 221, 222; relations of Great Powers with China crystallized in, 234; first time invoked, 240; failure of signatories to support U.S. nonrecognition note, 241
1915 treaty, *see* Twenty-one Demands
1931, dividing line between interwar periods, 3; tragic year against which crisis must be considered, 4
Nonni River crisis, U.S. concerned over reports, 124, 125; fighting over bridge, 125, 130; bridge blown up by Ma, 129; Lytton Commission's account, 130; Stimson reassured by Debuchi re, 131; Paris meeting of Council a consequence of, 131; Dawes not in favor of forcing Japanese withdrawal, 198
Nonrecognition, source of idea, 151; most powerful form of moral pres-

sure, 154; Stimson's note of Jan. 7, 223, 226, 232, 234 ff.; his decision to make restatement of principle of, 233; note handed to Debuchi and Yen, and later to other signatories of Nine Power Treaty, 234; *text*, 234*n*; British rebuff convinced Japan that U.S. was without support in advancing doctrine, 238; in tradition of American policy in Far East, not in that of Great Britain, 240; resolution introduced by Simon adopted by Assembly, 242, 248; a dead-end policy, 254

Norway, refused to minimize principles of Covenant, 202

Observers, neutral: contradict rumors of concentration of Chinese forces at Chinchow and Shanhaikwan, 188; Japan opposed participation by, in Chinchow, 204; *see also* Commission of Enquiry

Official Journal, 105

Olds, Robert E., 214

Open-door policy, 35, 235*n*

Orient, effect of British rebuff to U.S. upon Anglo-American cooperation in, 238

Oulahan, Richard V., 164

Pact of Paris, *see* Kellogg-Briand Pact

Panama welcomed by Council of League, 23

Paris Journal, The, excerpt, 81*n*

Paul-Boncour, Joseph, 242

Peace, a strong independent China essential to in East, 16; Council's duty to safeguard, 58; first great battle for world, lost, 80; cornerstones threatened, 97; indivisible, 180; historic milestones on path to organization of, 252; international organization which will include all nations imperative, 262

Peace treaties, means considered to compel Japan to respect, 148

Pearl Harbor, road from Manchuria lead to, 237

Pearson, Drew, and C. Brown, 31*n*

Peffer, Nathaniel, 50*n*

Peitaying, Japanese attack on, 20

Peking-Mukden Railway, British protest against Japanese advance along, 190; traffic disrupted, 230

People, *see* Public

Personalities, importance, 7

Philip, P. J., quoted, 166

Philippines, U.S. left position in, without further fortifications, 247*n*

Police force, international, for Manchuria, suggested, 139*n*

Police measures, international police force suggested to replace Japanese troops, 139*n*; Japan's demand for right to take, against bandits, 204, 205; Cecil and Madariaga on, 211; pledge against renewed hostilities vitiated by reservation as to, 222; Yoshizawa's reservation, 223

Politis, Greek delegate, 250

Powers, growing cleavage between great and small, 202

Pratt, Sir John, 249; on Foreign Office communiqué, 240, 241; refuted charge that no answer was made to Stimson, 244

Press, reports on sanctions strictly anonymous, 140; dispatches re disturbances in Manchuria, 188, 189

—— American: acrimony developed in British and, 244

—— British: attacks of Beaverbrook and Rothermere papers on Council, 138, 141; stunning rebuff to Stimson, 235; encouragement to Japan, 236; acrimony in American and, 244

—— French: attitude toward Japan, 8, 132

—— German: opinion that League had failed, 81*n*

—— Japanese: interpretation of American attitude, 45; attitude toward invitation to U.S., 103; War Office through press aroused animosity against all who opposed them, 134; belief that Japan should withdraw from League, 137; indication that opinion not uniformly behind military, 139*n*; on report of diplomatic withdrawal, 141; jingo papers inveighed against Stimson, 191; anxiety as to reaction of public opinion in U.S., 192; claim Council's action as victory for Japan, 229; interpretation of resolution of Dec. 10, 230; *see also* Asaki; Ji-Ji

Problems of Lasting Peace, The (Hoover and Gibson), excerpt, 152

Public, great mistake of keeping in ignorance of true state of affairs, 260

Publicity, Stimson's threat to invoke sanction of, 146, 178; value of in diplo-

Publicity (*Continued*)
macy: one of merits of League system, 256*n*

Public opinion, Stimson's attitude toward keeping, informed, 69, 79, 88 ff., 223; would have supported him in a sterner attitude towards Japan, 79; distrustful of periods of inactivity, 82; in Britain and U.S. did not favor economic sanctions, 142; U.S. confined itself to reliance upon sanctions of, 144, 146, 152, 154; pressure of, in behalf of China suggested, 147, 148; unguided and voiceless, 177, 255; Kellogg's advice to mobilize, of world, 179; need for lead in right direction, 180; publication of resolution of Nov. 25 meant to marshal, 201; first steps in educating, 221; would not have supported Stimson in a drastic action, 254; why needed, 255; *see also* Sanctions, moral

Rapidan declaration, 235

Reading, Lord, head of British delegation, 7, 95; re invitation to U.S., 107, 108; idea of American participation, 112; Foreign Office believed had gone too far in support of League and China, 236

Republican Party, isolationist sentiment precluded cooperation of U.S. with League, 53 f.; *see also* Isolationists

Roberts, Owen F., 142*n*

Robinson, Joseph T., isolationist sentiments, 180, 196

Roosevelt, Franklin D., frank character of utterances, 141; wanted to fortify Guam: appropriations refused by Congress, 255

Roosevelt, Theodore, 247

Rothermere papers, attacks on Council, 138, 141

Russia, absence from League when tragedy opened, 15; hostilities between China and, in Manchuria, 33; France's hostility to Soviet Union, 132*n*; relations with Japan strained, 230

Russo-Japanese War, 16

Salisbury, Laurence E., *see* Salisbury-Hanson Mission

Salisbury-Hanson Mission to Southern Manchuria, 70, 88, 110, 258

Salter, Sir Arthur, 7*n*

Salt revenues of China seized, 128

Sanctions, economic, 139-55; no government willing to assume responsibility for initiating, 140; policy of press, 140; public opinion in Britain not in favor of, 142; groping for a substitute for, 232, 234

—— moral: developed by Hoover and Stimson, 144, 146, 150, 152, 153, 154, 178, 261

Schnee, Heinrich, 231

Secret diplomacy, Chinese fear return to old methods of, 171; Japanese desire for, 172; time for, in grave instances, past, 179

Secret protocols of 1905, 173*n*

Selden, Charles A., quoted, 138, 162*n*

Shanghai, outbreak of violence, 225, 228, 231

Shanhaikwan, rumors of anti-Japanese disturbances, 188; Japan demanded Chinese withdrawal from Chinchow to West of, 193, 194; and Shanhaikwan Pass in Japanese hands, 229 f.

Shantung, compensation to Japan for return of, to China, 16

Shaw, G. Howland, 158

Shegemitsu, Japanese Minister to China, called upon Soong, 37; suggested mixed Sino-Japanese commission, 38

Shidehara, Kijuro, Japan's Foreign Minister, 10, 69, 77*n*, 127, 128; liberal position, 13; attitude toward China denounced by Minami, 26; slight to authority: control of foreign policy passed into hands of army, 26; Stimson's desire to avoid action in support of military against, 30; policy, 31; labored against pressure of army leaders, 32; strong stand by U.S. and League would have aided, 34; Stimson's fear of throwing difficulties in path of, 48; cause of fall, 50, 227; Stimson's oral message to, 78, 79; excuses for Japanese action, 78; yielded to military, 82; showed no desire to persuade army to recede from its position, 91; good record in international affairs, 94; no longer counseled moderation, 95; U.S. association with League resolutions announced to, 124; rejection of Briand's arguments, 136; rejection of proposal for League supervision of evacuation, and of China's offer to submit to arbitration, 137; on occupation of Tsitsihar, 177; declared Japanese would not attack

Chinchow, 189; ordered retreat of military from Chinese territory, 190, 192; *see also* Japan, Minseito Cabinet

Shiozawa, attack on Chapei, 242

Shiratori, Toshio, Japan's Foreign Office Spokesman: illiberal position, 13; policy of dividing Great Britain and U.S., 14; career, 14*n*; re agreement on fundamental points, 137; quoted, 138; discourteous remark about Stimson: retraction, 191

Simon, Sir John, 113, 129, 159, 161, 171, 184, 202*n*; determined British policy, 7; attitude toward League, 8; opposed to sanctions, 154; believed time limit clause for Japanese troop evacuation unwise, 162; approved plan for simultaneous and parallel negotiations, 173; Dawes's contacts with, 213; opened door for appeasement of Japan, 235; believed Cecil and Reading had gone too far in support of League and China, 236; Stimson's telephone calls and cable to, proposing joint invocation of Nine Power Treaty, 243; fear that action might lead to use of fleets, 244; would not step from behind shield which League membership afforded, 246; motives back of introduction of nonrecognition resolution, 248; lip service to League and cause of collective security, 250

Sino-Japanese commission, suggested by Shegemitsu, 38; Sze's suggestion for, 63; opposed by Yoshizawa, 63, 66

Sino-Japanese Controversy (Willoughby), 250

Sino-Japanese War, results, 16

Sloan, Alfred P., 142*n*

Small Powers, refuse to exert pressure on China, 201; omission from investigating group, 231*n*; constant fear of, 246

Snowden, Philip, repudiated by Labour Party, 5

Sol, El, 197

Soong, T. V., Shegemitsu's call upon, 37; out of office, 228

South Manchuria Railway, explosion on rails, 19; authorities of, demanded repair of Nonni River bridge, 129; *see also* Nonni River crisis

Spain, held office of president in 65th Council, 9 (*see also* Lerroux, A.); Consul-General in Shanghai to investigate situation in Manchuria, 88*n*;

notes to China and Japan, 114; refused to sacrifice principles of Covenant, 202; road from Manchuria lead through Ethiopia to, 237; *see also* Madariaga, S. de

Stimson, Henry L., U.S. Secretary of State, 3; knowledge of Far East, 11; held back action in Manchurian crisis, 12, 86; asked Debuchi to defer leave, 24; quoted, 25, 30, 31 ff., 45, 70, 71, 78, 100, 122, 157*n*; ignored China's appeal, 29; position in re Mukden incident, 30 ff.; memorandum to Japan, 44; put end to early sending of commission of enquiry to Manchuria, 47 ff., 76, 77; policy of conciliating Japanese, 48, 50, 59, 148, 233; stand strengthened hands of military, 51; notes to China and Japan, 54; Chinese and Japanese replies to notes, 67 ff.; failure to take public into his confidence, 69, 79, 88 ff., 223; change in attitude toward Japan, 71, 155; policy of silence, 77, 178; conferences with Debuchi, 77, 177; did not confer with Yung Kwai, 77, 233; oral message to Shidehara, 78, 79; mistake repeated: cable to Drummond, 84; confidence in Debuchi's assurances shattered, 85; first conference with Yung, 85; urged Hoover to agree to request that U.S. sit with Council in discussion, 86 f.; stern admonition to Japan, 87, 138; refusal to take initiative in invoking Kellogg Pact, 100; choice of representative to sit with Council, 101; choice of Kellogg Pact as agency for collaboration, 102; delay in collaborating with League, 114; instructed Gilbert to leave Council table, 122*n*, 163; Council looked to, to fulfill promise: disturbed by his silence, 123; "aide-memoire" commenting on Japan's reply to invocation of Pact of Paris, 124 f.; doubt of sincerity of, 142; authoritative discussion of position of U.S., 143, 144; summary of failure of efforts at conciliation, 145; conference with Hoover on sanctions, 145; attitude on sanctions, 146 ff., 178; on Hoover's attitude toward international cooperation, 153; delegate to London Naval Conference, 158; believed time limit clause for Japanese troop evacuation unwise, 162; emphasis on independent position and separate judgment of

Stimson, Henry L. (*Continued*)
U.S., 164, 165, 168; on Dawes's non-attendance, 167; reserved liberty to publish communications with Japan, 178, 255; strong statement from, needed to guide public opinion, 180; indignation expressed in message and press conference, 190; outraged by Japanese dual diplomacy: press release, 191; on U.S. approval of resolution of Nov. 25, 199; suggestion that Briand read Dawes's statement to Council, 215; on resolution of Dec. 10, and American relation to case, 220; note to Japan on his apprehension over situation in Manchuria, 223; non-recognition note of Jan. 7, 1932, 223, 226, 232, 234 ff.; faced with new problems, 226; hope of action in Japan vanished, 232; note of Jan. 7, handed to Debuchi and Yen, 234; *text*, 234*n*; looked for British cooperation, 235; stunning rebuff by British Foreign Office and press, 235; mistake in timing, 236; what British moral support of, would have meant, 237; proposal for a joint invocation of Nine Power Treaty, 243; British reluctant to join in, 243; anxious to cooperate with, 245; open letter to Borah, 245, 247, 250; on motives back of Simon's introduction of nonrecognition resolution, 248; disturbed over reports that Britain might not support resolution, 248; position supported by Eden and Thomas, 249; timely action brought incorporation of nonrecognition principle in resolution of Mar. 11, 250; note of Jan. 7 became historic milestone on path to organization of peace, 252; result of failure to publish notes on Japan, 256*n*

Streit, Clarence, 195, 201; quoted, 24, 209; on Dawes, 196*n*, 213
Stryder, R. E. L., 142*n*
Sugiyama, Lieutenant-General, 26
Swanson, Claude, 158
Sweetser, Arthur, 167; official liaison between Dawes and Council at Paris, 10, 158, 172, 175, 213
Sze, Alfred Sao-ke, Chinese representative at 65th Council, 9; report to Council on Mukden incident, 23; argument between Yoshizawa and, 35 ff.; attempt to keep discussion on local incident at Mukden, 36; request for immediate action by Council, 36; demand that *status quo ante* be restored, 37, 71, 74; request for a commission of enquiry, 38, 42, 46, 56; asked Council to order withdrawal of Japanese troops, 42; reaction to Lerroux's proposal, 43; proposal for local arrangements, a committee "on the spot," 46, 65, 74; request that Chinese reply to Council note be read, 56; note of prophecy in comment on Yoshizawa's statement, 57; ready to invoke Article 15 of Covenant, 57, 144, 175; effort to win support of U.S., 62; suggestion for organization of Sino-Japanese commission, 63; demand for immediate cessation of hostilities and withdrawal of troops, 67, 71, 184, 185, 187; interpretation of Council's draft resolution of Sept. 30, 1931, 74; not satisfied with resolution, 75; asked that Council be summoned forthwith, 90; almost immediate answers reported by, 94; prophetic appeal for preservation of structure of collective security, 97; discussion of bases of China's acceptance of draft resolution of the "Twelve," 118; opposed to meeting in Paris, 132; letter regarded in Tokyo as repudiation of 1915 treaty, 133; arbitration proposal, 135; ready to invoke other articles of Covenant, 143; desire for open meetings of Council: feared return to old methods of secret diplomacy, 171; withdrew demand for public meetings, 174; pled for immediate application of antiwar treaties by League and U.S., 175; raised spectre of sanctions, 175; response to Briand's appeals, 183, 186; on Yoshizawa's failure to mention suspension of hostilities, 184, 185; summary of oral reservations to his acceptance of Yoshizawa's proposals, 187; asked for neutral zone occupied by neutral detachments, 192; Yoshizawa's failure to trap, 195; refusal to compromise on evacuation of Chinchow, 205; reservations and comments on resolution of Dec. 10, 210; quoted, 212; Dawes's contacts with, 213

Taft, Charles P., 2d, 142*n*
Tahsing Station occupied by Japanese forces, 130
Tanaka, Giichi, 13, 14; lost ground to

liberals, 17; policy re Sino-Japanese relations, 33
Tanaka Memorial, 127
Taonan-Anganchi Railway, bombing of bridge on line of, 125, 129 (*see also* Nonni River crisis)
Tariff barriers, growth of, 5
Telephone diplomacy, 244
Thomas, British Secretary of State for the Dominions, 249
Thompson, J. D., 69
Tientsin, outbreak of trouble, 130; Japanese troops in, 189
Times, London, excerpts, 66, 96, 236n; encouragement to Japanese, 236
Times, New York, 104, 124; excerpts, 27, 30, 35, 60, 61, 69, 83, 88, 89, 96, 133, 142, 162n, 165
Toynbee, Arnold J., 4; quoted, 248
Trade, decrease in 1931, 5
Trans-Pacific, 205; excerpts, 47n, 78, 206, 207; on cause of fall of Minseito Cabinet, 50, 227
Treaty of Versailles, 144
Tsitsihar, endangered, 125; fall, 126, 131, 133; Japanese Consulate in danger of attack, 130; Debuchi's statement, 131; Honjo's advance on: Sze's declaration in response to, 175; Yoshizawa's demand for a new treaty, 176; U.S. protest to Japan: Shidehara's reply, 177
Turkey, 112
"Twelve, The," meeting called: disputants excluded, 106; draft resolution, 116; Gilbert's role at meetings, 122; effort to reconcile opposing views, 173; re liaison between neutral observers and Japanese commanders, 204; declaration along lines of Stimson's note, 241 f., 245
Twenty-one Demands, 16, 98; Manchurian quarrel over, 133; treaties based on, rejected by China, 173

United States, propaganda for those who would divide Great Britain and, 4; files of State Department closed to research in 1939, 4; crisis of 1931: split in Congress, 6; observers at Sept., 1931, meetings of Council, 11; conflict of personality and opinion in State Department, 12, 260; absence from League when tragedy opened, 15; effects of estrangement between League and, 15; China's appeal to, under Kellogg Pact, 22, 28; no answer made to appeal, 29; desire to avoid misunderstanding with Japan, 30; attitude in Mukden incident, 30 ff.; treatment of subject of Japanese immigration by Congress, 32; importance of position adopted by, 34; effect of uncertain policy concerning League, 34; prestige in Far East at stake, 35, 232; question of cooperation with League, 41, 99, 176, 195, 212-24; Japan's effort to keep out of League, 43, 45; interpretation of attitude of, by Japanese press, 45; opposed sending a commission of enquiry to Manchuria, 47 ff., 76; sympathetic attitude toward Japan reported by Debuchi, 47n; promise of diplomatic support of Council, 51; isolationist sentiment precluded cooperation with League, 53; result, 54; optimism re amicable solution of Manchurian clash, 60; opinion that League, in following advice of, abdicated its duty, 67; warned that Japan was up to no good, 82; Cabinet's first discussion of Manchurian affair, 85; Hoover's restraining influence on policy of collaboration with League, 86; asked to sit jointly with Council, 87; requested by China to send representative to Manchuria, 88; compliance considered unnecessary, 89; negotiations re invitation to send a representative to Geneva, 100; Gilbert authorized to accept, 101; shift from Nine Power Treaty to Kellogg Pact as agency for collaboration, 102; Council's decision to extend invitation to, 104; real advantage of presence at Council table, 105; Yoshizawa refused to consent to presence of, at Council table, 106; invitation to, based on Pact of Paris, 107; abnormality of position vis-à-vis League, 110; representative received by Council, 110; Gilbert's statement as to part U.S. would take in Council deliberations, 111; delegates' idea of American participation, 112; decision as to capacity in which representative should act undoubtedly Hoover's, 113; change of attitude: League circles disturbed, 123; policy of strict neutrality, 124; concerned over reports of Nonni River crisis, 124, 125; lame-duck Congress, 129; tendency toward appeasement, 138; rumor of formula for settlement, 139;

United States, (*Continued*)
position re sanctions, 139-55; urged to stronger action, 142; position far from clear, 143; trade with Japan, 145; idea that Japan could be trusted to regulate situation, 155; felt that setting date for evacuation was unwise, 155; isolationist sentiments of Senators, 155, 180, 196; withdrawal of representative from Council table, 163; emphasis placed on independent position and separate judgment of, 164, 165, 168; aloofness damaging bad situation, 165, 169; rumors re attitude helpful to Japan, 166; protest to Japan on occupation of Tsitsihar, 177; relations with Japan strained, 191; difficulty of co-ordinating efforts with those of League to maintain peace, 195; position as viewed from Paris, 196; part in drawing up tentative draft resolution released Nov. 25, 197; approval of tentative draft resolution of Nov. 25, announced, 199; political and economic situation, Dec., 1931, 217; Hoover's special message to Congress on Manchurian crisis, 218, 222; early support of, needed to stem tide of Japanese aggression, 220; attitude re treaty commitments defined, 220 f.; strain in British-American relations, 226, 232, 235 ff.; three necessary steps to meet changed conditions, 233; responsibility for failure to stop Japan divided between Great Britain and, 238; consular official beaten by Japanese at Mukden, 238; agreed not to erect additional fortifications in Far Eastern possessions, 247*n*, 248; continued its cooperation at Shanghai and in work of Lytton Commission, 251; appropriation to fortify Guam refused by Congress, 255; Senate Foreign Relations Committee's request for papers re Manchurian controversy, 257; summary of causes of failure to collaborate with League, 259; *see also* Castle, W. R.; Dawes, C. G.; Gibson, H.; Gilbert, P.; Hoover, H.; Stimson, H. L.; Wilson, H.; Wilson, W.

Versailles, Treaty of, 144

Wakatsuki, Reijiro, Prime Minister of Japan, 32, 127; liberal position, 13; yielded to military, 82; lack of disposition to persuade army to recede from its position, 91; cause of fall, 128, 227
Wang, C. T., attacked by students, 70; succeeded as Foreign Minister by Koo, 191
Wang I-Cheh, 20
War and Peace, 1931-1941, 258
Warren, Lansing, quoted, 176 f.
Warsaw, 237
Washington Conference, 1922, 147
Washio, S., 205
Western powers agreed not further to fortify Pacific possessions, 16
White, William A., 142*n*
Wilbur, Ray L., and A. M. Hyde, 143; quoted, 149, 150
Willoughby, W. W., 209, 250; quoted, 44, 194*n*, 252
Wilson, Hugh, U.S. Minister to Switzerland, 30, 46, 50, 53, 101, 102, 160; on Massigli, 9; an observer at Council meetings, 11, 15; quoted, 11, 93*n*, 157*n*; could not attend secret meetings, 105; conferred unofficially with members of Council, 159; active role, 214; better to have sent to Paris, 217*n*; on British reaction to Stimson's proposal for joint invocation of Nine Power Treaty, 243; on telephone diplomacy, 244; on wisdom of course followed by League and U.S., 253 f.
Wilson, Woodrow, founder of League of Nations, 15; tragic history not forgotten, 140
Wood, Edward (Lord Halifax), 8
World War, first: treaties growing out of, 16
World Wars, interwar periods: phases: dividing line, 3

Yangtse, naval vessels sent to, 91
Yen, Ambassador, China's representative on 66th Council, 234
Yoshizawa, Kenkichi, head of Japanese delegation to League, 9; loyalty to army group, 10, 94, 126; report to League Council on Mukden incident, 23; diplomatic pressure brought to bear upon, 24; words taken at face value, 25; argument between Sze and, 35 ff.; stress on entire Manchurian situation, 36; insistence on direct negotiations between parties, 36, 37, 39, 55, 67, 90, 91, 103, 206; warned Council to

keep hands off controversy, 38, 39, 44; re Japanese interests in Manchuria, 41; reaction to Lerroux's proposal, 43; opposed invitation to U.S. to sit with Council, 43, 94, 104; effort to obtain further information from Japan, 43; defiant: informed U.S. disapproved Committee of Enquiry, 47; proposal to send a commission of enquiry to Manchuria and to China, 49, 143, 184, 185; quoted, 56; opposition to Sino-Japanese commission, 63; interpretation of Cecil's suggestion, 65; misinterpretations of Chinese proposals, 66; acceptance of Council's draft resolution of Sept. 30, 1931, 73; unable to accept Sze's interpretation of draft resolution: succeeded in having vital points eliminated, 75; tactics of delay and confusion, 93, 94, 99, 104, 108; turned down every compromise offer, 94; questioned accuracy of Sze's statements: lapse of memory, 98; warned not to create an irremediable situation, 99; refusal to consent to presence of U.S. at Council table, 106; re constitutional and legal right of nonmember to sit with Council, 107; proposed committee of jurists to settle constitutional question, 108, 109; proposal rejected, 109; why he fought invitation to U.S., 110; unyielding position, 115, 187; refusal to discuss "fundamental principles" with Council, 119, 120, 126; asked to withdraw proposal: refusal, 120; why he would make no concessions, 127; request for open meeting withdrawn, 171 f.; asked what treaties fifth fundamental point referred to, 174; upset all calculations, 174; refused to explain "treaty obligations," 175; position contradicted Matsudaira's assurances to Dawes, 175; demand for new treaty, 176; response to Briand's appeal, 183; restrictions on Commission of Enquiry's field of endeavor, 184, 187; failure to mention suspension of hostilities, 184, 185; Briand's warning to: his disturbing response, 186; failure to trap Sze, 195; reservation as to police measure, 210, 223; made Minister of Foreign Affairs, 226; severely criticized at home, 226*n*; insolent reply to Stimson's note of Jan. 7, 238

"Young Marshal," *see* Chang Hsuehliang

Yung Kwai, Chinese Chargé d'Affaires, 13, 69, 86; not received by Stimson, 77, 233; first opportunity to outline Chinese point of view to Stimson, 85